D1256617

MOSCOW
TOKYO
LONDON

Twenty Years of German Foreign Policy

by

HERBERT VON DIRKSEN

UNIVERSITY OF OKLAHOMA PRESS

NORMAN

Copyright in the United States 1952
by the University of Oklahoma Press, Publishing Division of the University
Composed and printed at Norman, Oklahoma, U.S.A.
by the University of Oklahoma Press
First American Edition

Preface

This book was written in English in the years 1947–1948. Originally it was conceived on a larger scale and tried to give a comprehensive description of the life and work of a man coming from the German eastern provinces—from Prussia. As the manuscript proved too long for publication, it had to be limited to its political core. I am greatly indebted to Mr. F. A. Voigt for having edited and condensed the manuscript to its present form. I also wish to express my gratitude to Professor Haferkorn in Hamburg for revising the English text.

Being a refugee from Silesia and, consequently, unable to consult my private archives, I had to rely on my memory for writing this book. Only the chapter dealing with my activity in London has been written after I had studied the documents recently published by the American, British, and Russian governments.

The aim of this book is to give an account of a political career spent almost exclusively in Eastern European and Far Eastern countries. The question, raised so often nowadays, whether the task of an ambassador is limited in our technical age to that of a letter-carrier, and, consequently, whether his memoirs are worth reading or not, need not be discussed in detail. The answer to this question depends largely upon the personality of the man concerned and upon the political situation of his country and the country to which he is accredited. As to the tasks which came my way, the reader may come to the conclusion that I played an active rôle in Moscow, whereas in Tokyo I was merely an observer.

The task assigned to me by Hitler in London was that of a letter-carrier. My efforts to break the shackles imposed on me and to oppose a policy which was bound to lead to the catastrophe of the Second World War proved futile.

HERBERT VON DIRKSEN

Bergen, Upper Bavaria, February, 1951

v

Contents

List of Illustrations

MOSCOW, TOKYO, LONDON

TWENTY YEARS OF GERMAN FOREIGN POLICY

Introduction

It is important for the author of a book written in a foreign language for readers of a country not his own to begin his narrative with a short description of his background; more important than for a writer who addresses his own countrymen. I shall therefore begin with a brief description of the family from which I am descended and of my life before I entered the Diplomatic Service.

The Dirksens were Mennonites of Dutch stock. Owing to religious persecutions in the 17th century, they emigrated—with thousands of their countrymen—to settle in Danzig and along the borders of the Lower Vistula. My ancestors, well-to-do merchants, stayed in the city. When Prussia became a kingdom and the first kings built up the new State on the basis of a powerful army and a Civil Service, my ancestors entered the service of the Kings of Prussia, mostly as lawyers.

From then on up to this day hardly one member of my family has chosen any profession other than that of permanent civil servant. My great-grandfather, professor of law at the universities of Königsberg and Berlin, was one of the foremost authorities on Roman Law of his time. My grandfather, a judge, retired early in order to devote his life to the administration of the considerable fortune and of the estate which his wife had inherited.

My father, having passed his legal examinations, entered the Foreign Office. But apart from two years in London he remained, throughout his career there, head of the Department for International Law. A passionate collector of medieval art, he furnished with exquisite taste the Berlin house which he had built near his father's house in the Margaretenstrasse. He indulged the same passion when he bought a beautiful estate in Silesia, at Gröditzberg. Then he retired from office and spent the rest of his life administering the estate. He continued to be a member of the *Reichstag* and of the *Herrenhaus,* the Prussian House of Lords.

Whereas my father's family lived in Prussia and was thoroughly Prussian in its inner structure and tradition, my mother's family came from Western Germany. The Schnitzlers belonged to the oldest families of Cologne. For more than 150 years members of the family, together with representatives of another patrician family of Cologne, the Steins, have been partners of the well-known bank I. H. Stein. My maternal grandparents lived in their dignified old house near the cathedral during the winter, whereas the summer was spent in their villa in Rolandseck, one of the most renowned beauty spots on the Rhine.

The tradition of my family preordained my career. Being handicapped by ill-health—I suffered from asthma—I spent a childhood well protected by nurses and tutors. I went to the same school as my father and was trained by the same teachers who had taught him. I passed the final examinations without difficulty, compensating for a hereditary weakness in mathematics with a flair for history and languages.

I did not have to worry about shaping my future. The training of a civil servant was invariably conducted in three stages, entirely different from one another but converging to the one important point of producing officials of the highest ability for the service of the state. These three stages were: study at a university as a member of a students' *Korps;* military service; and preparatory courses as a junior official of the Civil Service.

I began my studies in Heidelberg and entered a students' *Korps.* These students' associations have been subjected to heavy criticism for being reactionary, for encouraging heavy drinking, and for preposterous duels. While the charge of drinking was justified, the duels were not more brutal than boxing matches and had the same effect of producing courage and manliness. As to the charge of being reactionary, it is refuted by the fact that these *korps* elected their presidents by secret ballot. I may mention, moreover, that the number of casualties (in both wars) in the *korps* of which I was member equalled and even exceeded the number of those killed in action from all other German *korps.* One-third of my fellow students of the Heidelberg days were killed in the First World War.

I finished my studies in Berlin and, thanks to an efficient crammer, passed my first law examination. This I followed up by acquiring the degree of doctor at the university of Rostock.

Before entering into the service of the State as a junior civil servant, I served for one year as *Einjährig-Freiwilliger* (volunteer for one year) with the Third Lancers of the Guard in Potsdam. Having got used to the rigors of military life, I really enjoyed it. (After this year I had to

4

serve two more terms of two months each as sergeant and sergeant-major. When I was made an officer of the reserve, four further terms of service, lasting eight weeks each, followed until war broke out.)

My training proceeded according to the rules. I switched from law to the Civil Service and had to work for several months in the *Landsratamt* (District Commissioner's Office) and in the *Bürgermeisteramt* (Mayor's Office) before my education in theoretical problems advanced to wider responsibility. Finally, I passed the rather difficult examination and was then assigned to the District Chief at Bonn as a fully fledged Higher Civil Servant. I was in Bonn for four happy years and was eventually transferred to the Prussian Ministry of Commerce in Berlin. However, I did not spend more than a few months in the new job, as I had to join my regiment on the fourth day of mobilization after war had been declared.

These years dedicated to the service of my country were, nevertheless, interrupted by some personal enterprises. With a cousin of mine I made a trip round the world. We started with German East Africa, where my family owned plantations. Then we kept to the beaten track, enjoying a hunting expedition in Ceylon and finishing with South America. A second transatlantic voyage followed a few years later, in 1912, again to German East Africa, and then home via the Victoria Falls and Cape Town.

Two other events of this period have to be recorded. I married Baroness Hilda von Oelsen, the daughter of a landowner who owned a beautiful estate near Küstrin, eighty kilometres east of Berlin. And I took to writing. My interest in politics being roused, I started writing articles for reviews about such problems as the theory of imperialism, the Monroe Doctrine, and similar subjects.

Since then the writing of political articles—in the official form of reports or the private one of articles for newspapers—has developed into one of the absorbing passions of my life.

During the 1914–18 war my regiment belonged to the Cavalry Division of the Guard which formed a part of the First Cavalry Corps. This unit crossed the Ardennes, advanced through Northern France and, by-passing Paris, to Château Thierry. In September we had to retreat to the Aisne, and then, marching on the extreme right wing of our armies, we tried—in vain—to envelop the French left wing. At last the Channel stopped us near Ostend. We had marched 3,000 kilometres in three months. We went into billets between Ostend and Ghent.

In the spring of 1915 my regiment took part in the second offensive of Field Marshal von Mackensen's army against the Russians in Galicia. We marched up and down Eastern Galicia, from Yaroslau to Cholm and Brest-Litovsk. Then I was transferred to the High Command of the

5

Army as an *Ordonnanz-Offizier* (Staff Aide). I served for several months with Field Marshal von Mackensen and the Chief of Staff, General von Seeckt, in Eastern Galicia and Southern Hungary. Then the Civil Service of the occupied countries claimed me and I was appointed district chief of Namur (Belgium).

The important turn in my life arrived when a friend of mine, Baron von der Heydt, asked for my services in the English Office at the German Legation in The Hague. He had organized it, and he was in charge of it. Here we had to fulfil the duties which, in normal times, fell to the German Embassy in London. We had to report on political developments in England and in the Empire.

In May, 1918, Herr von Kuehlmann, the Secretary of State for Foreign Affairs, asked whether I was prepared to join the Foreign Office. I replied in the affirmative and was assigned to the German Legation in Kiev. That was the beginning of my career in the Foreign Office.

I

In the Foreign Office

1918–1925

When the First World War was approaching its end, I was a member of the German Legation at Kiev, the capital of the short-lived "Government" which had been formed by the Ukrainian *Hetman,* Skoropadski. In October, 1918, I was transferred to Berlin, together with some officers of the German High Command. We arrived on the 27th of that month. It was not long before I became convinced that Germany would have to accept an armistice on terms dictated by the Allied Powers and that she was heading for revolution. The lack of guidance displayed by the leading men was the surest and most sinister sign of impending disaster.

General Groener replaced General Ludendorff, whose departure was no great loss. He had shown himself to be dictatorial but without any foresight. He had refused to recognize even the possibility of collapse in September, and yet, within a few weeks, he had demanded an immediate armistice.

The new democratic Government formed by Prince Max of Baden was under intolerable pressure from within and without and unable to negotiate with the Allied and Associated Powers on the basis of the Fourteen Points proclaimed by President Wilson. Far worse even was the apathy and the increasing disintegration which prevailed on the Home Front.

In that critical hour the Emperor failed to stand the test. He shirked his responsibilities by abandoning his post in Berlin. Had he remained, he would have been able to give the decisive commands which could have preserved public order and have averted rebellion and civil war.

It was no wonder, therefore, that the lesser men in Berlin and elsewhere failed when their War Lord and Supreme Commander forsook them. A great number of the 2,000 officers in Berlin who were on leave volunteered for the formation of a battalion of officers to suppress rebellion. But instead, revolutionary propaganda was allowed to continue unhindered and among the war-weary troops it made headway, chiefly amongst those who were not serving at the front. The navy acquired the sorry privilege of taking the lead in subversion (ever since the Battle of Jutland the big men-o'-war had remained inactive in port). Sailors everywhere paraded with red flags and led the dregs of the army in marches along the main roads and towards Berlin. Early in November Magdeburg was "conquered," and it was only a question of days before Berlin was to meet a similar fate.

Unperturbed by these surging floods of revolution and defeatism, the Government offices in Berlin continued their routine work. I attended conferences in the "Foreign Office" and in the Ministry of War, and was entrusted with taking over the huge tasks of the High Command of the army in the Ukraine in civilian matters. But I received no specific instructions to liquidate the various enterprises and it was left entirely to the discretion of the Legation at Kiev whether this was to be done or not.

My work in Berlin having been done, the question now arose: was I to return to Kiev? It seemed senseless, since the dissolution of the vast war machine was imminent and the evacuation of the Ukraine merely a matter of weeks, or at the most of a few months. Moreover, a rising on the part of the Poles was expected, in which case the German troops in the Ukraine would be cut off. After much heart-searching I decided to do what I considered to be my duty and return to Kiev.

I left Berlin on November 7th and the spectacle presented by the German capital on the evening of that day remains deeply impressed on my memory. The streets were thronged with silent crowds, milling along in a mood of despair and apathy, oppressed by some invisible, inescapable, and yet unknown fate. Some stray shots in side streets provided an almost welcome interruption to the ghastly silence. The train, which was well heated, although almost empty, left punctually. The journey to Warsaw and then on through Poland to the Ukraine passed without incident and I reached Kiev punctually. Two days later the revolt broke out in Warsaw. Railway communication was interrupted and we in Kiev were caught in a trap.

Events now began to move rapidly in the Ukraine. It was evident that the days of the *Hetman* régime were numbered. The German occupation troops grew restless and this unrest was accentuated by the creation of Soldiers' Councils. But this instrument for undermining the morale of the army did not work so well in the Ukraine as it did elsewhere. The average soldier was sufficiently intelligent to realize that without strict discipline he would be completely lost hundreds of miles away from home. The older age groups behaved comparatively well and the active regiments were fighting units of the first order. But it needed some responsible men in Kiev, among them the *Chargé d'Affaires,* Count Berchem, to explain to the men with infinite pains at numerous meetings with the "Soldiers' Councils" that they must hold out in this remote outpost until their turn came to be evacuated. Aware of the increasing menace of Bolshevism, they readily acquiesced.

The first stage of the internal collapse in the Ukraine produced a radical Left-wing Nationalist movement there which was headed by the two popular leaders Vinnitchenko and Petljura. They had formed a kind of army consisting half of regular soldiers and half of partisans. Similar insurrections flared up in various parts of the country headed by local robber chieftains. The Ukraine has had many such leaders, half patriots and half robbers. In Odessa an Allied naval detachment had taken possession of the city, but the Allied commanders cautiously refrained from advancing further into the country. Although some insignificant French Vice-Consul made some pronouncement from time to time, our hope that he or some other Allied representative would negotiate with the German High Command or with the Legation for a speedy evacuation of the Ukraine remained unfulfilled. We had hoped that some arrangement might be reached by which power would be handed over to the Allies, so as to avoid the anarchy out of which the Soviets were to emerge. But nothing of the sort happened.

In the meantime the overthrow of the *Hetman* régime became inevitable. The only people who were prepared to risk their lives for him were a few thousand former Russian officers and non-commissioned officers, commanded by a valiant old Tsarist cavalry general, Count Keller. The German troops had to remain neutral and only gave support one way or the other when they or the vital interests of the occupation forces were menaced. The conquest of Kiev by the Ukrainian nationalist army under Vinnitchenko and Petljura, therefore, was rather a tame affair, although there was some sporadic street fighting and artillery fire. The *Hetman* sought refuge in the German Legation. This was a strictly guarded secret which, if revealed, would have meant certain death for him and grave danger to the Legation itself. A week later, disguised as a wounded German Army surgeon, he was taken to Germany in a Red Cross train. He was granted a comfortable allowance by President Hindenburg and lived in a pleasant villa at Wannsee. How he fared in the catastrophe of 1945 I do not know.

The Vinnitchenko "Government" was short-lived. It comprised well-meaning men who were opposed to Bolshevism. But they lacked anything which might have enabled them to stem the Red tide which was rolling pitilessly in from the East. They had no capable men, no regular army, no money, no organization. All they had was patriotism and goodwill.

During those weeks when we were cut off from Berlin, we lived in utter seclusion and received neither telegrams from the Foreign Office nor any mail, as all means of communication were interrupted. The Ukrainian newspapers provided us only with little and unreliable news about the Armistice and about the revolution. At long last, however, telegraphic communication with Berlin was restored and the first code telegram from the Foreign Office arrived. I remember how we opened it with trembling fingers, expecting it to contain some momentous news, only to find some routine communication that something or other had happened in Spitzbergen or Greenland. But this was soon followed by more serious news about a renewed revolt in Berlin with fierce fighting in the vicinity of the Friedrichstrasse Station. And so we began to wonder in what state we should find the capital on our return.

By the beginning of the New Year the evacuation of the Eastern Ukraine by the German troops had been completed. The Soviet forces exerted severe pressure on Kharkov, and this important center was captured in the first few days of January. The German High Command resolved to evacuate Kiev and the Western Ukraine. On January 12th we members of the Legation staff entrained in a special train with Ukrainian personnel. We were doubtful whether we should reach our first goal, Brest-Litovsk, unmolested. But the journey passed off without incident. Huge crowds assembled at the intermediate stations and stared malevolently and suspiciously at the *bourgeois* foreigners, without, however, trying to molest us.

On arrival at Brest-Litovsk we drove to the headquarters of a German division which had remained at its post and thus kept the way to East Prussia open for the evacuating units. The main railway line from Brest-Litovsk to Warsaw and Berlin had been interrupted by the Poles since November, and the German divisions stationed there had deserted their posts and returned home. We crossed the German frontier at Prostken in East Prussia and managed to catch a train to Berlin. I bought a newspaper at the station and it contained the news of the murder of the revolutionary leaders, Rosa Luxemburg and Karl Liebknecht. President Ebert had fixed a date for a general election. This news confirmed my hope that Germany might be spared the horrors of Bolshevik rule which I had been able to observe so closely during the preceding months.

In Berlin I found everything entirely unsettled and on the brink of collapse. Order had been restored somehow; there was no more street fighting. But the general mood of the Leftist radicals was provocative. The workers were restless and were often incited to strikes by subversive elements. The morale of the returning troops was good, but they were without firm guidance and soon gave way to the irresistible desire to go home. The new Government, with President Ebert as chief of the State and under the dominant influence of the Social Democrats, fought valiantly to stem the Red tide. But they were hampered by the necessity of retaining the allegiance of their principal followers, the moderate part of the working population, and by accusations that they were reactionaries and traitors to the cause of the revolution. After the election of the Constituent Assembly, which had clearly indicated that the majority of the German people were opposed to a Bolshevik revolution and in favor of progressive evolution, things settled down a bit in Berlin.

By and by, resolute and popular officers, mostly holding the rank of colonel or captain, assembled some hundreds or thousands of faithful men from their units and formed so-called "Free Corps" which were resolved to fight the revolutionary bands in a more or less close subordination to the Government. It took some pains and much diplomacy on the part of the regular army, the *Reichswehr*, which was in process of slow formation, and its commander, the loyal and able General von Seeckt, to persuade these adventurous men to refrain from counter-revolutionary violence and to amalgamate with the regular troops. In these years the Social-Democratic Minister of Defence, Noske, rendered invaluable services to his country by trusting to the loyalty of his generals and declining every opportunity to seize the reins of the Government himself as dictator.

Though the immediate and deadly peril of a chaos receded slowly into the background, the general situation throughout Germany was far from normal. Again and again violent outbursts flared up here and there. The Communists seized power in some parts of the Reich—in Bremen, in Saxony, and in the Ruhr. In Munich a fully fledged Soviet Republic was established which the Bavarians were not able to cope with. They had to fall back on the help of Prussian troops, who suppressed the revolt in a short time.

Berlin offered the most depressing and disgusting aspect to the visitor by a blend of decay, riot, and frivolity. At noon a detachment of revolutionary soldiers paraded the streets, a huge sailor marching in front and waving a red banner. The very dregs of the slums from the eastern suburbs mingling with demobilized or deserted soldiers in their dirty and neglected uniforms gave the streets the dominant note. All the more repulsive was the impression of vice and licentiousness obtruding itself to the onlooker. Everywhere night clubs sprang up mushroomlike. The great hall in the fashionable Hotel Kaiserhof was transformed into a gambling casino. Private society seemed obsessed by a hysterical craving for dancing and parties.

Amid this unsavory mixture of vice, rioting, and decay, with which

11

a high percentage of despair was mingled, the bureaucracy continued its work unperturbed. But the Foreign Office had also received an injection of revolutionary medicine, with the result that it became more bureaucratic than ever. The revolution was personified by *Geheimrat* Schuler. He shattered the old historical structure dating from Bismarck and built up a new organization big enough to be the political brain of a victorious World Power. The sanctum of the old diplomacy, the Political Department, the domain of Holstein, was abolished. The Foreign Office was divided into geographical departments: Western European, Eastern European, and American. In these departments both political and economic affairs were dealt with. To almost every country one official for political affairs was assigned, and one for economic affairs. There were special departments for personnel matters and for legal and general economic questions, such as the conclusion of commercial treaties and tariffs. There was much to be said for the concentration of political and economic affairs in one department, but the whole apparatus grew very unwieldy, and foreign policy, which can only be handled in an efficient way by a few able and experienced officials, was diluted and became the object of mass conversations. Besides, the introduction of a huge bureaucratic apparatus was most untimely, when Germany had suffered a crushing defeat and had passed out of the world-wide political scene. One of the old janitors of the Foreign Office remarked skeptically: "I don't know what is going on. The German Reich is growing smaller and smaller but the Foreign office bigger and bigger."

There was still another reason which deterred free-lances from rushing into the posts of ambassadors and Ministers. They soon found a fly in the ointment: the outwardly so brilliant life of a diplomat was soon discovered to be an arduous one, demanding a considerable knowledge of history, economics, law, and a mastery of several languages. But above all it demanded a great sacrifice: the renunciation of political influence at home. The ambassador and minister loses his grasp of home affairs by continued absence from his country. It demands some inner independence and character to stand on one's own legs, being devoid of the support of parties and press at home. That was a sacrifice which most of the amateur diplomats were not prepared to make. So they retired from these outposts into the more profitable realm of home politics.

After my return from Kiev I was assigned to the Eastern Department under Herr Nadolny, who later on was Ambassador at Ankara and Moscow, and German delegate at the Disarmament Conference. He entrusted me with the sub-department for the Baltic. Nadolny did not remain my chief for long. After a few weeks he was transferred to the office of President Ebert. His deputy functioned as his intermediary successor; an elder consular official, amiable, but lacking the qualities for so important a department in such troubled times. Thus we three chiefs of the three sub-departments—Russia, Ukraine, Baltic—were pretty autonomous and enjoyed it.

The three newborn Baltic States, entrusted to my political care—Latvia, Estonia, and Lithuania—soon developed into a hotbed of international politics. One of the first major clashes with Bolshevism happened there. After the evacuation of Estonia and Eastern Latvia by the German troops, Soviet troops occupied these territories and the beautiful ancient capital of Riga. By their terrorist methods they succeeded in keeping down the majority of the population which abhorred Bolshevism. In the western parts considerable detachments of German troops under the command of General Count von der Goltz had remained on the request of a rightist Latvian Government formed by anti-Bolshevik Latvian elements and backed chiefly by the Balts. They had promised the German soldiers who were willing to help them in their fight against Bolshevism to give them land and to accept them as permanent settlers.

In view of the general conditions prevailing in Europe as a consequence of the breakdown of Germany, such a scheme was bound to prove unworkable in the long run, the more so as the rightist Latvian Government was just as little representative of the country as the leftist in Riga; and the German Balts, the backbone of active resistance against the Bolshevik invasion, were unpopular with the Latvians, as former overlords and alleged suppressors. In these troubled times, however, the average German soldier believed in the promise of getting land as a reward for his services, and was ready to fight, to die, and to suffer hardships for the liberation of the country.

By a bold surprise attack Riga was liberated in the spring of 1919, and German and Baltic troops pushed the Soviet forces back to a line well within Estonia. But soon the situation grew extremely complicated. The rightist Latvian Government was overthrown, and a more leftist Government took its place. The Estonians were just as opposed to Bolshevik as to German occupation. The Allied Powers grew aware of the situation and tried to find a way out of the dilemma. They wanted the Germans to leave the country, but they did not want to reinstate Soviet rule. Consequently they started their counteraction with a mild pressure; but the screw of protests was tightened with ever-increasing vigor.

The German Government was almost helpless. Though perfectly willing to comply with the Allied demands, it lacked authority over the recalcitrant troops in the Baltic and had no means of coercion whatsoever. Count von der Goltz remained adamant, and the rank and file were firmly convinced that the Latvians should not be allowed to cheat them by depriving them of the price for their continued fight—the promised land. More and more they split up into single units under popular commanders. Here also, as in Germany, numerous "Free Corps" were being founded. They were still more recalcitrant than the old units.

At last General von der Goltz gave in. But he took the most ominous and unsoldierly resolve imaginable: he submitted to the order of the Berlin Government to return home, but he came to Berlin, without making the least attempt to persuade his troops to follow him. Probably they would have done so, as he enjoyed great authority among them. Instead of choosing either alternative—to induce his troops to follow him home or to disobey Berlin and stay with his men to the bitter end—he left them without leadership and turned up alone in Berlin.

The inevitable result was that most members of the "Free Corps," who had more and more developed into a kind of foreign legion or *lansquenets,* ready to fight for the sake of fighting, remained stubbornly in the Baltic and insisted on the promised land: the more orderly of the "Free Corps" had already started to settle and had organized some agriculture and farming. The commanders, some of whom came to see me in the Foreign Office, showed not the least inclination to obey the order from Berlin.

In this emergency the German Cabinet resolved to invite an International Commission, which was to examine the situation on the spot and find a way out of the deadlock. The Allied Powers accepted this proposal and appointed a Commission composed of a French, a British, an American, a Japanese, and an Italian general; the President was to be the French General Niessel. As president of the German Baltic Commission, Admiral Hopman was to act with Major von Kessler as Chief of Staff and with myself as delegate of the Foreign Office. Several German officers from the General Staff, among them Captain—later Field Marshal—von Küchler, were also assigned to accompany the delegation. The choice of Hopman and Kessler was made because in 1918 they had been cut off with numerous units of German troops in Southern Ukraine, had been interned and had skilfully performed the repatriation of these troops by negotiating diplomatically with the Inter-Allied authorities. Thus they had some training in the difficult task awaiting them.

On a rainy November day in 1919 the train with the Inter-Allied Commission and numerous personnel was due on the Bahnhof Friedrichstrasse. I had been requested by Baron Maltzan, the new chief of the Russian Department, to welcome the delegation together with Captain von Küchler. I loathed this task, as I felt intensely the shame and humiliation of Germany, which had to submit to the orders of enemy officers. Besides, General Niessel had the reputation of being gruff and rabidly anti-German. My anger was roused still more when the train stopped and French *poilus* in full war outfit rushed out of the train and guarded the entrances to the cars. I squeezed myself through the narrow dark corridor leading up to the room where the Commission was assembled at a round table, like a Ku-Klux-Klan court passing its verdict on a criminal. My brain worked feverishly on how I could demonstrate to Niessel my thorough dislike of this job.

I resolved to address him in English, legitimately, as the majority of the members of the Commission spoke English. My scheme worked. Niessel turned red in the face and, stuttering with anger, requested me to speak French. After a lengthy pause I complied with his demand. I did not mention this insignificant episode to anybody, but fifteen years later I was to acquire some fame by it. In 1934 General Niessel published his memoirs about the expedition to the Baltic and described this incident in detail. When the German press got hold of the book one East Prussian paper dug out this episode and printed it with a glaring headline, "Proud and manly behavior of a German Counsellor of Legation." I got this clipping in Tokyo and was highly amused. Apart from this episode Niessel mentioned me in a decent and fair manner in his book.

During a conference of the two delegations the procedure for the work of the "Inter-Allied Baltic Commission" was settled. Both Commissions, the German and the Inter-Allied, shared the opinion that successful work could only be performed on the spot. It would be necessary to talk matters over with the most diverse authorities, persons, and units—German provincial officials, Latvian and Lithuanian representatives, and, above all, with the commanders of the German "Free Corps." The transport and communication facilities were so unsettled that it was senseless to establish standing headquarters at Berlin, Königsberg, or Riga. Consequently it was decided that the work of both Commissions should be done in a train which might move to all the spots where troubles had arisen and quarrels were to be settled.

Thus one of the most extraordinary and singular international actions was started and completed. For six weeks a long train with many wagons was our habitation and with it both Commissions roamed through troubled Eastern Europe with its undefined boundaries, uncertain little governments, uprooted transport facilities, and unruly military detachments, trying to get about 60,000—70,000 disappointed, disgruntled, desperate German soldiers out of a foreign country defended by them against Bolshevism, and to repatriate them.

The collaboration between the German and the Inter-Allied Baltic Commission was far from satisfactory at the beginning. The Inter-Allied generals, above all Niessel, had still to learn their lesson. They came to

Germany with the conviction that as victors all they had to do was to give some orders, and then all would be well. By and by they learned that in such chaotic circumstances they were helpless. They met with a bitter disappointment at the start. The first stage of our expedition was at Königsberg, where a conference of the provincial authorities and of the *Reichswehr* officers had been convoked in the old historic castle where the Kings of Prussia had been crowned. The *Oberpräsident* of the province, Herr Winnig, being a Social Democrat, General Niessel had anticipated the very subservient and obsequious attitude of this official; he speculated on making a lasting impression by a truculent and dictatorial attitude. Winnig, a proud and patriotic man, was in no way impressed, but gave unmistakable vent to the exasperated and bitter feeling of East Prussia, which—as a consequence of being cut off from the Reich by the "Corridor"—felt forlorn and menaced. The conference ended in total failure. Somewhat subdued, the Inter-Allied Commission proceeded to Tilsit. It deemed the attitude of the local press entirely unsatisfactory. Some commanders of the "Free Corps" who followed the summons for a conference were disinclined to obey a French general. Niessel telegraphed to Paris that he was unable to bring about the evacuation of the Baltic without an army of 75,000 men.

Then the dramatic turn came. The "Free Corps" broke down. The hardships of winter made further resistance impossible. Hungry, starved, without winter equipment and provisions, in turn all the "Free Corps" declared their readiness to go home. It was a great triumph for General Niessel. Now the second part of his task began: to organize the evacuation and the transport to Germany of the different units. It was a most complicated task which demanded hard thinking, much organization, and never-ending negotiations. The heaviest part of the task lay on the shoulders of the German delegation, especially of Major von Kessler, the Chief of Staff. As he was familiar with the Eastern theater of war and had some authority over the "Free Corps," it was he who had to advise Niessel. It was amusing to observe how the soldiers of both nations got on increasingly well with one another, speaking the same military language.

The following weeks we travelled to and fro in East Prussia, Latvia, and Lithuania. We stayed some time at Tilsit and Tauroggen and other places famous in the Napoleonic wars. Then we drove into Latvia or Lithuania as far as possible. Suddenly the tract was interrupted. There was no communication between the two small countries. Lengthy negotiations followed. The Inter-Allied Commission wanted the different units of the "Free Corps" to proceed on certain roads and was suspicious lest they change their minds and stay in the country or start a counter-revolution. The "Free Corps" preferred to choose their own way home. The so-called

Avalov-Bermont Army proved to be a most unruly and riotous crowd. Avalov-Bermont, an adventurer from the Russian Army, had, being a Georgian, promoted himself to the rank of Prince. "Prince" Avalov had assembled a crowd of similar adventurers who proclaimed that they would liberate first Latvia and then Russia from Bolshevism. He was on variable terms— sometimes friendly, sometimes in bitter enmity—with the Latvian Government and the German "Free Corps." His men, robbers and daredevils, strongly opposed to being disbanded, mutinied against the Inter-Allied Commission. Our train had to pass stations occupied by these men with full speed because sometimes they fired or threw hand grenades.

Other urgent problems arose. Some places, like Schaulen in Lithuania, were full of refugees from the country. Communications were interrupted, the sanitary and feeding conditions deteriorated, and something had to be done. One morning a *draisine* (an open platform car, running on rails and set in motion by pushing a handle to and fro) was started with a mixed crew: a German major, a French colonel, a Lithuanian officer, a railway official, and myself. We "rowed" the 30 kilometres to Schaulen, got hold of some officials, and arranged everything for opening up the line.

There was behind the attitude of the "Free Corps" and that of certain German individuals and officers a vague hope or expectation that German troops and the "Free Corps" might be called upon by the Allied Powers to fight Bolshevism and to join the detachments of these Powers or the White Russian armies which were trying to overthrow the Soviet Government. It was well known that Mr. Churchill favored similar plans and that the Latvian and Lithuanian forces were not deemed reliable. There was even a faint hope that General Niessel, himself a rabid anti-Bolshevik, might be won for this idea. But nothing came of it, and the "Free Corps" had to go home and were disbanded, but only perfunctorily. They retained a certain comradeship. They went into action in Upper Silesia when Korfanty started his insurrection there in 1921. They were revived when the French entered the Ruhr in 1923, and they soon took sides with National Socialism, of which they became the first and most ardent supporters.

The Baltic Commission, having fulfilled its task, proceeded, just before Christmas, to Riga for some formal negotiations with the Latvian Government. That gave me the opportunity of getting acquainted with this charming old town, one of the very jewels of medieval German Gothic brick architecture. To walk in the narrow, snowbound streets, lined with little homes, the bells ringing solemnly from the church steeples, was like a fairy tale. In the opera we enjoyed an excellent performance of Tchaikowsky's *Pique Dame*. The concluding chapter of our expedition was a short stay in Kowno, the face of which bore the familiar marks of the ordinary Russian provincial town. After the return to Berlin the Commissions were disbanded, though much work was left to be done in the following months to bring this political episode to a conclusion.

Meanwhile, my new chief, Baron von Maltzan, had installed himself firmly as head of the Russian Department. He was an old friend of mine since our university days, as he was a member of the *Borussia* in Bonn. I had met him often during my Berlin years, and later on in The Hague. He was one of the most forceful personalities of post-war Germany. Very intelligent, though not learned, he blended an iron will and energy with a great subtlety and flexibility of method. His great intellectual qualities were somewhat discounted by a cynicism and an outspoken disdain of the inferior people with whom he had to work; and as such he regarded almost anybody whom he met. He was handicapped by a sort of superiority complex and by the fact that the ethical part of his character was not up to his intellect and political courage. He was to play a great part during the following years as head of the Eastern Department, and then as Secretary of State and Ambassador in Washington, until he was killed in an airplane crash in 1927.

As Baltic politics receded into comparative insignificance during the following months Maltzan deemed it advisable to transfer me to another post. So in March, 1920, I was appointed First Secretary to the new German Legation at Warsaw. After a short interval, when a free-lance diplomat had represented Germany after the Armistice at the newly founded Polish Government, diplomatic relations had been interrupted between both countries. Now a new effort was to be made to establish them on a more lasting basis.

I left the Foreign Office in a more consolidated state than I had entered it a year before. Preparations for the peace negotiations in Versailles, which had played a predominant part, had ceased with the signing of the Versailles Treaty, or *Diktat*, as it was immediately called in Germany. But the controversies about the question, whether it was right to sign or whether signature had to be repudiated regardless of the consequences, still divided public opinion and proved to be one of the major stumbling-blocks of the Weimar Republic. Count Brockdorff-Rantzau, the Foreign Minister, had resigned over this conflict and had retired into private life for the time being. This retirement deprived Germany of a strong and brilliant director of foreign policy. I was in too subordinate a position to have entered his orbit. It was some years later that a close and intimate co-operation started between us.

The general situation in Germany was far from settled. Before I left Berlin, a dangerous crisis shook the Republic to its foundations; the so-called Kapp-Putsch. The attempt of rightest elements to seize power was thwarted. As officials and officers remained loyal, even the initial attempt to capture the machinery of government in the capital failed. The Cabinet, which had managed to escape from Berlin, organized counter-measures from outside. Even without the general strike proclaimed by the workers, the insurrection would have broken down. But the reper-cussions were to be felt for some time after. The Communists seized this welcome opportunity to start new revolts and strikes in the industrial areas. Political murders, perpetrated by Nationals—the murder of Erz-berger above all—were sinister omens. The ever-present danger of a French march into Germany across the Rhine became manifest in the occupation of Frankfurt under a flimsy pretext.

I was full of disquiet when I left Berlin early in April, 1920. It was evident that my work in Poland—a country with which our relations were so hardened by mutual age-long antipathy—would be extremely difficult. Everything had to be built up from scratch, as there had been no legation up to now in Warsaw. It was an omen of the abnormality of the situation that I had to proceed to Warsaw via Danzig, the direct line Berlin-Posen having not yet been re-established.

2. WARSAW, 1920–1921

The Foreign Office had requested me to do all the preparatory work for the installation of our Legation, above all to find rooms for the office and, if possible, to buy a house as a permanent residence. The first steps having been taken, the newly appointed Minister, Count Oberndorff, was to follow me. I had known Oberndorff for very many years. His parents had lived in Heidelberg in an old house overlooking the Neckar and had often entertained the members of my corporation. In the Foreign Office he had worked in my father's department. He was the prototype of the diplo-mat of the old school, cultivated, amiable, speaking excellent French and convinced that by personal contact between *grandseigneurs* of different nations the outstanding differences would be solved.

Having arrived in Warsaw, I went to the Polish Foreign Office with-out having secured a room in a hotel, as they were all crowded and I still lacked, at that time, the technique of bribing the porter. The amiable *Chef de Protocole,* Count Przezdiecki, ordered a youthful secretary to go with me. He found two rooms for me and my man servant in a third-class hotel in the ghetto district. It was infested with bugs. The next day I called on the German passport officer, who had been in Warsaw several weeks;

a former merchant from Poznania, he helped me to find a few furnished rooms which the cultivated Jewish occupant of the flat was prepared to sub-let. Thus it was possible for my wife to join me later on.

Even the question of finding rooms for the Legation was solved more quickly than I had anticipated. An elderly couple, proprietors of a dignified house in one of the side streets of the main street of Warsaw, the Ujasdowska, were willing to sell the house, even to the German Government. I closed the bargain as soon as possible in view of the declining value of Polish currency. The proprietors evacuated some rooms as offices for the Legation, and later on, when I had found a convenient flat for them, the whole floor.

It took me, however, one year to get the upper floor cleared of its inhabitants, and I succeeded only because of the help of the acting Foreign Minister, M. Skirmunt. Then new rooms were built for the office in the stable, which adjoined a small garden. Thus when I left Warsaw eighteen months later the Legation was quite presentable and worthy of the general political status of Germany. Our Ministers, who served many years in Warsaw, my friends Rauscher and Moltke, were quite satisfied with my purchase even in times when the Legation, and later on the Embassy, became one of the centers of social life.

I made contact with the political department of the Polish Foreign Office. Its chief, Cajetan Morawski, a wealthy landowner from Poznania, and a clever, agreeable, and not too chauvinistic man, informed me, when I first saw him, radiant with joy, that Marshal Pilsudski had conquered Kiev. An old dream of Polish imperialism had come true! The entirely unmotivated attack on the Soviet Union had paid handsome dividends for the prestige of the new army and for the aggrandizement of Polish territory in the east. In the Ukraine the Poles had vast interests as owners of a considerable part of the great estates which were also model farms being administered mostly by Germans or Czechs.

After having made the necessary preparations and established the indispensable contacts, I wired to Count Oberndorff, the lately appointed German Minister, that he might now start his mission. He arrived in due course with a Secretary of Legation and some personnel. He had to stay in a hotel. We had no motor-car. Everything was primitive and temporary. The Minister soon took up his duties and, being a Westerner at heart and soul and abhorring Bolshevism with an almost physical antipathy, he started his political task by offering to the Polish Government and his colleagues of the Diplomatic Corps the collaboration of Germany in the fight against Bolshevism. He met with no response at all.

Within a short period the Poles were in dire need of foreign help. The advance to Kiev had overtaxed the strength of the young Polish

Army. The Russians, with their traditional faculty for deploying their full military power only when attacked, had assembled considerable forces to expel the invaders from Russian soil. The Soviet Union succeeded in winning the support of many thousands of former Tsarist officers and non-commissioned officers who overcame their dislike of Bolshevism in order to help expel the Polish invader. Under the fierce blows of their attacks the Polish Army broke down and fled. Within a short time the distant front came alarmingly near to Warsaw. Refugees thronged the railway stations. And though an elegant crowd with numerous officers filled the restaurants and streets, preparatory steps for an evacuation had to be taken, at least for the *Corps Diplomatique*. We received neatly printed evacuation certificates from the Ministry of Foreign Affairs.

The Legation had secured from Germany a train for the transport of our nationals. In June when the Russians were twelve miles from Warsaw the moment came to evacuate the members of the Legation to Posen. Only the *Chefs de Mission* were to stay, but a few days later they followed us, greatly relieved.

So there we were in Posen, which had belonged to Germany for 150 years until eighteen months before. Outwardly it was "Polonized." The street names and the signposts were in Polish. But everything else—the cleanliness of the towns and their architecture, the neatness of the villages, the agricultural standard of the country—was Prussian. So was the mentality of the population. Although the most anti-German population of Poland, it was nevertheless permeated by the Prussian spirit with its craving for order and efficiency. The Poznanians were the Prussians of Poland and keenly felt their superiority over the backwardness of the *Kongressuwki*, as the inhabitants of the former Russian part were called. Though the Prussian administration had not been able to inspire love for Germany, it certainly had created a flourishing and highly educated middle class in the towns, forming the backbone of the intelligentzia of all Poland, which, on the whole, lacked this part of the social structure; and also a peasantry which was superior in agricultural efficiency to all the rest of the Polish peasantry.

The Polish nobility everywhere had the same high art of life. The *grand seigneur*, and even more so the Polish *grande dame*, has been one of Poland's most valuable assets in building up national prestige abroad. In the Diplomatic Service and as private citizens the Polish nobility have, by their adroitness, good manners, and looks, and by their sportsmanship, been effective propagandists for their country. There was tension prevailing also in Posen in the presence of coming events. Would the Soviet tide be stopped? Red troops were approaching the boundaries of East Prussia. Some units were pressed against the frontier and had to cross it. They

21

were disarmed. Would the Red Army overwhelm Poland and push on into Germany? And what would happen then? Would there be a Communist uprising or a fraternization of rightist elements with the Russians for a common fight against the West? Or both? In Danzig the dock workers had downed tools and refused to load ammunition and war material for the Poles in the war against Communist Russia.

Then the turn of the tide came. As in all successful battles, there was keen competition as to who had done the job, the "mircle of the Vistula"— Weygand or Pilsudski or some other Polish general? The answer is probably the same as that which General von Hammerstein gave when the question was discussed as to who had won the battle of Tannenberg in 1914; whether Hindenburg or Ludendorff or Hoffman or General von François had merited the highest decoration, the *Pour le merite*. Hammerstein answered, "Rennenkampf (then Russian Commander-in-Chief) has merited it." And so probably the Polish victory was due to the Russians themselves. They, probably, were too inexperienced to be able to concentrate their troops at the decisive points. Budenny had made his own war in Galicia. The Russian advance had exhausted itself; the Russian lines of communication were too long; and it needed only a slight impact to force the tide to run backwards. Thus the chase through the eastern parts of Poland started for the third time within a few months. When it came to a halt, both parties were ready to negotiate.

The weeks in Poznan, which after the first tension had turned out to be rather idyllic, soon came to an end. We had met some German friends who were still in the country; especially we had befriended a German wine merchant, who, intending to leave the country, had decided to liquidate his stock on the spot. As Hungarian wines were appreciated highly in Poznan, our friend excelled in these brands, and we spent the better part of some nights in drinking them. We were highly amused when the Polish secret police believed themselves to be on the track of a secret German plot on account of the light in our friend's windows.

Count Oberndorff did not return to Warsaw with the Legation, but went home on leave and then to Berlin for some conferences. In autumn he resigned his post and came back to Warsaw only for a short time to take leave. I had to act as *Chargé d' Affaires* until a new Minister was appointed. But as German-Polish relations deteriorated, the Foreign Office did not deem it appropriate to send a fully fledged Minister to Warsaw. I was entrusted to represent the Reich as *Chargé d'Affaires* for a longer period. Thus it turned out that a heavy responsibility was laid upon my inexperienced shoulders for a whole year.

When the Polish Government and the *Corps Diplomatique* had reinstalled themselves in the capital, things settled down to a more normal

Dr. Herbert von Dirksen

course. I was able to take stock of the situation and start regular work. But relations between the two countries were far from normal. For 150 years, since the partition of Poland, no sovereign Polish State had been in existence. During the war Pilsudski, the most popular leader in Poland, had backed the Central Powers and had with newly organized legions fought on their side. In 1916, Chancellor von Bethmann Hollweg had pleaded for a resurrection of Poland, and a Polish Government, with Pilsudski at its head, had been proclaimed. The wisdom of this step had been doubted by influential political circles in Germany and Austria. It was argued that thus a separate peace with Russia had become impossible and that, on the other hand, the Poles would never be satisfied with their dependence on the Central Powers. That is what happened.

The relations between Pilsudski's Government and its sponsors became more and more unsatisfactory. At last a break was unavoidable. Pilsudski was arrested and honorably imprisoned in the fortress of Magdeburg, a measure which (as Pilsudski remarked humorously in later years) made it possible for him to become the head of the new Polish State, as the slur on his reputation, the collaboration with the Central Powers, had been removed. The problem why Bethmann's experiment of a Polish State, sponsored by the Central Powers, failed is a too complicated one to be treated here. Probably it would have been insoluble even if it had been handled with greater statesmanship and adroitness from both sides.

The formation of the Polish State by the Allies after Germany's downfall created an unbridgeable gulf between the two powers. The feeling of being menaced by a resentful neighbor within striking distance—about sixty miles—from Berlin created an atmosphere of distrust from the beginning. By the cession of the "Corridor" to Poland, the German East was broken up and East Prussia was severed from the Reich.

More than two million Germans came under Polish rule, which they found unbearable. A million returned home and swelled the ranks of a discontented population. The remaining million were subjected to harsh and discriminatory treatment by a Polish Government which was resolved to retaliate for the harshness of Prussian rule—a harshness which had been considerably exaggerated, as a well-to-do middle class in the cities and a prosperous peasantry in the country testified. Polish greed for German territory spread to East Prussia and Silesia. As the population of Masuria, the southern part of East Prussia, had voted for Germany, this danger spot was removed, but the Silesian problem loomed, unsolved, in the background. A huge amount of inflammable material was piled up between the two nations.

I do not hope to give an objective and comprehensive survey of the German-Polish problem by these remarks. It is extremely complicated and obscured by life-long mutual antipathy, the more deep-seated as without doubt a feeling of superiority over the Pole is inherent in the German and keenly resented by the Pole. The difficulty of peacefully living side by side is further complicated by the fact that the two countries are not separated from each other by clear-cut boundaries, and that both nations are closely interlocked with each other. It is impossible to draw a line of demarcation separating the two nations. Islands of the other population are bound to remain and to create ill-feeling. What I want to point out for the sake of my narrative is the fact that sufficient explosive material was assembled to endanger, again and again, the establishment of peaceful and conciliatory feeling. From the German side the dominant factor to be taken into consideration was that the "Corridor" moved German public opinion to its core even in the period of deepest prostration. Germany has always been unanimous in claiming a just settlement of the "Corridor" problem.

Things might have been easier if the newborn Polish State had been a healthy, strong, well-administered structure, as, for example, Czechoslovakia soon became, although Czech hatred of the Germans equalled that of the Poles. But the national characteristic of the Poles, their historic past, and the delimitations of their new State prevented this. It was a superhuman task to weld together the three different components of the new Poland: the well-to-do and highly cultivated Prussian, the easy-going Austrian, and the backward Russian part. The inherent disunity in the Polish character which had so much favored the partitions had been intensified by existence for 150 years under three different sovereignties.

The National Democrats, led by Roman Dmowski, were intensely nationalistic, and rather more favorably inclined towards Russia than Pilsudski and his huge following in Eastern Poland and Galicia, which hated Russia. Both parties disliked each other intensely. The feuds between them made up the internal history of Poland between the two wars. What Pilsudski ordered was not obeyed in Poznania; and when the Endecja, or National Democrats, were at the helm of the Government, they had nothing to say in *Kongressowka*, in Eastern Poland. The separatist feeling went so far that the military adherents of Pilsudski favored the round-cap—the *Maciejowka*—with their uniform, while the National Democrats preferred the *Konfederatka*, the high cap with its four corners. That Poland was infiltrated with about 33 per cent foreigners—Germans, Russians, Ukrainians, Jews, Lithuanians—did not add to the strength of the newborn State, but increased its suspicion and the tendency to oppress the minorities.

If Poland had produced a real statesman with clear vision and moderation as its leader—a Masaryk or Kemal Pasha—things might have taken

24

another turn. But Marshal Pilsudski lacked these qualities. Perhaps he was the most fascinating, interesting, tragic, and inspired leader amongst European statesmen. He was a passionate patriot with a clear vision of his nation's shortcomings—shortcomings which were also his own. He was utterly unselfish. He had boundless courage. But he was a romantic adventurer and his very nature made his unable to develop steady and moderate national leadership. He started his reign with the adventure of the war against the Soviet Union, he continued with the *coup de main* against Vilna, he suffered Korfanty's attack on Upper Silesia, in 1926 he started a revolt to seize power, in 1933 and 1936 he proposed to France a war of aggression against National-Socialist Germany, and in the meantime concluded a pact of friendship with Hitler. There was always a touch of romanticism and adventure in his acts, while his adversaries excelled by stubbornness and narrow-mindedness which were just as detrimental to a creative policy.

Thus the foreign policy of the new State lacked firmness and steadiness. Of course, a close alliance with France formed the cornerstone of this policy. But France did not encourage her ally to seek conciliation with its neighbor. Poland was intended to be the gendarme watching the suspect German evildoer even then when she was sincerely willing to be co-operative, as during the Weimar Republic. Relations with Soviet Russia remained uneasy and strained; an improvement generally was due to entirely opposite motives, not a tendency to reconciliation and friendship. Fundamentally the alliance with France was unpopular with most Poles, who resented the too evident tutelage of their Western ally. A hearty dislike between Czechs and Poles was one of the unavoidable ingredients of Eastern European politics. Thus the stage was set for one of the most menacing coalitions—the German-Russian friendship, based on a common dislike of the common neighbor, Poland.

Events had not progressed so far while I was in Warsaw. The Soviet Union was entirely out of the picture, and Germany then such a political nonentity that consideration of her was not deemed to be necessary. Thus I had to work under very trying circumstances. Even the technical conditions were inadequate. It was almost a year before the Foreign Office put a car at my disposal. Neither the personnel of the Legation nor the office rooms were adequate for the ever-growing amount of work to be done. To establish contacts with my colleagues from the Diplomatic Corps or Warsaw society was made impossible by an almost total boycott to which the German Legation was subjected. There were no invitations and no visits. *Agents provocateurs* were sent to the Legation. Abusive language was used by anonymous telephone callers. But we were on terms of close friendship with the Austrian and the Hungarian *Chargés d'Affaires,* the small

German community, and some courageous Poles. Daily life did not offer many distractions either. Warsaw still bore the marks of a Russian provincial town. Its surroundings did not invite week-end visits or excursions. Even with a car the bad roads prevented extensive trips. The theaters did not tempt us, as we did not understand Polish, and it was hard for an outsider to secure a ticket for the opera. Life was rather dull, and I was grateful to my wife because she never complained and made our home life as agreeable as possible in the circumstances.

Political excitement had to compensate for the dullness of everyday life. My routine work, it is true, was unsatisfactory and barren. The notes of complaints and protest which I had to transmit grew to mountains on the tables of the harassed officials of the German department. Even when dealing with the most conspicuous cases of violation of the rights of the German minority, they could not pierce the wall of ill-feeling and incompetence of the local authorities. The newly appointed head of the Department, Jackowski, a wealthy landowner from Poznania, was pleasant and helpful. I met him frequently during the following years, when he was appointed Polish Minister to Berlin, and we became good friends.

But with regard to foreign policy in general and internal development Warsaw was a most interesting post of observation. There was always some excitement in store. Either General Zeligowski marched into Lithuania and conquered Vilna, or some little revolt was started by Prince Sapieha or other members of the Opposition, or a change of Cabinet was due, or the peace negotiations with the Soviet Union in Riga were on the brink of breaking down, till—at last—the peace treaty was signed on March 18, 1921.

Unhappily the enterprising mood of Marshal Pilsudski and the Polish Government turned against Germany. The Poles, far from being satisfied with the huge cessions of German territory in the east of the Reich, claimed more Prussian provinces as ancient Polish territories. They contended that the Masurians were of kindred race and that, consequently, the southern part of East Prussia belonged to them. The same demand was claimed for Upper Silesia. The Versailles Conference had decided that the inhabitants of both territories should be called upon to vote about their destiny. The Masurians had declined the Polish by a vote of no less than 98 per cent in favor of Germany at elections controlled by Inter-Allied Commissions in the summer of 1920. This result deeply disappointed the politicians in Warsaw, and they had decided to take recourse to their old tactics of shock treatment, that is a *coup de main,* the use of armed force, in order to create *faits accomplis* by surprise. This scheme had worked well in General Zeligowski's attack on Vilna, and it was resolved to repeat it on a larger scale in Upper Silesia.

The preparations for a *coup* were clearly discernible for many months in Warsaw. Being cut off from sources of information, I resolved to call on those officials who might be supposed to grant an interview. Not that I thought that they would give me frank and truthful answers; but I guessed that by comparing the different subterfuges by which they would try to evade the truth, I should gather some valuable clues as to what was going on. I had conversations with Witos, the President of the Cabinet, a crafty peasant in jackboots, with some Ministers and other influential Poles within my reach. I expressed my concern about the atmosphere of enmity towards Germany and about adventurous plans with regard to Silesia which were discussed or hinted at in the press. The answers were not reassuring. The manner in which the more frank of the men reacted with embarrassment, the craftier in evident divergence from the facts, forced me to draw conclusions which I confided in several reports to my Foreign Office.

The scene became more and more lively. Detachments of troops passed the Legation, marching, cheered by the crowds, and carrying flowers in the muzzles of their rifles. If these demonstrations were meant to provoke the German Government to rash acts, they failed. Early in May the fuse in Upper Silesia was touched off. Korfanty, a leftist demagogue, leader of the Poles in Upper Silesia, and former Member of the Reichstag, started an insurrection with Silesian and Polish bands, well armed through direct and indirect help from Warsaw. Numerous acts of violence and arson, a wholesale persecution of the German population, followed. Of the detachments of the Inter-Allied troops the Italians offered some resistance and tried to restore order. They suffered some losses. Then the German population organized a resistance; thousands of war veterans from Silesia assembled in Breslau and were organized into poorly armed units of some kind; "Free Corps" from other parts of the Reich joined them. An embittered and murderous guerilla war ensued. The German volunteers succeeded in pressing back the Polish insurgents and, at last, in defeating them.

This time the Poles had overplayed their hand. The high-handed breach of peace in the face of Inter-Allied authorities and occupation troops was too flagrant to be allowed to pass unnoticed and be sanctioned silently as the capture of Vilna or the attack on the Kiev had been. World opinion was roused and reacted strongly, above all that of the Italians, whose soldiers had been killed. I had an exciting time in Warsaw in this period of undeclared war. I had to declare the responsibility of the Polish Government for Korfanty's insurrection by proving the active collaboration of military and semi-official departments. My relations with the authorities were still more restricted and strained than in ordinary times. But, on the other hand, I got into touch with my colleagues of the Diplomatic Corps, who were now willing to listen to the information I had to pass over to them about the events in Silesia. I had some conversations with Sir William Max Müller, the British Ambassador, a son of the famous German savant, with the Italian Ambassador, Tommasini, and with the apostolic delegate, Achille Ratti, later on Pope Pius XI.

At last, after two months, the storm subsided in Upper Silesia. The insurrection was quelled, the Poles had to submit again to the authority of the Inter-Allied Commission, which started to fix the frontiers allegedly according to the result of the vote of the Upper Silesians, of whom somewhat more than 60 per cent had taken sides for Germany.

My official work again ran on ordinary lines. I had to have conversations with M. Olszowski, the head of the Department for Economic Affairs, about negotiations to be started in order to settle the numerous economic problems which the foundation of the Polish State had created.

When everything was quiet again on the Polish front, the auspicious moment neared when I would be relieved from my arduous task in Warsaw. Already in spring I had insisted in Berlin that a regular Minister should be appointed to Warsaw. The Foreign Office agreed in principle, but Korfanty's insurrection reduced mutual relations to freezing-point. But when I repeated my request Herr von Schoen was appointed and arrived in Warsaw. I introduced him everywhere and took leave myself. I was given a very pleasant farewell lunch by the Ministry of Foreign Affairs and at least had the gratification of having made some personal friends. Then my wife and I hurried away from Warsaw—or, at least, we tried. Up to the last moment Warsaw held us in its grip. A railway strike broke out, and we had to postpone our departure for a day or two. At last, with a sigh of relief, we left the station.

3. THE POLISH DEPARTMENT, 1921–1922

After my return to Berlin in October, 1921, I was told in the Foreign Office that a new and important task was awaiting me. I was to become Chief of the Polish Department. This was one of the biggest and liveliest sections with some thirty or forty officials and employees. Most of them had to deal with Upper Silesian affairs. This appointment was meant to be a promotion and a reward for my work in Warsaw. But I was thoroughly tired of the task of handling our relations with Poland, a most depressing and negative affair. The wounds inflicted on our eastern frontier were still bleeding, and now the same operation had to be performed in Silesia. There was, however, no other choice left to me than to shoulder this task and to do my best to help my country.

The Foreign Office had settled down to more normal conditions during the last year. Herr von Haniel was Secretary of State for Foreign Affairs, a career diplomat and scion of a well-known dynasty of industrialists, an amiable man, with no passion or ambition for politics, but very fond of a gay, social life. As chief of the Eastern Department the Foreign Office had secured the services of an old, respected Jewish grain merchant, Herr Behrendt, who retired soon into private life and was replaced by the dynamic personality of Maltzan. The Polish press made guesses about the meaning of the nomination of the "moderate" Herr von Dirksen together wtih that of the activist Baron von Maltzan. Of course there was no sinister plot behind these appointments; it was simply a matter of routine on the part of the personnel department. That Maltzan steered his own course in Eastern policy was as great a surprise to the Foreign Office as to the rest of the world.

The looser the contact between the Ministers of Foreign Affairs with their Ministry became, the more these Ministers changed. The Foreign Office became a *rocher de bronze,* whereas the chiefs were reduced to the rôle of figureheads who had to rely on the experience and disinterestedness of the permanent officials. This they did and fared well with it.

During this year of my activity in the Foreign Office the foreign affairs were dominated by Chancellor Josef Wirth and the Foreign Minister, Walther Rathenau. Wirth, a schoolteacher from Baden and *protégé* of Erzberger, was an interesting personality. There could be no doubt he was endowed with an innate gift, amounting to a spark of genius, for foreign politics. He was a brilliant speaker and a good tactician on the parliamentary chessboard, but somewhat unbalanced and impressionable.

Rathenau, by his life, his books, and his tragic death, has become a statesman of world fame, and I need not dwell on the character and qualities of this brilliant and complicated man. He was charming and sympathetic, clever and skeptical, but I doubt whether he would have developed to a great and forceful statesman if a longer life had been his lot. He has been compared to a tree covered with blossoms, but bearing no fruits.

As my father had offered us a flat in the Margaretenstrasse, we settled down there with our two servants in some small rooms on the second floor. It was a *ménage à la bohéme,* but it was enough for our needs. We had no social duties to fulfil, as Berlin had not yet developed the turbulent social life of the outgoing twenties; and I had a subconscious feeling that my stay in the Foreign Office would be short-lived. Thus we limited our social life to seeing a few friends and making some new ones, among them Georg Kolbe, who was to be the greatest German sculptor of this time, equally impressive by his art as by his character and personality.

I can survey my official activity with some perfunctory remarks. Not much impressed itself on my memory during this period. It bore the hallmark of transition as far as German-Polish relations were concerned. On the one hand the consequences created by the war and the Versailles Treaty were put into practice; on the other, a start was made to come to normal relations with the new neighbor.

The delimitation of the new frontiers in Upper Silesia was repulsive from the German point of view. The partition of a homogeneous country on a 64:40 basis, according to the result of the plebiscite, was a hopeless task on the whole, but it could be performed with common sense in regard to the details. The Inter-Allied Commission excelled in finding solutions which made daily life a burden to the population and spread seeds of discontent. A waterworks was severed from the town. Workers had to cross the frontier twice or thrice on their way to the factories. That the workers did not live in the same country in which their factory was situated was a common occurrence. Mostly the Poles succeeded in singling out objects which they coveted—factory or hospital or mine—and the frontier was drawn accordingly. Besides, the Commission, when starting its work, was wholly inexperienced. When they arrived at the castle of Prince Biron von Kurland at Gross-Wartenberg early in their work, they inquired what was the geographical situation of the place and asked for a map, as they had not—so they confessed—the faintest knowledge of the country.

The theoretical foundations of the partitioned country were laid in Geneva by the League of Nations. Though the German Government was not, as far as I remember, officially invited to take part at the deliberations of the statute, representatives of the population were heard. The chief delegate for Upper Silesia was Count Welczeck, later Ambassador to Madrid and Paris. He acted courageously and adroitly on behalf of his country. After discussions and conferences lasting for many months a statute of the size of the Versailles Treaty emerged. It provided at least some international supervisory authorities as cushions destined to soften the full impact of the Poles. M. Calonder, from Switzerland, and M. Kaekenbeeck, from Belgium, did useful and disinterested work for many years and tried to find a solution for an insoluble task.

The constructive approach to normalize Polish-German relations was inaugurated by negotiations about the different questions to be settled, above all economic problems. I accompanied a technical commission of the Foreign Office on their voyage to Warsaw as their political adviser. In the meantime, Herr Rauscher had been appointed as our Minister to Poland. A South-German intellectual, a good writer, a member of the Social-Democratic Party, he enjoyed the special favor of President Ebert, who insisted on his nomination to Warsaw. Rauscher was one of the few outsiders who turned out to be a success. He developed into a most successful representative of his country in a difficult and thankless post over a period of eight years. He was popular in Warsaw society. He was one of the few Germans with *esprit*. We became very good friends. His sudden death from tuberculosis of the larynx saved him from the ignominies which would have awaited him in the Third Reich.

In Warsaw we fixed everything for the official beginning of the negotiations to be held at Dresden in the autumn. The President of the Polish delegation, M. Olszowski, an experienced and very witty man, and his opposite number, Herr von Stockhammern, one of the old guard of the Foreign Office experts for commercial negotiations, plunged into a sea of intricate problems which kept them busy—I don't know how long, probably years, as all these Eastern negotiations continued interminably.

At the most important event for the Eastern Department during this period—the Treaty of Rapallo—I was only an onlooker. It created an enormous sensation in the Foreign Office, as Maltzan had negotiated everything personally during the Conference at Geneva. Before this Conference there were—as far as I remember—only preliminary conversations with Soviet representatives in Berlin without, however, suggesting the conclusion of a political treaty. Military relations had already been resumed between the *Reichswehr* and the Red Army; and a German military mission headed by General Hasse, with Admiral Wülfing von Ditten as a member, had already paid a visit to Moscow. An economic agreement had been concluded in 1921.

The Foreign Office was dumbfounded. I am sure it was hardly informed about what was going on. I, personally, was rather enthusiastic, for I looked at this treaty as the first sign of a reviving national self-consciousness and as the only means of impressing the Poles. I was therefore highly amused when, at the daily morning press conference, to which all the heads of Departments gathered, I wanted to congratulate the Chief of the Russian Department; he apologetically shook his head and uttered, somewhat embarrassed, *"Ich wasche meine Hände in Unschuld"* (I wash my hands in innocence).

I soon had the opportunity of looking more closely at the proceedings in Geneva. I was summoned to Geneva for a conversation with the Polish Minister of Foreign Affairs, M. Skirmunt. There I met the whole delegation—Wirth, Rathenau, and a host of other politicians—who, with the exception of Maltzan, of course, had not quite recovered from the courage of their own initiative in the face of Lloyd George and the raging French delegation. The Genoa Conference and the preliminaries of the Treaty of Rapallo, with their hectic behind-the-scene intrigues, and the Soviets playing off one against the other till the German delegation outpaced and outwitted the others (above all Lloyd George) and concluded the deal, has been an object of thorough historical studies. That the German delegation resolved to conclude the treaty was solely due to Maltzan's energy and skill. He was not only the author of the political combination involved in this treaty, he was also the pilot who steered this frail boat through the shallow waters of his own delegation. First, he succeeded in winning over Chancellor Wirth, who was unprejudiced and politically minded. The main obstacle was, of course, Rathenau. He was a Westerner to the very core of his being, a refined and cultivated man who abhorred the Russian Method of ruling and terrorizing. He was at last persuaded, with the help of Herr von Haumer, to give way. Von Raumer, *Reichstag* member of the right-wing Liberal Party, was one of the most witty and brilliant men of the Weimar period. He gave Rathenau some courage by drawing an analogy with Bismarck in a similar situation. Rathenau signed the next day.

Two months later he was murdered by some fanatic nationalist, and the process of appeasement within Germany was again interrupted. The funeral ceremony for Rathenau in the Reichstag was one of the most impressive I have ever witnessed.

In the early autumn of 1922 a brighter prospect for my career seemed to develop. I seized my opportunity with doubled zeal as it offered me the way out of a task which I loathed. Our Embassy to the United States was to change its provisional post-war status to a permanent one. I was designated by the Foreign Office to be Counsellor of the Embassy. Maltzan had agreed to let me go. The Secretary of State, Haniel, the personnel department—everybody supported my nomination. But opposition came from quite an unexpected quarter. Chancellor Wirth had taken a liking to me and had the intention of appointing me as the first post-war Ambassador in Moscow. This nomination would, of course, have been a serious blunder, as I was much too young, too inexperienced in Russian affairs, and as I lacked the personal prestige which was indispensable to impress a government so susceptible as that of the Soviet Union. But it was very hard to get this idea out of Wirth's head, and six years later when I was appointed Ambassador to Moscow he congratulated me and reminded me of his initiative.

At the same time, however, he was opposed to my appointment to

Washington. He wanted a member of the Catholic Center Party in this post. The Consul he had in view, being a co-patriot from his native town Freiburg, was utterly unsuited. The Foreign Office objected. A compromise was found by appointing Herr Dieckhoff, who was a Catholic, though not a member of the Center Party, but very able and perfectly fit for this responsible post. I am dwelling somewhat more explicitly on this unimportant episode, as it illustrates the cross-currents and difficulties which an inexperienced parliamentary system created for the routine work of the permanent officials.

The net result of this muddle for me was that I found myself "between two stools." I was neither appointed to Washington nor to Moscow. I did not wait for the result of the dispute between Wirth and the Foreign Office, but—with the blessing of the latter—took a long leave designed to show my disgust at the methods of bungling important issues and to give me the opportunity of enjoying the hunting season in Silesia. My father put at my disposal a charming little baroque house at one of the farms of Gröditzberg, his estate in Lower Silesia. We moved our furniture there and enjoyed—for the first time since 1914—having our own home. My wife and I both loved country life, and I was perfectly prepared to go to the country for good and to administer a part of my father's estates. My father was very helpful in installing me in Adelsdorf without trying to secure my permanent stay in the country. So we enjoyed our independence and visited relatives and friends. I went to the Riesengebirge on a skiing tour. We had my father's horses at our disposal and waited for something to turn up.

After some months, in February, 1923, Maltzan wrote that he wanted to send me to Danzig as Consul-General. I was in no way delighted by the prospect. I was again tied to the Polish sector of our foreign policy. The scope of my activity was narrow. The nearness of Berlin—many members of the diplomatic profession thought it important to be near the capital—was more a liability to me than an asset. After some arguing, I agreed. In the beginning of May we started for Danzig.

4. DANZIG, 1923–1925

With our arrival in Danzig two of the happiest and most harmonious years in my diplomatic career began for my wife and me. Not that our personal life corresponded with the position of the representative of the old mother country in a state which had been carved out of German soil. Far from it. There existed no official residence for the German Consul-General. The house which had been bought for this purpose was still inhabited by its former residents. I had rented a flat in the seaside resort of Zoppot, but it was no more than a suite of furnished rooms with a malevolent landlady who interfered with our daily life. Entertaining even a few guests was a complicated and impersonal matter. We had no motor-car at our disposal and had to fall back on the railway or on the kindness of friends or colleagues to give us a lift in their cars. As the social life of Danzig spread over its suburbs—Langfuhr, Oliva, down to Zoppot—all this was rather arduous, especially for my wife, during the winter months.

It took me a year to settle comfortably in Danzig. Then we moved with our furniture into the meanwhile evacuated official residence, and a motor-car was financed by the concerted efforts of my father and the Foreign Office.

We soon felt at home in Danzig, where my ancestors had lived for 100 years and where the graves of some of them still were looked after by my father and me. But quite apart from these personal ties, everybody who had a sense for beauty had to love the Free City and its environs. It is a matter of European knowledge that Danzig was one of the jewels of medieval architecture. The proud old Gothic cathedral, the Marienkirche, whose dark red bricks glowed in the evening sun, testified to the pious religious feeling of the old German merchants of the Hansa as deeply as the Marienburg near by testified to that of the Knights of the Prussian Order.

But it was the characteristic trait of the old Hanseatic town that bygone centuries survived into the 20th century not merely in single monuments, scattered over the city among modern buildings. Danzig in its entirety formed a harmonious whole. A dozen other Gothic churches and chapels competed with the Marienkirche. The city hall, with its elegant, needlelike tower, dominated the Marktplatz, the rhythm of which was further stressed by the dignified Artushof. The massive *Krantor* still served to load and unload ships and shared the vicissitudes of its mother town through 500 years. There were not a dozen patrician houses which

34

had survived—there were hundreds of them, street after street, laid out and built according to one homogeneous plan, with front stairs and gracious ironcast rails—the so-called *Beischläge*. The tradition of these stately patrician mansions was upheld through the centuries, from the sterner Gothic houses to the gay luxury of the baroque *Uphagen-Haus*. Nor were these churches and representative buildings empty shells, walls dating from old times with modern cheap, pseudo-artistic furniture. They were decorated and enlivened by the refined taste and the exquisite workmanship of the generation which had constructed them.

The beautifully carved galleries and choirs of the Katharinenkirche competed with the stern luxury of the Artushof. One of the most precious treasures of the Marienkirche was the collection of ecclesiastical garments worn by the bishops and ecclesiastics of those centuries. And the famous painting by Memling, *Füngstes Gericht,* recalled the warlike and adventurous part of the Hanse City; it had been robbed by a freebooter captain, and had been recaptured, after bitter fighting in the Baltic, by the Danzig Admiral Benecke.

Prussian administration had enlarged and widened the city towards and along the sea-coast. A wide avenue of beautiful old ash trees opened the way to Langfuhr, the garrison of one of the crack cavalry regiments, the Death's Head Hussars, in which the Crown Prince had held the rank of Colonel. Oliva followed Langfuhr, leaning against the slopes of the Uralo-Baltic hills which run along the coast of the Baltic Sea. And then came Zoppot, an elegant and lively seaside resort with a long pier and a newly constructed *Kurhaus* and Casino where the gamblers of Eastern Europe gathered. Embedded between sea and beach and oak woods which covered the hills, it was the Dieppe or Brighton of Eastern Germany. Not far from Zoppot an obelisk indicated the frontier of Poland. A few kilometres further the small village of Gdingen was being built up in feverish haste by the Poles as a first-class harbor destined to compete with Danzig. It had been assigned to Poland as harbor and outlet to the sea, as its situation on the mouth of the Vistula was ideal for this purpose.

The hinterland of the Free State was well worth seeing, too, though its beauties were not so spectacular as those of the coast. The two *Kreise* (districts) which had been joined to the Free State were entirely agricultural and inhabited exclusively by Germans, many of them of Dutch origin. They were fertile marshes, comparable to those of the Netherlands and dominated by the sea and by the Vistula. It is a dangerous and treacherous ally, this stream, and the high dykes which follow its course were not always impenetrable. Blocks of ice piled up with terrific force when the thaw set in, and the floods often tore gaps in the dams and inundated the fertile soil. With justified pride my namesake, Dirksen, the *Deichhaupt-*

mann of the Marienwerder dyke system, showed me round and explained the intricacies of dyke strategy.

In the plain protected by these dykes rich peasants settled, living in spacious houses with front porches, the number of which testified to the size of the estate. Each estate was the equivalent of 100 acres.

Danzig and its hinterland were hemmed in on all sides by the compromise-seeking solutions which had been worked out at the conference table at Versailles. The "Corridor," with all its intricacies and absurdities, was firmly impressed on the memory of every traveller from Western Germany to East Prussia and to the Free State. There were some through-trains which crossed the "Corridor" under special rules, hermetically closed doors and windows and comparatively little delay. But woe to the traveller who went to the Free State or wanted to leave the train at a station in the "Corridor"! It took hours to go through the different customs and to travel on a slow train. So as not to make things too simple and let the boundaries coincide with the course of the Vistula, the makers of the peace treaty had carved five villages on the other bank of the river out of Prussian territory. They were completely isolated without hinterland, their only communication with the outer world being across the Vistula, and a dangerous communication at that during the highwater period. No more efficient means of propaganda as to the nonsense of the "Corridor" was possible than these five villages.

But Danzig was a hybrid also, and had evidently been created only with the intention of furnishing complicated themes for academic theses or scientific works for experts on the international law. Everywhere in the administration privileges granted to the Poles interfered with ordinary life. The railways, the post offices, and the harbor administration offered incessant objects for petty quarrels. Even the bookstore at the station was divided into a German and a Polish section. On the Westerplatte, a part of the harbor, special rights were conceded to the Poles, and when they installed an ammunition depot there, an outcry of indignation forced the Senate to bring the matter before the League of Nations.

One day, by a surprise move, the Poles extended their postal privileges, which had been limited to their official mail, to the territory of the city by establishing letter-boxes in Danzig. Another outcry against this attempt to eliminate the postal privilege of Danzig, and another complaint in Geneva! The international authorities charged by the League to supervise the smooth working of this complicated machinery, the High Commissioner, and the President of the Joint Board of the Harbor Administration proved less and less able to cope with these conflicts, and the number of questions in dispute engrossed in a mounting degree the agenda of the Council of the League.

The government of the Free City, represented by the Senate and its President, proved equal to their responsible and delicate task. President Sahm developed into a statesman who won the esteem of the Poles as well as of the League. More than six feet tall, silent, friendly, honest, thorough, and a good speaker, he represented Danzig during more than ten long difficult years. He was then elected Lord Mayor of Berlin, was transferred to the Diplomatic Service by Hitler, and died as minister in Oslo in 1939. Herr and Frau Sahm became intimate friends of my wife and myself. The members of the Senate, corresponding to ministers in an ordinary State, were mostly former Prussian officials converted into Danzigers. They were able men, and one of them, Volkmann, the Minister of Finance, was brilliant. The success of the first great experiment of stabilizing currency was his achievement.

Danzig, with its Reichsmark-currency, suffered from the mounting inflation just as severely as the Reich itself. In the summer of 1923 the bottom was knocked out of the mark as a consequence of the failure of the passive resistance against the occupation of the Ruhr by the French. The interruption of normal economic life, the financing of unemployment pay, and the other huge expenses merely by the printing press had sent the mark to incredible heights. Senator Volkmann resolved to start a special currency for Danzig. By very clever and adroit handling, by negotiations with London, by securing the services of a first-class currency expert from the *Reichsbank,* he succeeded in creating the Danzig guilder which was linked with the pound. Everything went well, the guilder remained stable from the first day to the last, and a wave of relief, comparable to the awakening from a nightmare, swept over Danzig. Then it became evident to me how far-reaching the social and political effects of such a monetary reform are. I made detailed reports to Berlin about that aspect of the problem.

It was my task in this transaction to allay the concern of the Berlin authorities, lest the new currency in Danzig mean a loosening of the ties connecting this part of Germany with the Reich. It was simply a matter of trust, and I was convinced that we could trust Danzig.

To preserve cultural unity between Danzig and the Reich, to resist the feeling that the city was being abandoned and forgotten by the mother country, to maintain the circulation of persons and ideas from East Prussia through the Corridor and Danzig to the Reich and to Poznania across the artificial boundaries of Versailles—that was, of course, the great task which was set before me and to which I had to devote myself. Disunited, disrupted as Germany was after the First World War, she was united in the unshakable conviction that the truncation in the East had created an intolerable situation, and that the laws of humanity and the Fourteen

Points of President Wilson had been violated; that the Corridor and the greater part of Poznania had to be restored one day, and that the world in general had to be convinced and won over to this viewpoint. With the exception of a few ultra-nationalists nobody thought of war. The idea that a close understanding with the Soviet Union was the most efficient means of pressure on Poland and the rest of the world was gaining ground slightly.

There were many ways of maintaining the circulation of German sentiment through the veins of former Eastern Germany. I continued the work already begun and added new methods of my own. The exchange of students and university professors between the Reich and Danzig was an important part of cultural relations. Numerous visits and lectures by professors were useful. Danzig became a center for congresses, for sport, for the gathering of the *Vereine* (clubs) from the Reich; the circumvention of the land frontiers of the Corridor by a mailboat service of new, comfortable ships and the installation of airlines helped greatly. The mailboat service alone took years to accomplish. Danzig was visited by famous Germans: Hindenburg, Admiral Scheer, Count Dohna of *Möwe* fame.

I thought it would be useful to keep personal contact with the different parts of East Germany. Frequently we were in Königsberg, where I made friends with the university professors and the authorities; Goerdeler was in these years Deputy Burgomaster. One of the most impressive festivities at which I participated was the bicentenary commemoration of Kant's birthday. I often went to Pommerellen and Poznania to see my friends—most of them friends from Heidelberg and Bonn and now leaders of the Germans in Poznania and Pommerellen; we went to their balls or gatherings in Brombert or to their country houses. We arranged similar gatherings in Danzig. The human contact is the most important factor in politics also—that has been my conviction throughout all the decades of my public service.

It was not only a stern duty which I fulfilled circulating thus throughout Eastern Germany. I had also a lot of fun. I took up shooting again. I had some of the most exciting and charming shooting parties with my friends; in the princely estate of Runowo, belonging to my *Korpsbruder*, von Bethmann Hollweg; with Count Limburg-Stirum and Herr von Witzleben. The bag was 400–500 or more, and a very mixed one at that—hare and pheasant, rabbit, fox, and snipe.

The nobility played a great rôle in creating a feeling of cohesion between the derelict parts of Eastern Germany, but not all of them were prepared to come out in the open as protagonists of German culture, as some of my above-mentioned friends did who risked retaliatory measures from the Poles. In the vicinity of Danzig three noble families which had intermarried played a dominant rôle: Count Keyserling, Count Krockow and von Below. The Keyserlings owned a large estate, Neustadt (Weierowo), and were also prominent by reason of their high cultural and artistic standing. Countess Keyserling had published a masterful translation of the English poet Browning. Her younger son—the eldest had been killed in World War I—was an accomplished pianist and concerts were arranged for him. He died miserably in a Polish concentration camp in 1945. His brother-in-law, Count Krockow, represented the type of the country squire who successfully administered his estate which had been owned by his family for 500 years. Three of his sons were killed in the First World War; one survived. The Belows were an old, refined, and amusing couple, having spent many years in the German foreign service. Many years abroad had not been able to efface the unusual and charming personality of Frau von Below. She was cruelly murdered at the age of eighty in the first days of the Russian invasion in 1945. It is regrettable that all those who are abusing Prussian "Junkers" as reactionary, medieval, lacking in culture and refinement, never got to know the country seats and characters I have mentioned, as well as many others in the Eastern German territories.

The social life in Danzig proper was lively and harmonious. Around the sovereign of the Free City, the High Commissioner of the League of Nations, a small but homogeneous society gathered, enlarged by occasional participants. Mr. MacDonnell, a British colonial Civil Service official, occupied the difficult and responsible post of High Commissioner. Quiet, sympathetic, a good sportsman, musical, and, with Mrs. MacDonnell, a very good host, he enjoyed great popularity. We were on very friendly terms with him, played bridge, badminton, and tennis together and tried our luck in skiing on the hills between Danzig and Oliva. His A.D.C., the Hon. A. M. Bertie, was just as popular. Other prominent members of our society were the Danish Consul-General Koch and his wife. Their spacious and well-furnished house was a social center in Zoppot. They were the most experienced members of our skiing club. From the Polish Mission, Mr. and Mrs. Kermenic and Mme Gorka participated with some other members in our sporting excursions. We were on very friendly terms with the chief of this mission, Cajetan Morawski, an acquaintance of mine from Warsaw. Some younger couples and young girls from Danzig rounded out our circle.

During the brief summer months social and sporting life reached its peak. Zoppot had for years enjoyed fame as the center of Eastern German tennis and, even now, almost all the crack players assembled there for the tournament in spite of territorial obstacles. Yachting played an important part. Steeplechasing also attracted crowds. The beach was covered with bathers and visitors from Germany and Poland. The Casino was not the least of the attractions of Zoppot.

A musical and cultural event, unique to Danzig-Zoppot, at the height of the summer season, attracting thousands of visitors from afar, was the *Wald-Oper* of Zoppot—an operatic performance with stage and seats for spectators located in an old, beautiful forest. No ceiling protected singers or spectators from rain or amplified the audibility of the human voices and the orchestra. Arriving before sunset, the crowd enjoyed the rays of the sun, coloring the leaves of the beeches and dark firs. Of course there had to be fine weather. But, strangely enough in this wet and rainy climate, it was exceptional for performances to be postponed or interrupted on account of bad weather. The weather forecasts, which singled out the days of the performances based upon a statistic survey of the weather in the past decades, generally proved right.

Still more inexplicably, the acoustics of the opera didn't suffer from the lack of ceiling and walls. Evidently the forest formed a sufficient barrier against the dispersion of the human voices and the orchestra into the open. On the contrary, the singers' voices became more audible, whereas the orchestra receded somewhat into an accompaniment of the singers. Acoustic laws, inexplicable to me, must have prevailed to accomplish this marvellous effect.

It was no second-rate orchestra with provincial artists which performed these operas. The most prominent conductors and stars from the Berlin and Vienna opera gathered in Zoppot. The *Götterdämmerung* and *Siegfried* impressed their full majesty on the minds of the hearers amid this scenery. There were no rocks of papier maché, but real rocks which witnessed Siegfried's death. No Valkyries on dummy horses, or invisible, sang their "Hojotoho!" They were galloping on real white horses through a real forest. Returning by motor-car to Danzig after the performance, we would meet the Valkyries riding by twos in their police uniforms to their barracks. The Valkyries were nothing but mounted police. The singing had been done by singers on *terra firma*.

The longer we stayed in Danzig the more we loved it. My wife and I both wished that we might enjoy for years this life, which had the amenities of the town and also those of the country. But, in the meantime, the Berlin scene had changed, and a new chapter in my diplomatic career was due to begin before two years of my stay in Danzig had passed.

After passive resistance against the occupation of the Ruhr had proved useless, the Rightist Cabinet with Herr Cuno as Chancellor had been replaced by one of the "Great Coalition" extending from the *Deutsche Volkspartei* (the Right wing of the Liberals) to the Social Democrats. Gustav Stresemann entered the political scene in which he was to play a leading rôle for six years. Chancellor at first, he was shifted to the Ministry of Foreign Affairs; Herr Luther succeeded him as Chancellor. A currency reform stabilized the Reichsmark and ended the devastating inflation, which, in the meantime, had brought about a silent social revolution by destroying the financial basis of the middle class. The Dawes Conference in London had directed the irregular flow of reparations into normal channels. The U.S.A. had taken the lead in the financial reconstruction of Europe. A new era in post-war history had begun.

Stresemann had resolved to exchange his right-hand man, the Secretary of State Maltzan, whose dominating personality did not harmonize perfectly with his own outspoken character, for a more pliable official who would be easier to handle than the autocratic initiator of the Rapallo-policy. He was appointed Ambassador to Washington, to be succeeded as Secretary of State by Herr von Schubert. By this shift a gap opened in German Eastern European politics which had been directed by Maltzan. It was decided to fall back on me. I was to be appointed as deputy Director-in-Chief of the eastern department, but I was promised to be promoted soon as Chief Director, after the actual chief, Herr Wallroth, had been nominated Minister on some European post.

In view of the importance of the task and the promise of promotion, it was impossible to evade this doubtful honor conferred on me.

I was well enough acquainted with our Eastern problems, with the inner working of the Foreign Office, and with the parliamentary and general political situation, as to be fully conscious that a very difficult task was awaiting me. On the one hand, I doubted whether I would be equal to it; on the other, I was attracted by the prospect of being entrusted with a key position in Eastern affairs. Towards the end of February, 1925, I arrived in Berlin. My period as apprentice in diplomacy had come to an end. A severe test awaited me. A period of four years, perhaps the most interesting chapter of my life, was beginning.

II

The Eastern Department

1925–1928

I was not the only one who had been summoned from his post to the Foreign Office. The office was again slowly becoming a center of foreign policy. The fresh blood which had been infused into its alleged arteriosclerotic veins after 1918 by transplanting men from different walks of life—merchants, army officers, managers—to responsible posts had failed to produce wholesome effects. Now a new experiment was started by putting career diplomats in the posts of deputy chiefs of departments as nurses for their non-political chief. It was not a reinstallation of the old political department, sacrosanct in Bismarck's days, but a step back on this road. The newly appointed "Directors" were entrusted with important political negotiations. They accompanied the Minister to conferences, they drafted the notes, negotiated with the Embassies, and had direct access to the Secretary of State and the Minister. They were often party to the most secret affairs and were not allowed to communicate them to their chiefs. Schubert set up a so-called "Bureau of Ministers" in which these highly confidential matters were concentrated, but he shrank from the decisive step of forming a new political department.

The newcomers were Herr von Bülow, later on Secretary of State, as deputy chief for the League of Nations Department and other international affairs, and Count Zech, Minister to Helsinki, son-in-law of former Chancellor von Bethmann Hollweg, later on Minister at the Hague, who died miserably in 1945 in a Russian concentration camp. He was entrusted with Western European affairs.

The chief of Bülow and Horstmann was the genial, witty, and intelligent *Ministerialdirektor* Köpke, an old official from the Consular Service. The corresponding position in the Anglo-American Department, headed by *Ministerialdirektor* de Haas, also an old official from the Consular Service, was entrusted to Herr Horstmann, a man of the world with a good political flair and with the ambition to direct world politics by persuasion and sociability rather than by arduous work. He was married to the daughter of the well-known and very cultivated banker von Schwabach. Horstmann has been abducted by the Russians, and it is not known whether he is still living or dead. The chief of my Eastern Department, Herr Wallroth, a former member of a Chamber of Commerce, had a thorough knowledge of economic affairs, but lacked the gift for politics. He was an amiable, honest, and straightforward man, with whom I collaborated harmoniously. Tired of the strenuous work in the Foreign Office, he looked forward to an appointment as Minister to an agreeable post; but he and I had to wait three years more till this wish, cherished by both of us, was fulfilled. I was his deputy for the Near-Eastern Department (Russia, Poland, Baltic, and Scandinavian States), whereas Herr Trautmann, later on my successor in the Eastern Department and Ambassador to Nanking, looked after the Far East.

The key figure in the hierarchy of the Foreign Office was, of course, the Secretary of State, Herr von Schubert. Having been educated together, having visited the same school, and studied in Heidelberg and Bonn as members of the corresponding students' associations, we had inherited the friendship which linked our parents and our sisters.

Schubert—or "Carlchen," as he was nicknamed—was a strange and very complicated man. An outspoken gift for foreign politics was combined with very painstaking and conscientious routine work. Having no good looks, paunchy, with an eagle nose, he made up for it by a queer sort of humor, half sardonic, half ironic, and often directed against himself. He was suspicious, secretive, and lacked the gift of taking things easily and confining himself to the really important matters. He made life a burden to his collaborators, but still more to himself. He was passionately devoted to his task and believed that everything would be on the rocks if he were out of his office. A Westerner by birth and career, he was a convinced advocate of the pro-British school in the German foreign service. But he was sufficiently far-sighted and politically minded to take into consideration the duty incumbent on the conduct of German foreign policy: to counterbalance the Western influences by a good understanding with Russia. Nothing could drive him more mad than when I complained that he was all out for the West.

Being married to a *grande dame*, Countess Harrach, and the owner of a great fortune and of an estate on the borders of the Saar, where he grew an excellent but very expensive wine, he played a prominent rôle in the social life of Berlin and entertained the Diplomatic Corps often and lavishly.

Another key figure was Dr. Gaus, the chief of the legal department.

He was—there is no doubt about it—an eminent jurist who wrote in a brilliant style. A pupil, almost a slave, of his predecessor, Dr. Kriege, a stubborn and intractable old theoretician, he knew the ins and outs of everything connected with the law of nations. But he had the whims of a prima donna and his "No, no!" was dreaded by all those who wanted him to frame a political thought in legal language. Besides, he was ambitious and longed to exercise political influence. As there was a boom for jurists in this period, he succeeded in playing an important part in politics.

In the years following the Dawes Conference there was a general desire to rearrange the political scene and to fit Germany somehow into the European concert again. As outright political treaties were somewhat suspect, the nations turned to the expedient of giving assurances that they would not attack each other. This simple resolve could be carried out by an infinite variety of formulae, starting from a thinly veiled expression of distrust and mounting to the fervor of a military alliance. These non-aggression treaties were the happy hunting grounds of international jurists before and after Locarno. Gaus enjoyed the game thoroughly with his colleagues in the other ministries of foreign affairs.

But he did not avoid trespassing in the political arena. As these legal men are supposed to devise a waterproof and bomb-proof formula for every political trend and thought, they are not apt to take a definite and rigid political line. Thus a flexibility develops in the character of jurists which usually makes them unfit for political work.

Being a nervous, sensitive man, Gaus's unaided adventures into politics frequently proved disastrous. These characteristics, combined with a burning ambition, were probably responsible for his acceptance of National-Socialist foreign policy and Ribbentrop, which estranged him from most of his former colleagues.

Almost a collaborator of the then German Foreign Office, the British Ambassador, Lord d'Abernon, may also be included. His important political rôle in world political and economic affairs for some decades is common knowledge and well documented by his memoirs. Whereas Maltzan indulged with d'Abernon in a fine piece of fencing, Schubert was more inclined to stand at attention and *jurare in verba magistri*. The Ambassador played a decisive rôle in Berlin during the years 1925-26.

As further newcomers to the Foreign Office, two career diplomats occupied important posts: Herr von Stohrer, later on Minister to Egypt and Ambassador to Spain, as director of the personnel department; and Roland Koester, Stohrer's successor, later on Minister to Norway and Ambassador to France, as *Chef de Protocole*. Both were, like Zech and Bülow, close friends of mine. Thus the most important key positions in the Ministry were occupied by an almost homogeneous team.

The inner circle of the Foreign Office officials maintained very close contact. After having read the telegrams and urgent matters, they gathered at half-past nine with a larger circle of minor officials for the press conference, where the most important news and articles were summarized by the witty Dr. Schacht (no relative of the financial "wizard"!). Afterwards the chiefs and deputy chiefs retired to Schubert's room, where the more important overlapping questions were discussed. These little daily conferences were often important and mostly amusing. The political jokes current in Berlin were told, and, occasionally, Köpke imitated old Hindenburg or Stresemann. Then, sometimes, a *privatissimum* with Schubert and Gaus followed. In the Eastern department the *Referenten* for the single countries, Russia, Poland, Baltic, and the Far East, assembled for a short survey and the distribution of the more urgent tasks. Then the daily work began.

Often this routine work in the office was interrupted by conferences; conferences within the Foreign Office, or with other Ministries, or with representatives of the national minorities, or with industrialists; or by negotiations with a foreign power about technical matters, or by preparing answers to questions submitted by a *Reichstag;* or I had to participate at the regular session of the Inter-ministerial Economic Commission, where practically the economic policy of the Reich was decided upon during the Weimar period. The four representatives of the Foreign Office —the Ministries of Finance, Economics, and Agriculture—were so thoroughly skilled that the individual minister was generally outvoted by them and unable to override their vote; perhaps Schacht, himself a strong personality and a first-class expert, made an exception. Speaking generally, Germany during the Weimar period was run by the high ministerial bureaucracy. They enjoyed the confidence of the Ministers and of Parliament. They had close relations with the press and with the industrialists. They performed their task extremely well.

I ought to have started my account of the Foreign Office at the time of my entry by mentioning the most important person, the Foreign Minister, during the whole period of my sojourn in Berlin, Gustav Stresemann. But, somehow, I omitted it under the impression that he was not a permanent official and that the rôle he played transgressed so far the narrow bounds of one Ministry that he simply did not fit in the frame of a bureaucratic institution. On the other hand, his connection with the more important members of his Ministry was so close, and he was more and more involved also in routine matters, that I should like to add a few remarks concerning his rôle as Minister of Foreign Affairs in connection with the Foreign Office.

Stresemann, a member from the lower middle-class in the eastern suburbs of Berlin, was, when he took office, not altogether free from suspicion and a sense of inferiority towards the nobility and the diplomats. But soon he became convinced of the loyalty and the devotion of the Foreign Office staff. A feeling of mutual trust, amounting to friendship, developed between him and his colleagues. The personnel of the Foreign Office and of the missions abroad were too many, and he himself too much absorbed by manifold other duties, to enable him to come into close contact with most of the people. It was his weakness and his strength that the leadership of his party, his work in the *Reichstag,* and in the Cabinet, absorbed most of his time.

As the influence wielded by a Minister of Foreign Affairs depends mainly on the strength of his internal political position, the Foreign Office and our foreign policy benefited vastly from the fact that he played a predominant rôle in the *Reichstag* and in German public life as a whole. Besides, he was fond of the theatre and interested in literature. He enjoyed parties and seeing people. But the routine work of a complicated bureaucratic machine bored him, and he would have tried to evade it even if he could have spared the time for it. He was thoroughly unbureaucratic, and he could drive his subordinates to despair by his failure to keep appointments or draw up minutes of his conversations. His foremost characteristic feature was his genius for grasping political ideas and adapting them to the domestic and foreign problems in any particular situation. He was perhaps not a creative genius in forming political plans, but he had a stupendous flair, springing more from inspiration than from intellect, for moulding an idea presented to him into something startling, convincing, and acceptable. During the sessions of the council of the League of Nations he startled his colleagues, who had prepared careful notes for the agenda, by the ingenuity with which he disregarded the trend of thought presented to him and stated the case in an entirely different, unorthodox way. And his method nearly always proved to be successful. He was greatly aided in these tactics by his prodigious oratorical gift.

His successes on the rostrum of the *Reichstag* were all the more admirable, as he lacked the personal charm and the insinuating, almost musical voice of Briand. But the genuine passion and the evident sincerity which inspired his speeches never failed to evoke the enthusiasm, or at least the admiration, of his hearers. Throughout the almost four years of my work in the Eastern Department I enjoyed his confidence, which developed beyond official work to closer human relations. It was he who entrusted me with the responsible and difficult post in Moscow. His political courage and an idealism which was admirable even if it was disappointed are the deepest and most lasting impressions of my association with him.

46

2. RELATIONS WITH RUSSIA

Since Maltzan had been its chief, the Eastern Department enjoyed a special position within the Foreign Office. It was somewhat aloof, almost autonomous; a cloud of secrecy, amounting to magic, surrounded it. Among Foreign Office officials there was a feeling of relief not to be involved in the mysteries of the Eastern world and its politics mingled with the satisfaction of knowing that there were men ready to do the job and that they should be left alone. To a certain extent this mentality stemmed from the simple human fact that Western politics were much more easily understandable as to language, tradition, and thinking; and last, not least, that the diplomatic and consular posts in the West were so much more agreeable and comfortable than those in the East. There was a feeling that one would have to stay indefinitely in the Eastern realm if one had proved efficient in this department.

But quite apart from these career tactics, the relations of Germany with the Eastern European nations failed to evoke the sympathy and understanding which are prerequisites for devoted and successful work. Everything concerning Poland was unsympathetic from the start; the relations with this country troubled by the care for the German minorities depressing; its capital and the seats of the consulates loathsome. But also our policy towards the Soviet Union did not evoke much sympathy from the members of our foreign service. To foster friendly relations with a government whose methods were so repugnant and linked with the underground activity of the Comintern seemed almost perverse. The representatives of the Bolshevist creed in Germany did not inspire sympathy either. Better keep your hands off—that was the simple formula to which the general feeling towards the Eastern Department boiled down. This restraint was a blessing in disguise for those who had to handle this distasteful task, for it gave them real independence.

The main problem of the Eastern Department was the Soviet Union. The center of policy-making with Russia was not the Foreign Office but our Ambassador to Moscow, Count Brockdorff-Rantzau. There was, since Maltzan's departure, nobody in the Foreign Office in close contact with the Ambassador.

To grasp these three fundamental facts did not take me long. Russian politics had remained outside my orbit so far, or had been limited to perfunctory glances from Kiev or from Poland. I had had no personal contact with leading Soviet statesmen. Still worse, my contacts with Count Rantzau were almost nil.

The problem of my relations with the Ambassador found a speedy solution by his initiative. He let me know that he trusted me and intended to collaborate closely with me. Thus I experienced one of the foremost traits of this remarkable and striking personality: the boundless trust or the unlimited distrust which characterized his intercourse with human beings. In distributing his favors or disfavors he was less guided by his intellect than by emotions or by a sensibility which strangely contrasted with a piercing, analytic, and caustic intellect. To be shifted from one category to the other amounted to an impossibility. Whoever was classed among the unreliable ones was persecuted by his untiring hate, by a biting irony, till the elimination at least from his sphere of influence was attained. Just as firmly seated were those classified as reliable. Even if they had failed, his faith in them was not shaken. Thus the collaboration established between him and me was the most gratifying aspect of this period of my career.

A scion of an ancient and noble family from Schleswig-Holstein—one of his ancestors was a *maréchal de France*—Count Rantzau was, physically and mentally, the very incarnation of an aristocrat. In fact, he often reminded me of a solitary rock left over from prehistoric ages in an utterly changed world. Proud and dignified, he had nevertheless a gift for making contacts with men from the most different walks of life—workers, Socialists, industrialists. If he liked them personally and if they were useful for his purposes, it did not matter whether they were of noble birth or commoners. But in his innermost soul only those counted who could prove their sixteen or thirty-two noble ancestors.

Also his diplomatic technique belonged to a bygone era. He has been criticized for putting his money on one horse only, of concentrating his entire energy and attention on one man—generally the Foreign Minister —as on Scavenius in Copenhagen or on Tchitcherin in Moscow—and of neglecting the other important elements that form a modern State. Nevertheless, he had the luck, or the ability, to achieve by this method the results he desired. He was also of the old school inasmuch as he loathed great gatherings and speeches. Being most brilliant in private negotiation and quick in repartee, writing a most carefully worded, classical style, he was a failure in public discussions and oratory. This weakness was reinforced by his way of life. He preferred seclusion and used the night-time for his work. He rose about noon, had lunch with some guests, worked in the afternoon in his private rooms—without ever setting foot during six years in the office building of the Embassy—and started real work and serious conversations at ten o'clock, working, talking, and drinking brandy till

48

two or three o'clock in the morning. I used to say that it would be easy to get rid of Rantzau: it was only necessary to convoke a session of the Cabinet at ten in the morning and then to ask him to give a survey of the political conditiohs in the Soviet Union, and he would have failed ignominiously. But in small company and in carefully-drawn-up memoranda, he was not to be beaten.

He was a master in creating an atmosphere comparable with that of a royal court. He picked his entourage carefully and took good care that none of the minutiae of the protocol was violated. If he wished to transmit really important letters or memoranda, he had them written out beautifully by hand, a task performed by an old clerk who was a member of his staff. He insinuated, though he never pressed the point, that his only superior was the President of the Reich, and that if he sent a copy of his reports to the Foreign Office, he did so only as a matter of courtesy.

He was very careful not to lose touch with Berlin. This contact was meticulously organized. His twin brother, devoted to him, lived in Berlin, a courtier in the time of William II, with a mustache and a Napoleon on his chin, and nicknamed "Knave of Spades." Lacking the brilliance of his brother, he knew his defects and was fond of understating his qualities. He acted as his brother's Berlin ambassador and kept him informed about everything, especially about intrigues against him. When Brockdorff-Rantzau came to Berlin, he lived in his brother's comfortable flat in the Viktoriastrasse. An excellent cook provided the possibility of entertaining *en petit comité*. Important and often strangely assorted guests assembled here, such as the Apostolic Delegate (now Pope Pius XII) and Tchitcherin.

Rantzau's voyages were a problem for Stresemann and the Foreign Office and all other persons concerned. The day of his arrival was known, but never the day of his departure. He insisted on staying an indefinite time in order to strengthen his position and his policy, to annihilate intrigues spun against him. The most complicated schemes and ruses were invented to get him out of town, as nobody had the courage to tell him frankly that his official duties demanded his presence at his post.

The paramount and decisive fact of his career and his life was Versailles and the negotiations, or rather the dictated peace, when he was Minister of Foreign Affairs. Passionately patriotic, personally proud, he never could forgive or forget the humiliations which he had to undergo as a nobleman and a representative of his country. He accepted the consequences and resigned when the Cabinet had rejected his proposal not to sign the draft treaty imposed on Germany. He lived and worked exclusively for the purpose of undoing the shame of Versailles.

The Treaty of Rapallo seemed to offer an opportunity to realize this idea. He therefore willingly accepted the post of Ambassador to Moscow, offered to him by Maltzan and the Chancellor. Fully conscious of Bismarck's policy of friendship, he created the myth of Rapallo, which found expression in the two slogans of "Rapallo-spirit" and of the "common destiny of the two great, vanquished nations." Lip service was paid to this formula by numerous people in Germany for some time. I am convinced that many Russians, of whom Tchitcherin was one, approved this concept, as it coincided with their own inclinations, though many made frequent use of the phrase to further their own political ends. Bitterly they reproached every slip of tongue in the German press or *Reichstag* while they themselves conferred high decorations on the German bandit Max Hölz or started an insurrection in Saxony and Thuringia.

In spite of "Rapallo-spirit" and kindred slogans, it was an uphill fight which Count Rantzau had to wage on behalf of his policy. How thin the ice in Germany was on which this Russo-German friendship skated I soon perceived when I took stock of the foundations for co-operation with Russia. And this impression grew stronger the longer I was in Berlin.

The basis of the policy leading up to the Treaty of Rapallo was the sentiment prevailing in Germany as well as in the Soviet Union that both countries shared the same fate. Both had been vanquished in the war, both were being treated as outcasts by the Allied Powers. Both felt resentment, or enmity, towards their new neighbor Poland, who was being used by French policy to keep both at bay. Both were convinced that a give-and-take would be mutually advantageous. The general mood of the average German towards Russia may be summed up in the simple phrase: whenever we were good friends with Russia, everything went well with both of us, whereas we both suffered by enmity.

In this phrase the memory of Bismarck's policy and of the close ties connecting the Hohenzollern and Romanov dynasties became vivid again. Sentimentalists remembered the somewhat apocryphal words ascribed to the Emperor William I on his deathbed: "Don't disrupt the wire to Russia!" Anyhow, these were the considerations and sentiments leading up to Rapallo and to its most important clause, by which the reparation claims were waived, thus clearing the way for unfettered economic intercourse.

The warmth of political friendship between two nations will always vary according to the events of the day and the strength of foreign pressure. The newborn Russo-German friendship was all the more susceptible to such climatic influences, as one of the partners was an emphatically novel and revolutionary State and the other fragile in its structure by reason of social upheaval, a crushing defeat after an exhausting war and control by foreign powers. Slowly the doctrine developed that the relations with the Soviet Union were to be managed strictly on a two-road basis: on one road political friendship and economic exchange were fostered; on the other, a life-and-death struggle encouraged unrest, trouble, and chaos in Germany, with all the constructive forces in the country reacting against this subversive activity with all the vigor they could muster. It was difficult for the politically minded amongst the Germans to grasp these facts, and impossible for the man in the street. Thus the mutual relations were liable to abrupt changes, the thermometer falling overnight from warm friendship to cold disgust whenever the Comintern had its own way.

The Soviet Union, on its part, plagued us with an indestructible distrust. Being conscious of Germany's central position in Europe, she was haunted by the fear that Germany might be lured or threatened into the Western camp, which made her (Germany) a potential enemy in an aggressive war against the mother of the world proletariat. According to tactics which have since become world famous, this concern manifested itself in a blend of insolent and slanderous press and radio campaigns, and by earnest and insistent reproaches *et petit comité*. The great and difficult task that fell to the Foreign Office was to keep the Russo-German home fire burning in spite of these obstacles.

There were comparatively few pillars on which the edifice of stable and good relations could be erected. The "Rapallo-spirit" was a somewhat doubtful asset, as has been explained above. Military relations proved to be of a more permanent value. So long as confidence was shown to the other partner on this delicate field there was no real danger of a thorough change of policy. This argument was, and remained, one of the most convincing. Besides, on the German side, General von Seeckt and the *Reichswehr* were the most stable and reliable adherents of friendship with Russia.

Economic relations never reached the strength of a solid pillar; or at least not before the great credits were granted and business done on a big and secure scale. Our industries recovered only slowly, and the banks, preferring great gains with no risks, turned a cold shoulder to Russia.

Of the political parties only the *Deutsche Volkspartei*, the Right-wing Liberals, showed understanding for the importance of Russia in Germany's game of international politics. One of the most brilliant deputies, Herr von Raumer, was a great help. The Right, the *Deutsche Nationale*, disliked closer economic contact with the Soviet Union because they feared the potential competition of Russian grain. The Catholic Center party loathed the Bolsheviks on account of the persecution of the Church. The Social Democrats were afraid of Communist competition. And the German Communists did more harm than good to the kindred party on account of their clumsy tactical behavior and their incitement to strikes and uprisings. Thus there were in the *Reichstag* only individual members, like Professor Hoetzsch of the *Deutschnationale*, von Raumer and Baron Rheinbaben of the *Deutsche Volkspartei*, with Wirth of the *Center*, who could be relied upon as supporters of an understanding with Russia. The same remarks applied to the press. Here it depended on individual editors or Moscow correspondents how long and whether individual papers would advocate the Rapallo-policy or at least economic co-operation. So long as Paul Scheffer dominated the correspondents in Moscow and was in favor with the *Narkomindel* (the Ministry of Foreign Affairs), the influential *Berliner Tageblatt* was a great help. But when diplomatic relations between both powers had been broken off because Scheffer was refused a visa to re-enter Russia, this paper also went into opposition.

When I appeared on the Berlin scene, the Rapallo-ideology had worn rather thin. The honeymoon of the first year had been brought to a premature close by the Communist risings in Saxony and Thuringia during the year 1923. While the Comintern generally tried to keep up appearances, it dropped the veil entirely at that time. With the Hitler Putsch in Munich, inflation at its peak, and the collapse of passive resistance against the invasion of the Ruhr, the opportunity for starting a definite revolution and overthrowing the bourgeois and semi-bourgeois elements in Germany seemed too good to be missed. Radek told me himself later on in Moscow how, during this uprising, he happened to stay (with a faked passport, of course) in the Hotel Europäischer Hof in Dresden, where the General commanding the *Reichswehr* who was to quell the rebellion had established his headquarters. One of the most dangerous terrorists, who had been helped by the Soviet Embassy in Berlin (I have forgotten his name, it was something like Pavlovsky), had been caught by the police and was in jail, awaiting his trial (later on we bartered him away for some Germans held in Soviet prisons, one of those unpleasant deals unavoidable in diplomatic intercourse with Moscow).

Economic relations were disappointing. The economic honeymoon was inaugurated by Lenin's NEP (New Economic Policy), which he started when he had reduced Russian agriculture, industry, and commerce to ruin by his strict application of his theories. Then, clever tactician that he was, Lenin made a *volte-face*. His principles went overboard for the time being. He introduced free commerce again and encouraged the inflow of foreign capital by promising the grant of concessions and of a special régime for the establishments concerned. Profit-hungry capitalists arrived only in limited numbers from Germany, let alone from other countries. As capital was scarce in Germany, and the industrialists concerned had counted on making huge profits without investing much money, whereas the Soviets had just the opposite idea of the bargain, there was disappointment from the beginning. Under this scheme of concessions the Junkers Aviation Corporation had built a huge aircraft factory in Fili, near Moscow. Otto Wolff had a concession. A firm of timber merchants from Freiburg had been granted a timber concession *Mologda*. Krupp had started an agricultural concession in the northern Caucasus, near the Kuban. Two other German landowners had followed suit. And quite a series of other concessions were in the making, down to a button factory and a fur concession, which, however, with the years, shrank (almost symbolically) to the utilization of mouse skins.

The Soviet Government, wishing to demonstrate its respectability, wanted to conclude a comprehensive economic treaty with Germany. Not only trade questions proper were to be settled, but consular and juridical questions also. We agreed. A commission was dispatched to Moscow with one of our most hardened negotiators, Herr von Körner, as Chairman. This was a tempting opportunity. An interminable number of new difficulties arose the longer the negotiations dragged on. There was no end in sight after six months' haggling, when I joined the Eastern Department.

Russo-German relations were bound to be put to an acid test by a new turn of our relations with the Western Powers. The Locarno-policy was beginning to shape itself and was to compete with the Rapallo-policy.

---

3. THE ROAD TO LOCARNO

After the Dawes Conference in London a feeling prevailed in the Foreign Office that something should be done to bring Germany back into the comity of nations. The dictate of Versailles ought to be replaced or supplemented by a genuine understanding. It is almost impossible to decide whose head first conceived this idea; probably Gaus and Schubert, inspired by Lord d'Abernon, invented it. The rôle of Stresemann was more that of a nurse taking care of an infant than that of a parent. Quick to grasp a political idea, he immediately realized the importance of normalizing the relations of Germany with the outer world. Farsighted and courageous, he was prepared to run the risk of tactical disadvantages, such as internal political fights, in order to reach the strategic aim of re-establishing Germany as a great power.

From these roots sprang a note which he addressed in the beginning of February, 1925, to Great Britain and France, proposing a guarantee of Germany's western frontiers by a common treaty between the adjacent countries. The leading principle of his proposal was a renunciation of Alsace-Lorraine by Germany, whereas the problem of the eastern frontiers was left open. But, even with this limitation, Stresemann's offer meant a huge concession made in advance, whereas the compensation, the evacuation of Western Germany by Allied occupation armies, remained undecided. Only by being aware of the intensity of feeling in Germany about the dictated Treaty of Versailles and about the cession of territories considered to be German, is it possible to gauge the audacity of Stresemann's offer.

The note was kept strictly secret, and so were the ensuing *pourparlers* and exchanges of notes. Conversations dragged for months, interrupted by long intervals, and speeded up by renewed German initiative. The British Government grasped the importance of the issue and was co-operative, whereas in Paris doubt, suspicion, and the legal formalism which are so characteristic of the Quai d'Orsay prevailed. In the early autumn matters had crystallized so far that the scheme of the Locarno Conference was agreed to. I need not go into details, as these negotiations are now common knowledge, and as I was involved in them rather as a spectator and observer than as a participant.

When I assumed my post in the Foreign Office at the end of February I was initiated into this secret by Gaus and Schubert, and also into their concern as to how the Russians would react. The Russians were kept informed from that time onwards and reacted with mounting vigor. Their ever-present distrust rose to a pitch. They had no confidence in Stresemann, whom they suspected of being a Westerner. But quite apart from the personal issue, their inborn suspicion was bound to be aroused by negotiations between Germany with the Western Powers, the more so when they sprang from German initiative and not from Allied pressure. The motive of this initiative could be nothing but the intention of the German Government to abandon the Rapallo-policy and to turn to the West.

More to the point, and better founded, was their anxiety regarding another problem: they foresaw that the German-Allied negotiations would somehow end with Germany becoming a member of the League of Nations. And that raised a problem of immense importance to them: the problem of Article 16 of the Covenant of the League, which imposed upon members the obligation to join the sanctions which might be decided upon against a recalcitrant member or an aggressive non-member—or, at least, the members had to tolerate the march of the sanction contingents through their territory. And here the nightmare of an attack of the capitalistic states against the protector of the proletariat revived again. If such an attack were planned and executed, Germany would be forced willy-nilly to participate, or at least to tolerate the passage of forces acting under the League. This was the *leitmotif* which was reiterated for months with ever-increasing vigor and in all its variations.

The Signing of the Berlin Treaty, April, 1926
Left to right: von Schubert, Gaus, Wallroth, von Dirksen,
Stresemann, Krestinski, Bratman-Brodowski, Jacubovich

Solemn denials of even the remotest inclination to depart from the spirit of Rapallo, uttered and reiterated by all the Ministers and officials concerned, proved entirely ineffectual in allaying Russian anxiety. In vain was it explained that, after all, Germany could not and would not remain an outcast in Europe, that she had to try to find a *modus vivendi* with the West, seeing that she was situated in the center of Europe, that this did not mean taking sides, that all questions relating to Eastern Europe remained open and would be tackled only in harmony with the Soviet Union. The stumbling-block of Article 16 turned up in later stages of these conversations as the junction between the Treaty of Locarno and membership of the League was established by the Western Powers.

The initial conversations with the Russians led us to the conviction that some political equivalent would have to be offered to the Soviet Union in order to re-establish the equilibrium between East and West. This idea developed into a project ending in a political treaty in which the unaltered friendly attitude of both powers should be restated and some sort of guarantee be given to the Kremlin against potential dangers arising from Article 16. In a word—the Rapallo Treaty was to be rejuvenated. This was the trend of thought that led to the so-called Treaty of Berlin.

It was a long and arduous way to this goal. The distrust of the Kremlin was not to be allayed easily. Things were complicated by the fact that Count Rantzau shared Russian anxieties and was bitterly opposed to Stresemann's initiative. He felt esteem and some sympathy for the Foreign Minister, but did not trust the strength of his character if tempted by the Western Powers. He frankly disliked Schubert, who reciprocated this feeling. The Ambassador argued more as a spokesman of the Russians than as one who explained the German point of view to the Russian Government.

During one of Count Rantzau's prolonged stays in Berlin the combined efforts of Stresemann, Schubert, Gaus, and myself convinced him that at least an attempt should be made to induce the Soviet Government to accept our point of view and also the draft of the treaty which was under discussion. Gaus had invented a new formula which, he said, had a magic effect on the Russian mind. I was initiated into the deepest secrets of every word, for the Ambassador's mind, being averse to the principle as such, did not react to such subtleties. At last the plans crystallized. I was to accompany Count Rantzau to Moscow and explain everything to Tchitcherin. Rantzau willingly agreed and postponed his threat of resignation.

There was still another string attached to my somewhat precarious mission to Moscow. The negotiations about the conclusion of an economic, consular, and juridical treaty were held up. The President of our delegation, his Excellency von Körner, who was seventy-two years old, insisted on interrupting the talks on a fixed date. We in Berlin were plunged into deep despair by his resolve, because we regarded these negotiations as the most efficient means of filling the gap till the political treaty was secured. At last I discovered the motive of Körner's stubbornness: his wife had secured a room in Bad Gastein and had ordered him home. By defraying the costs, the Foreign Office succeeded in persuading Frau von Körner to postpone her voyage for some weeks.

The third purpose of my voyage to Moscow was that Count Rantzau should be induced to return to his post. Through weeks he had disappointed the hopes of all concerned that he would relieve Berlin's Ministries from the pressure to which he exposed them.

At last we started, not on the direct road via Warsaw, which Count Rantzau loathed for some reason, but via Riga, where a special car awaited us. During the trip I tried to train him once more for the coming conversation with Tchitcherin by explaining Gaus's magic formula. But in vain. He requested me to do the talking while he would stand by and give the political background to the technical discussion.

The atmosphere in Moscow could not have been worse for our purposes. The suspicion of the Russians at the double deadlock of both negotiations was unabated, whereas our anger was stirred to boiling point by a propagandist display which was staged by the Comintern at our expense. It was the first of the mock trials which became such a characteristic feature of Soviet politics. This time the victims were two German students, Wolscht and Kindermann, who, having started a trip to the Soviet Union out of sheer curiosity and interest, had been arrested by the G.P.U. and were being tried on the customary charges of high treason, espionage, and so on. Perfectly harmless boys as they were, they had not lived up to the intricacies of G.P.U. *agents provocateurs,* and had been caught in the trap. But worse than that, the Comintern deemed it profitable to involve the German Embassy in this alleged plot. It was hinted that Herr Hilger, one of the most reliable officials of the Embassy, perhaps the foremost expert in everything concerning Russia, had given advice to the students and had directed their plot. Whereas we were furious at being used as guinea-pigs for the Bolshevist experiments in show trials, it was maddening that they dared to attack an Embassy which had been the most eloquent interpreter of the Soviet attitude ever since Count Rantzau took over his office.

Soon after our arrival the first conference of the Ambassador and myself with Tchitcherin started. The reception by the Commissar of Foreign Affairs was decidedly friendly. He listened attentively to my explanations and replied, in his high-pitched voice, with some searching questions.

A prolonged discussion followed with Count Rantzau contributing some political remarks couched in the "Rapallo-spirit." Tchitcherin, of course, could do nothing but think matters over—which meant that he had to report to the Politburo. But at least the ice was broken and conversations resumed. Count Rantzau was kind enough to send a highly laudatory telegram about my efforts to Berlin.

Then I turned to the economic side of my mission. There were some members of the German delegation still left, most of them representatives of the Ministries concerned, and, the most important person, Consul-General Schlesinger. Not being a full-fledged official, the Foreign Office had secured his services because of his vast knowledge both of the Western and the Eastern mentality, and had bestowed the title of Consul-General on him. This had the inestimable advantage of freeing him from bureaucratic fetters and providing the opportunity of starting him to work wherever it was necessary. His fertile and imaginative brain produced solutions for the most hopeless deadlocks. Besides, he was unselfish, extremely witty, and a devoted friend. We had known each other vaguely for some years, but from now on we were on very cordial terms and collaborated successfully for many years. During this period I also made friends with another of my closest colleagues in Russian affairs, Hilger. He was loyal and reliable, and his knowledge of the Soviet Union was of great value to me and my successors.

I soon made the acquaintance of my opposite number in the negotiations, Fürstenberg-Ganetzky, an official of the Commissariat of Trade; no proletarian, but a scion of a wealthy family. That he was personally a polite and well-educated man did not affect our conversations, for he simply had to execute the orders given to him. That is what makes negotiating with Soviet representatives so thankless a task: they proceed full steam on one track like a steam engine, and nothing can deflect them from their course. And never is it possible to talk matters over with the really authoritative person. Your opposite number is generally running for a 100 per cent victory, because his career, and maybe his freedom or life, may depend upon it. *"Post equitem sedet atra cura."*

My negotiations with Tchitcherin and Fürstenberg-Ganetzky dragged on for about six weeks. It is entirely unnecessary to go into details, quite apart from the fact that I do not remember them. Russia was striving for a most comprehensive treaty, which was to become their show-piece for negotiations with other governments. We were still living under the illusion that we would be gainers if a compromise clause were elaborated. It was a bitter but inescapable disappointment when we found that the working of such a treaty did not depend upon the concise wording of the clauses but upon the political atmosphere prevailing for the moment. If relations were friendly, then the Consul would be allowed to visit a German citizen imprisoned by the G.P.U. If not, the most exasperated protests were of no avail. To fulfil obligations incurred by a treaty was simply a matter of expediency with the Soviet Union, as with dictatorships in general.

The political conversations of Rantzau and myself with Tchitcherin were also held up. The Foreign Commissar did not yield to the lure of Gaus's formula, and a prolonged exchange of telegrams with the Foreign Office failed to produce satisfactory results. What was I to do? Continue talking or return empty-handed to Berlin? After serious consideration I chose the latter course. Disagreeable as this was for me at that moment, my resolve proved to be the appropriate one from a tactical point of view. Clinging too tenaciously to negotiations is interpreted by the Soviet mentality as a sign of weakness. It was also right to stick to my resolution once I had taken it and not be persuaded to prolong negotiations by vague promises that a way might be found by further talks. Once a sleeping-car is ordered for the return trip, one ought never cancel the order. That is one of the most important principles in negotiating with the Soviets. Thus I left Moscow without positive results.

Nevertheless I look back on these weeks spent in Moscow with satisfaction and gratitude. I had acquired a pretty thorough knowledge of Soviet Russian affairs. I had grown acquainted with the strange atmosphere of the Russian capital. And, above all, the frequent conversations with Count Rantzau had created a sympathy and a trust between us which lasted until his death. I had widened my knowledge of everything Russian by talking matters over with Hilger, Schlesinger, and many other important and interesting men visiting Moscow—one of them being Frithjof Nansen, who was accompanied on this mission by Quisling, who was to become notorious in the Second World War.

The disappointment about the lack of positive results in Berlin was none too great. Everybody's attention was focused on the negotiations with the Western Powers. Besides, the Russians, in an afterthought, resolved to resume the negotiations by a more conciliatory attitude in the political and in the economic field. They may have been incited to this attitude by the growing concern that Germany was turning to the West for good.

As soon as the most dangerous stumbling-blocks between Germany and the Western Powers had been overcome and an agreement had been reached to fix a date and a place for a conference—the first days of October in Locarno—the Soviet Government started for an all-out offensive against the Wilhelmstrasse. A last desperate effort was made to keep Germany back from a road which was bound—according to the view of the Kremlin—to lead to disaster and to a break with the Rapallo partner.

Tchitcherin started on a voyage to Berlin which he linked with the extortionist gesture of staying a few days in Warsaw on the way, and of proclaiming his intention to visit Paris after his stay in the German capital. Thus we were meant to be intimidated by the prospect that the Soviet Union had political alternatives.

Especially in nightly talks with Stresemann, immediately before the departure of the German delegation, Tchitcherin exercised the highest pressure imaginable. He frightened Stresemann by allegedly secret pledges agreed upon by former German governments—a contention which was proved to be utterly unfounded when files and statements by the officials concerned were scrutinized. He had to be satisfied with the promise of the Chancellor, Luther, and of Stresemann that the German Government did not contemplate a change of its policy towards the Soviet Union; that the pact which was to be negotiated at Locarno would in no way contradict the words and the spirit of the Treaty of Rapallo; and that German statesmen would insist on safeguarding the common interest with regard to Article 16 of the Covenant of the League, in case Germany were to join the League.

On the day of his departure for Locarno Luther invited Tchitcherin, the Soviet Embassy, and numerous leading German Ministers and deputies to a formal lunch in Bismarck's Chancellery. Even my humble person was put in the scale in order to improve the equilibrium between East and West in Locarno. On the last day it was decided that I should join the delegation to allay Rantzau's and the Soviet's suspicion that Locarno was bound to be an entirely Western enterprise.

---

4. LOCARNO

I was spared the rôle of Banquo's ghost at the banquet during the Locarno negotiations. Luther as well as Stresemann were fully conscious of their duty not to disturb the precarious equilibrium of Germany's central position in Europe. The general situation was much too dramatic and enigmatic to be brought to a crisis by the desire to throw in our lot with the West whatever the costs might be. Seldom have statesmen been under such multilateral strain and pressure as the German delegates at the Locarno Conference. The offer made by Stresemann was, as such, a very risky one and apt to undermine his position in Germany. To offer a guarantee of the Western frontiers meant a voluntary signing of the dictate of Versailles, or at least an important part of it. Alsace-Lorraine was not so near to the heart of the Germans as the Corridor, and its severance from the body of the mother country did not create such a fatal wound, but there existed narrow bonds between the Southern German States and Alsace.

Lorraine was of inestimable value for our heavy industry. Above all, the feeling that the Versailles Treaty had been signed under duress, and was, consequently, not binding, restored at least some self-respect to Germany. This feeling was not seriously shaken by guaranteeing the Western frontiers. Besides, as Poland and Czechoslovakia were also invited to the Locarno Conference for negotiations about a non-aggression pact without guaranteeing the frontiers, public opinion in Germany grew suspicious lest the Eastern frontiers might also be bartered away. It was almost impossible to explain to the man in the street the intricacies of the formulas invented by the jurists. Even I, though somewhat trained in this secret science, had to ask Gaus again and again for explanations in order to be reassured as to the safeguarding of our interests in the East.

These considerations weighed all the heavier on the minds of Stresemann and Luther as the parties of the Right had been brought into the foreground by their sweeping victory in the elections to the *Reichstag* in December, 1924. The Cabinet was composed of members of the Right wing, together with the *Deutsche Volkspartei,* but without the Social Democrats. *Reichspräsident* Marshal von Hindenburg had been elected after the untimely death of President Ebert. This also added to the strength of the Right, though the old Field Marshal was never an outspoken party man.

I often wondered, during the Locarno days, how Stresemann did succeed to get the assent of his Conservative colleagues in the Cabinet to start and to continue his negotiations with Great Britain and France. I can only explain it by the fact that they simply did not grasp the implication of the offer made by Stresemann, who had presented his ideas to them with all his eloquence and aided by Gaus's hair-splitting juridical acumen. Anyhow, the Right wing in the Cabinet grew more and more restless during the negotiations and brought about a serious crisis.

The second pressure on Luther and Stresemann came from the other partners concerned in the Conference and from public opinion throughout the world. After all, the German delegation went to the Conference as the prodigal son who returns to his father's house to be pardoned. The world in general yearned for the restoration of real peace. Well-meaning people everywhere hailed the German initiative and eagerly awaited a real reconciliation at Locarno. The searchlights of press and propaganda were turned on the statesmen there. Every step of theirs was watched and commented on as when Briand and Stresemann had a talk, or when they and Chamberlain had a motor-launch trip on the lake. It was no easy resolve to break off the Conference and to reject an unsatisfactory compromise. It was hard to be the villain of the piece once more, to return home empty-handed, met by the sneers of one's colleagues and the inevitable invective of all those who dare not shoulder a responsibility. And as the third and greatest threat, the shadow of the Russian giant loomed over the sunny beaches of the Lago Maggiore.

Thus the fortnight of the negotiations was bound to be loaded with excitement, drama, and tension. The stage fitted well into the scene: the conference-room of the town hall with its round table; the delegates with their experts; no crowd of spectators, not the unrest of the sessions in Geneva. The main actors of Locarno had a setting which displayed their character and personality with the utmost lucidity. From the beginning Briand and Stresemann dominated the scene. Sir Austen Chamberlain, by his nature and by the rôle assigned to Great Britain, limited himself to the part of the conciliating *père noble,* to the *Attinghausen* in Schiller's drama *Wilhelm Tell* and his exhortation, *"Seid einig, einig, einig!"* (Be united!) Mussolini, who made an appearance, remained silent and had to be satisfied with the publicity. To have witnessed the oratorical duel of these two great orators, Stresemann and Briand, was unforgettable. Never did I hear Stresemann defending and pleading for his ideas and the interests of his country with more courage, oratorical skill, and brilliance than during the Locarno debates. The very essence of his speeches was to demonstrate the necessity for Germany to obtain a guarantee against the potential consequences of Article 16, of the sanctions which might involve the Reich in a war or, at least, in becoming the battleground in an East-West conflict.

The rôle of Briand, who had to profess the peaceful intentions of his country and to persuade his opponent to join the comity of peaceful nations, was less thankless and difficult. The beautifully formed phrases also responded to the eminent oratorical qualities of his character and to the persuasiveness of the French language. Stresemann had to overcome the disadvantage of his somewhat husky, almost hoarse voice, and of an outward appearance which did not win sympathy at first sight. But when he warmed up, and the genuine pathos of a great and idealistic mind came to the surface, he was equal to Briand and carried as much weight and persuasiveness as the French statesman. I personally was bound to follow the debates with the closest attention, as it fell to my lot to draw up the minutes.

After many dramatic debates and private conversations, the most important of which was held during an excursion on the motor-launch *Orange Blossom,* an agreement was reached which satisfied our demands and represented a compromise between the maintenance, in principle, of

Article 16, while giving us sufficient loopholes to evade consequences which might endanger our relations with the Soviet Union.

The main obstacle having been overcome, the further proceedings went off more smoothly. The conclusion of non-aggression treaties with Poland and Czechoslovakia attached a string to the original conception of the past which it was hard for the German delegates to agree to, though our right to demand a revision of the clauses concerning our Eastern frontier remained unimpaired. But the outward appearance was somewhat nasty to swallow. The disappointment deepened when it became known that the Western Powers had granted to Poland a semi-permanent seat in the Council of the League of Nations. After all, the German Government had not taken the initiative for the Locarno Pact to help Poland to the rank of a great power in the Geneva hierarchy. Besides, the obligation for Germany to apply for membership to the League of Nations was— from the internal point of view—far more of a liability than an asset.

A far greater danger for the German delegates emerged from the fact that the main problem for their country remained unsolved, and their hopes were disappointed, for the time being at least. This was the famous problem of the effects of Locarno which dominated the scene of German internal politics during the following years. Stresemann had not offered Germany's ideological surrender in exchange for being patted on the shoulder by the Western Powers and being hailed as a member of their club after ten years of exclusion. The German delegates went to Locarno with the firm expectation that the psychological reconciliation would be followed by an actual *détente;* that Germany would be acknowledged as a full-fledged member of the European comity of nations by relieving her from the most burdensome and ignominious clauses of Versailles, the occupation of her Western territories by Allied troops.

Equality of rights with regard to disarmament was both a sentimental hope and a practical demand. But neither Briand nor Sir Austen Chamberlain was prepared to give clear assurances as to the evacuation of the Rhineland, still less to fix obligations of this kind by an exchange of notes or by clauses in the treaty. Nothing else could be obtained but the vague assurances that the promotion of good will among the nations of Europe and the lessening of the tension would lead in the near future to the fulfilment of the German demands.

As the negotiations drew to a close, the formidable decision whether to sign the draft of the treaties could no longer be postponed without insisting on further improvements: to withhold signature pending a settlement of the evacuation issue; or to consult the Cabinet in Berlin. A more and more audible rumbling of discontent and doubt from Berlin warned Luther and Stresemann that a growing awareness of the implications of the pact had strengthened the hands of the diehard group in the Cabinet. The danger rose that a veto from Berlin might interfere with a successful close of the negotiations. On the other hand, the consideration that an exchange of opinions with Berlin and a formal approval of the draft of the treaties by the Cabinet would lessen their responsibility was bound to be tempting to men less courageous than the German delegates. At the same time such a move might impress the delegates of the Western Powers, who were also eager for a speedy conclusion, and might lead to further concessions. A mounting pressure was applied to Stresemann and Luther. The concentrated yearning of the world—made articulate by an impatient press—for a great peace demonstration weighed increasingly upon them, and so did the urgent and renewed inquiries by their colleagues. Even considerations of a sentimental kind were brought into action by the outspoken hint that Chamberlain's birthday was imminent, on October 16, and that the signing of the pact would be the nicest imaginable birthday present for him.

It is idle now to ponder over the problem whether tactics of procrastination would have resulted in a more favorable draft for Germany. Facts decide history, and Stresemann and Luther felt it more important for Germany not to disappoint the hopes which had been pinned on her initiative, and to secure the advantages of good will in the world which were to be expected from a voluntary reconciliation with the West and the outer world. Stresemann trusted the assurances given to him as to the after-effects of Locarno. He had delivered the goods and he was certain to get the equivalent later on. In that case he would be justified and his internal political position would be secure. In the meantime he would have to face opposition, doubts, and attacks. But he trusted to his ability to weather the storm until the reinforcement would come from the side of the Allies. So he signed.

The immediate result of the conclusion of the Locarno Pact was as he expected. A sigh of relief went through the world. The peacemakers of Locarno were praised by a war-weary humanity. Stresemann was applauded as one of the great European statesmen. This prestige enabled him to overcome domestic storms. It was the hour of triumph for him personally and the peak of his political career. But at the same time the tragedy of the rest of his life and of his death was set in motion. The hour of triumph was also the moment when the tragic conflict in the third act of the classical drama took shape, leading to death with inexorable logic.

A further analogy to the classical drama may be found in the fact that the following years were characterized by resounding successes, whereas the interior structure of his political achievement was being steadily undermined. Stresemann in Geneva, admission to the League, his friendship with Briand, the conference at Thoiry, his oratorical triumphs during the sessions of the Council—all these were unheard-of successes for a German statesman, six years after Versailles. But while the press and public opinion of Europe lavished praise upon him, he himself had to fight a battle on two fronts with diminishing physical strength. The glittering phrases of the Locarno-spirit were too empty to sustain the starved organism of Germany. With growing intensity the parliamentary opposition insisted on the promised "results" of Locarno. With ever greater urgency Stresemann reminded his Locarno partners to honor their pledges. The political atmosphere deteriorated steadily. After Briand's resignation the customary cold wind blew from Paris. And when, at last, Stresemann succeeded in extorting a *"beau geste"* as insignificant as the evacuation of the first zone, the psychological moment had gone by, the concession fell flat and failed to strengthen his position.

Thus, the fifth act of Stresemann's tragedy was inaugurated by his own admission in the session of the *Reichstag* in November, 1928: "Germany's right is violated so long as her claim on the evacuation of the Rhineland is not fulfilled." The leader of the Right-wing Opposition, Count Westarp, replied: "The episode of the so-called Locarno policy is finished. France threatens the security of Germany. She remains with troops on the borders of the Rhine; together with Great Britain she is organizing huge maneuvers on German soil." This was indisputable. The commanding generals of the occupying powers had started maneuvers with the strategic assumption of an eastward attack.

The constant and futile fight on two fronts consumed the physical strength of the Foreign Minister, who was suffering from grave kidney trouble. He might have prolonged his life by quitting his office and retiring to Egypt. He preferred to fight to the last. By the high ideals for which he fought, by the generous confidence with which he trusted that his sacrifices would be rewarded, by his failure, and by the valor with which he worked until his death, his memory will survive as that of a great and tragic political figure.

Another political reputation was impaired, almost annihilated, though not in so dramatic and tragic a manner as Stresemann's: that of Count Rantzau. It is true Stresemann had secured a satisfactory formula to allay the concern of Moscow. Count Rantzau could even boast of a little counter-Locarno. The negotiations concerning the commercial treaty had come to a successful end, as the Russians were at last abandoning their go-slow tactics for political reasons. The treaty had been signed with much pomp in Moscow on October 12 while the Locarno confusion was in progress. It is true that a revivifying injection was administered to the organism of Russo-German friendship and matters went on more smoothly. But the atmosphere between Moscow and Berlin had, nevertheless, changed fundamentally.

The romanticism of Rapallo had evaporated. The common destiny of the two great, humiliated, vanquished nations had been replaced on the part of Germany by a two-sided, well-balanced policy. This was utterly strange and repugnant to Count Rantzau. Locarno had brought about a fission in his policy. He had foreseen it, but he had acquiesced. He had been persuaded to stay in office. Now he regretted it. He continued his work in Moscow, but a cord of the instrument was broken. His friends agreed that it would have been more consistent with his career to retire. But fate was lenient to him. He did not have to live long in an utterly changed atmosphere. He died a few years later. His tragedy was not as striking as that of Stresemann, but a tragedy all the same.

Has the Locarno policy paid in the long run? I pondered over this question for years, especially so far as Russo-German relations were concerned. From a convinced supporter of Locarno, I developed into a skeptic. Discussing with Russian officials, also with Russophile Americans, the merits of Stresemann's policy, I used to stress the fact that Germany simply could not remain out in the cold, but that she was bound to find a *modus vivendi* with the Western Powers and to reassert her position as a Central European Power. I was refuted by the retort that Locarno was not necessary to achieve this end; that the settlement of the reparation problem at the Dawes Conference in London, 1924, or rather the re-entry of the United States into the arena of European politics, would have had just the same result as Locarno: to re-establish Germany's position in Europe. If we had been more patient, we might have saved the political expenses of Locarno and Geneva.

In a retrospective view I am inclined to agree with this opinion. The failure of Locarno—for a failure it was in the long run—evoked the most sinister consequences. It meant that Western European statesmanship had failed to reconcile Germany, to win her wholehearted collaboration in European reconstruction. She felt disappointed, almost cheated, as she had not received her reward for the goods delivered by her. It must be kept in mind that the German statesmen of this Weimar period cannot be blamed as Junkers, Fascists, reactionaries, crooks, or idiots. They were honest, capable, intelligent men, inspired by the one desire to restore their country, in collaboration with the other European nations, to an honorable position on the European continent. Their supreme effort to achieve this goal, initiated by the most capable of them, was Locarno. Together with Versailles, the non-fulfilment of President Wilson's Fourteen Points, and the breakdown of disarmament, the failure of Locarno was one of the roots from which National Socialism sprang.

5. THE EQUILIBRIUM BETWEEN RAPALLO AND LOCARNO

I have anticipated the ultimate effects of Locarno in order to give a comprehensive survey on one of the most important epochs of the Weimar Republic. When we lived through those years, these effects became visible only gradually. The immediate reactions of the swing of our foreign policy penetrated even to the Eastern Department, in so far as the Soviet Union ceased to play the predominant rôle in my work. As soon as Germany had entered the League, our minority problems on our Eastern border came to the foreground, for we, as members of the Council, had a platform on which we could plead for the Germans in the ceded territories.

The immediate aftermath of Locarno was, however, the straightening out of the remnants of distrust which the German escapade to the West had left in the minds of our susceptible Eastern friends. Boasting of the Article 16 formula, won at Locarno, we prepared for the resumption of the summer talks about the bringing up to date of our Rapallo-relations to a post-Locarno, Geneva level. Our hope that the Soviet Union would share our interpretation of the Locarno-formula concerning Article 16, and that she would abandon her suspicions, was doomed to disappointment. During the whole winter of 1925-26 the negotiations dragged on till at last the clauses of the treaty and the accompanying exchange of notes about the guarantee against the menace of sanctions were agreed upon. The non-co-operative attitude of Count Rantzau made the task of the Foreign Office still harder. An insurmountable aversion to the Locarno-policy, stemming almost more from sentiment than from intellect, and the conviction that the blow inflicted on the Rapallo-spirit was irreparable, prevented the Ambassador from a wholehearted co-operation, though he tried to force himself to be helpful. He even declined the proposal which I made to him that the pact should be signed in Moscow. He did not want to link his name with this transaction. This time he lacked foresight as to the effects of the treaty. It was to be signed in Berlin, and the date was fixed for April 26. The Soviet Government managed to give quite an effective setting by proclaiming this fact on the very afternoon of the signature at a session of the so-called parliament in Moscow, thus securing the re-sounding applause of the obedient deputies.

To invest the signing of the Pact with all the paraphernalia of ardent love and mutual friendship did not correspond with the intentions of Stresemann and Schubert. They regarded the whole matter rather as a ransom extorted to hush up an unsavory family affair. Thus the act of signing was reduced to the minimum of decent *mise-en-scène*. A perfunctory lunch, with some phrases of congratulation muttered by Stresemann, followed.

We never learned to make political hay out of the Moscow sunshine, and were in this respect outwitted by far by the Russians. After the Maltzan-Rantzau period and since the beginning of the Locarno-policy there was always a touch of bad conscience in our flirtations with the Russians. We always felt like the boy caught by his parents in a love affair. The Russians, entirely uninhibited by emotions of this kind, were well aware of our embarrassment and resented it. But they squeezed the last drop of propaganda value out of such opportunities. In April, 1932, at the ten-years' jubilee of Rapallo, Litvinov and the Russian delegation, staying in Geneva for the Disarmament Conference, met Chancellor Brüning. Litvinov proposed to Brüning an exchange of speeches at a lunch in commemoration of this jubilee. Brüning consented to the lunch but declined the speeches, as he was afraid that this might produce an unfavorable impression on the assembled Western world. An uneasy lunch was started. Brüning and Litvinov raised their glasses, drinking one another's health. Therewith the official part was terminated.

The romantic honeymoon of the Rapallo-spirit was gradually replaced by the matter-of-fact considerations of developing the trade between both countries. The German economy, having recovered from the disastrous inflationist period and having gained a firmer footing by the Dawes Plan and American credits, was on the lookout for exports. The Soviet Union continued its experiments for the economic rehabilitation of Russia. Lenin's startling *volte-face* from rigid Bolshevik doctrine to the free enterprise of the NEP had proved almost too good to be true. The *laissez-faire* policy had restored the free flow of goods within the country and had re-established some wealth. The fact that the peasants, born enemies of Bolshevism, profiteered from the NEP was causing some uneasiness, but, as yet, no drastic counter-measures. Russia's foreign economic policy, had, however, failed. The attempt to attract foreign capital by granting concessions had met with no response. German industrialists had shown readiness to do business in Russia, but with empty pockets. The German concessions in Russia began to wither as soon as the Soviet Government became aware that this scheme did not fulfil its expectations. True to its customary tactics, the Soviet Union managed to make life a burden to the concessionaires in order to get rid of them and the obligations involved. Inexplicable difficulties arose and prevented a successful working of the concessions. The workers demanded higher wages, the authorities ordered the construction of exorbitant social welfare institutions, the raw materials did not arrive in time or at all. To anybody familiar with the technique of Soviet tactics it became evident that the concessions would never become a going concern. New ways had to be explored.

The Russians wanted to buy, but not to pay cash down. They asked for long-term credits. The Germans wanted to sell, but had to insist on immediate payment, as the war and the inflation had deprived them of the financial basis for credits. Besides, as the economic prosperity of the Soviet Union was in no way assured, German firms deemed credits too great a risk. Moreover, the whole trend of economic mentality was being transformed from that of the individualist or banker with the courage of risking all on a great enterprise to the "managerial" type whose trend of thought and wish to avoid risks gave him the mentality of the permanent official. The "managerial revolution," described by Mr. Burnham, was already in full swing in Germany. Not that these industrialists and bankers were shy of making huge profits, but they preferred to place the risk on the shoulders of the State. That the State might be willing to take the risk for reasons of general economic policy, but that the price would be a strict control of private business—this reflection came to the German businessmen only when they were already half devoured by the Leviathan: *"Qui mange de l'état, en meurt!"*

The start of the credit business moved along traditional lines. A 100- or 150-million-mark credit in cash was granted to the Soviet Union by the four great German D-banks, to be paid back within a comparatively short time—six months or so. The credit was granted to the banks by the Reich. It took infinite pains to persuade everybody concerned to favor this new venture. I had to try to persuade the leaders of the *Reichstag* parties to give their blessing. It almost ended disastrously, as most of these men listened sullenly and were full of distrust of the Soviet Union in general and its economic good will in particular.

This short-term credit in cash gave satisfaction to nobody. Above all, the Russians raised objections. They accepted the credit merely to let the Germans commit the original sin of giving credits. But what they wanted was long-term credits so that the invested capital might pay interests in the form of goods produced by factories constructed with the aid of the credits. A long-drawn-out haggling ensued, until a new form was worked out: the so-called *Kredit-Ausfall-Garantie,* which means that the Russians got the machines ordered in Germany on credit, to be paid back after two years or so; that the financing was arranged between the individual exporting manufacturer and the German banks; and that in case of non-solvency on the part of the Soviet Union, the Reich or the Länder would step in and pay the German industrialist 70–80 percent of the risk involved. Thus practically the individual German ran only the risk of his profit, the more so as prices charged by the Germans were somewhat generous; whereas the Russians retaliated by discovering defects in the goods delivered and lowering the price if the exasperated industrialist lost patience or could not stand the financial strain any longer.

The whole scheme was a happy hunting-ground for discussions, for horse-dealing little short of sharp practice between industrialist and banker, between both and the representatives of the Reich and Ministries of the Federal States, and between all these and the Soviet Union. Infinite variations did not cease to creep in. If the Russians ordered machines to which we attached great importance, they insisted on a longer term; the Federal State where the factory was situated increased the pressure, so that the Reich authorities generally succumbed to this pincer. The first attempt was made with a 300-million-mark credit, financed by the *Ausfall-Garantie*. It worked satisfactorily and became the model for further transactions of the same kind. This was in 1927.

Whereas this difficult but constructive work interested me and gave me satisfaction, the routine work in Russian affairs consisted of an uninterrupted string of loathsome and exciting incidents which disturbed the political atmosphere and had to be settled somehow. Most of them lack general interest and have happily passed into oblivion—the failing memory in old age being one of the most gracious gifts of fate—but I recall two or three of them and I will narrate them here, for the sake of illustrating the relations between the two Governments. One day the Command of the Red Army bestowed a high decoration—something "red," the "Order of the Red Flag," I believe—on the former German bandit chief Max Hölz, who had robbed and killed in Saxony during the uprisings of 1921, though he did it in a certain romantic and gentlemanly way. This angered our military men, who trusted the loyalty of their Soviet comrades.

Another incident, with more serious consequences, was a second show trial, begun by the Soviet Government in the spring of 1928. Once more the German friend was singled out as scapegoat; and, in particular, one of the great firms which was displaying such an interest in the Russian reconstruction, the *Allgemeine Elektrizitätsgesellschaft* (A.E.G.). The purpose was to direct public attention in the Soviet Union to mismanagement of the coal mines. As coal production was lagging and a widespread discontent and embitterment threatened to turn against the Government, the Soviet authorities resorted to their old trick of diverting public opinion from the real causes—bureaucracy and red tape—and to fix the responsibility on some individuals, branding them as wreckers and saboteurs. Among the defendants—most of them Russian engineers and officials—some employees of the A.E.G., engineers and foremen, who acted as specialists and advisers, were put in the dock. They were accused of having participated in the sabotage, with the implication that the machines delivered by the A.E.G. were outmoded and of no use.

This time the Soviet tactics backfired. A wave of indignation swept Germany; a general outcry of scorn and criticism broke loose against the mock trials in particular and Soviet methods in general. Press, industry, trade unions, the *Reichstag*—all joined a bitter campaign of invective against Bolshevik rule, while the Soviet brazenly retorted and kept up its accusations. Official notes and protests were sent to Moscow. I took advantage of this occasion and advised the breaking off of negotiations, which were dragging on in Berlin, with a Soviet delegation about some minor technical questions. They were broken off in accordance with my advice, and this act produced the desired result of causing considerable uneasiness in Moscow. The trial terminated with the customary death sentences, while one of the German defendants was acquitted and two others were condemned to prison, all being released within a few weeks. By and by the excitement subsided and things settled down again. But lasting damage was inflicted on the economic relations between the two countries, and the willingness of German industry to co-operate was impaired. The firm German attitude may have helped to make the Soviet Union single out other nations as objects for its mock trials.

The Kellogg Pact, which was negotiated in Geneva during the summer of 1928, furnished another opportunity to the Foreign Office to demonstrate—though not publicly—one of its leading principles towards the Soviet Union. We never strove for a monopoly of friendship with the Union, but, on the contrary, tried hard to bring our Russian friend back into the comity of nations and to re-establish those links with other nations which had been interrupted by the Bolshevist revolution and the wars of intervention. We were guided by the reflection that a Russia which would again be a full-fledged partner among the great powers would carry more weight as an ally of Germany and that the world-wide suspicions against the dark Russo-German plot would then subside. It was also our hope that the revolution had to die down some day and give way to normal and ordinary relations without the Comintern and world revolution. We had first pinned our hopes on the restoration of free commerce. These hopes were bitterly disappointed, for the NEP was strangled for internal reasons, and so were our hopes in the coming years, just as those of the rest of the world were bound to be. But we thought we might try again.

We did help to overcome one obstacle.

For once we succeeded in winning over the Soviet Union. Litvinov's suspicions were overcome, and even the last obstacle surmounted. No diplomatic relations existed between the Soviet Union and Switzerland, for a Russian diplomat had been murdered in a Lausanne restaurant by a rabidly anti-Bolshevik Swiss citizen. Paul Scheffer, the well-known journalist, who at that time still enjoyed the confidence of the Soviets, acted as mediator between the *Narkomindiel* and the Swiss Government. At last, somewhat belatedly, the Soviet Union affixed its signature to this important document, which was greeted hopefully by the nations of the world.

The more colorful and varying part of my work in these two years of the post-Locarno period was shifted to an international forum, to Geneva. By joining the League of Nations as a permanent member of the Council the German Government was also to protect the German minorities in the territories ceded to Poland and Lithuania in a more efficient way than had been possible before. I was appointed by Stresemann to be a regular member of the German delegation, to act as expert in these problems. Thus I spent a considerable part of the year in Switzerland, as the Council held four sessions annually—in March, June, September, and December—each session lasting at least two weeks. The great gathering of the League in September lasted four or five weeks. As the delegation was composed of the same officials, quite a homogeneous body was formed out of this "travelling circus," as we used to call it, and we worked in perfect harmony. Stresemann and Schubert, Gaus and Göppert from the legal department, Bülow for general matters of League policy, and I for the Eastern affairs, formed the general staff of the delegation. Herr Redlhammer acted as *Chef de Protocole;* Herr Bernhard as personal secretary of Stresemann; Herr Strohm and Herr Trutter as secretaries of Schubert; some casual members were added according to the special needs of sessions.

For the *Assemblée,* the gathering of the whole League in September, five members of the *Reichstag,* representing all the parties (the Communists excepted), enriched the delegation. They were Herr Hoetzsch and Herr von Rheinbaben from the Rightist parties, Herr Kaas of the Center party, Frau Bäumer, Democrat, and Herr Breitscheid, Social Democrat.

Our last voyage to Geneva in September, 1926, was memorable and has left a lasting impression in my mind. At last all stumbling-blocks had been overcome, and Germany was to be admitted as a member of the League. The ceremony of this inaugural session, the solemn entrance of the German delegation, Briand's impressive speech, *"Pas de canons . . .,"* Stresemann's eloquent answer . . . this has been described again and again. A general atmosphere of friendship and conciliation prevailed and strengthened the resolve of all the Germans present to collaborate loyally with this world-embracing organization and to make it a success. I am convinced that the majority of the Germans shared this ardent and honest wish.

71

Geneva during the weeks of the Assembly was truly a gathering point for politicians and important persons—and those who thought they were important—from all continents. The delegations of fifty-two nations were composed of influential and outstanding politicians; the world press dispatched its most prominent representatives. A crowd of international sightseers, would-be politicians, and elegant ladies added some color to the drab seriousness of the sessions and to the Calvinist austerity of Geneva. Crossing the street, smoking a cigarette in the lobby of the Assembly, visiting a smoky little inn—everywhere one met interesting people and could start a conversation about international politics. For us Germans, having been secluded for more than a decade, this dazzling new world was quite a revelation. Whereas the first sessions of the League were being eagerly visited and the speeches listened to attentively, these debates receded by and by into the background, and the merry-go-round of worldly life prevailed. The delegations arranged individual receptions, dinners, or lunches for the journalists, for friendly delegations or "distinguished foreigners." The hospitable Swiss authorities invited their foreign guests.

There was an uninterrupted chain of social events, conferences, sittings of the delegation, excursions. We, the small fry of experts, did not take part in most of these festivities, as the number of the regular delegates already crowded the halls and rooms to overflowing. But we had our full share of the social events of our delegation, and arranged appointments with friends in one of the numerous little restaurants of Geneva. Then we discovered by practical experience that Switzerland produced splendid wines and is, besides, one of the greatest wine-producing countries. The Sunday was dedicated to excursions, mostly to France, to Annecy, or some place which tempted us by an exquisite cuisine, for Stresemann and Schubert were, happily, just as fond of a good dinner as I.

These weeks in Geneva were not exclusively filled with worldly life. Arduous and difficult work loomed in the background and kept us busy till late in the evening or the night. The complaints of the German minorities were numerous, difficult to handle, and in the limelight of European public opinion, especially German opinion. What made them so important was the fact that the treatment of these problems was for the average German the touchstone which was to prove whether the League was a serious institution and fit to re-establish justice, equity, and confidence towards the outer world—sentiments badly shaken in Germany by the non-fulfilment of the Fourteen Points. The other test case was the disarmament problem, which, however, played its decisive part later on and at special conferences in Geneva.

I cannot say that I was a popular member of the German delegation, let alone the secretariat of the League. I had to inundate both harassed bodies with intricate and highly contested questions lacking political glamor, but full of pitfalls, international as well as German. The minorities were not easily satisfied and the Opposition press was waiting eagerly for a weak spot to attack the Government. By attacking League proceedings they killed two birds with one stone; they weakened Stresemann's position, and they could also openly deplore Germany's entry into the League and its inefficiency.

To have gone through this acid test unharmed means to have added very much to one's experience in the diplomatic profession. That was the balance which I drew from my Geneva experience, and I was very well satisfied with this result and with the glimpse into the inner workings of a diplomatic machine. By and by a certain routine developed which started, immediately after the arrival of the delegation, with a conversation with our Consul-General in Geneva, the capable Herr Aschmann, and the German members of the secretariat. They had to furnish us with the "climate" of the secretariat; they had to listen to the different points to be brought forward during the session and to advise us how to proceed. Then followed a session of the German delegation; then conversations with the representatives of the minorities lobbying in Geneva in order to win over the members of the Council to their claims.

My efforts to convince them that cutting down the number of their complaints meant the strengthening of the remaining and more important ones generally remained fruitless. President Sahm, Danzig's representative, an amiable man, generally proved adamant. On one session of the Council, Danzig turned up with seven complaints, starting from the griefs of some schools menaced by Polish interference and mounting to the important quarrel of the Polish munitions depot on the Westerplatte. Everybody who just heard the word "Danzig" grew angry during this session. German representatives from Poznania and Upper Silesia had filed a suit against the Polish authorities accusing them—rightly—of an oppressive and discriminatory taxation of the Germans with the aim to annihilate them economically and to turn them out the cold way. Sometimes also Memel had some complaints against Lithuania. But generally we got along quite satisfactorily with the Lithuanian delegates in Geneva—sly M. Sidzikauskas, the Minister to Berlin, and Premier Woldemaras, a man as stubborn as a mule. Both parties were more united by a common antagonism against Poland than by the desire to fight each other before an international auditorium.

The preliminary preparations thus finished, the next step was a conversation with the officials of the secretariat of the League. The chief of the department of minorities was a Norwegian, M. Colban, later on, as Norwegian Minister, my colleague in London, and a Danish jurist, M.

Rosting; both clever, interested, and well-meaning men, but of course, both under the strain of their difficult position between the devil and the deep sea. Then some formula was being worked out which might be acceptable to both parties concerned. Hopefully I returned to the German delegations and tried to explain the intricacies of the compromise. It was very difficult to get hold of Stresemann, who loved to disappear, to take a walk or a drive or to drink a glass of beer with some friends or journalists. Generally he acquainted himself with the details immediately before the session of the Council.

The session itself was always a gamble. Everything turned out to be entirely different from the prepared and agreed schedule. The secretariat had met difficulties with other departments, or the Poles had taken quite a different turn, or Stresemann himself set aside the notes prepared for him and started with his genius for improvisation for quite another purpose. The infant born from this multiple effort was generally far from satisfactory even to its parents. But it had to be nursed as efficiently as possible. After the session I rushed to the telephone for a heart-to-heart talk with my colleagues in the Foreign Office. They had to be informed and soothed and put on the right track, as they generally were far from satisfied with the results obtained in Geneva; when they were in the know, they could pass on their interpretation to the press and deputies and the rest of the Berlin busybodies. This being done, I tried to buttonhole the German journalists present in Geneva; the same procedure of persuading and explaining followed. Then those of them who were not out to vilify Stresemann and the Government in any case gave our version of the matter to their papers, grateful that somebody else had done the thinking.

It was an exciting and interesting job for somebody whose passion is foreign policy; but disappointing and depressing for somebody who put his heart into his work and tried to undo, or at least make tolerable, the wrong which had been inflicted on millions of Germans.

The more intimate my knowledge became of the Geneva mentality and of the motives which prompted decisions, the more I grew conscious of the fact that the will to mete out justice was not the fundamental motive of this international institution. Its tendency was to hush up existing controversies, to come to a compromise at any cost, and to give the underdogs, the minorities, no more than a bone which would prevent them from barking while in Geneva.

Surveying the positive results obtained for the minorities during these two years of my intimate relationship with the League, I am bound to state that they were inconsiderable. In the long run I perceived that the Council of the League was not a court of justice, with judges high above party politics, intent to find out the real truth and to pronounce a just verdict, but a political body which, according to the strength of the political groups it incorporated, tried to shape a compromise sugar-coated with high-sounding phrases for public consumption.

It was dominated by France and Great Britain. The question of the minorities did not interest either of them. They were concerned with the Balance of Power and how much or how little must be conceded to Germany so as to restrain her from troubling the tepid atmosphere of Geneva. Those Germans who still believed in the justice of international institutions lost the remainder of their idealism when, some years later, the International Court in The Hague passed a judgment motivated by political reasons in the conflict about the Austro-German customs union proposed by Curtius, the German Foreign Minister, and Schober, the Austrian Chancellor, in 1931.

At the bottom of this estrangement was the defective statesmanship of the Western Powers during the period between the two wars. The disappointment caused by the League of Nations strengthened the feeling of frustration of which Stresemann's tragedy was a symbol. It was a contributory cause to the rise of National Socialism.

I was just about to leave Berlin for the customary session of the Council of the League of Nations in June when I received notice that my father was gravely ill. I hurried to Gröditzberg, but he had already lost consciousness and died twenty-four hours later. He bequeathed to me his estate Gröditzberg and appointed me executor of his will. Thus an additional burden weighed on my shoulders for many years to come.

Having returned to Berlin, I resumed my official work. In August Count Rantzau arrived for his leave. He was in poor health, and a few weeks later, on September 8, 1928, he succumbed to an angina. The nomination of his successor took several months, as President Hindenburg turned down the candidate presented to him by Stresemann, and vice versa. At last both parties, exhausted by their fight, dropped the candidates and looked out for a compromise. The compromise was that both agreed to appoint me, and so I was appointed to Moscow in the last days of November, 1928. After some hectic weeks of farewell dinners and private and official business, my wife and I started on January 6, 1929, for our new destination.

III

Ambassador to Moscow

1928–1933

When we reached the frontier station at Niegoreloye we changed over to the broad gauge of the Russian railways and boarded a train which had been placed at our disposal by the Soviet Government. It turned out to be the special coach which had belonged to the Commander-in-Chief of the Russian armies in the First World War, the Grand Duke Nikolai Nikolaevitch. In the drawing-room of the car a huge map on which the front lines of both armies had been marked could be pulled down from the ceiling.

After our arrival in Moscow things moved quickly in accordance with a carefully prearranged plan. I first called on Litvinov and then drove to the Kremlin to hand over my credentials to Kalinin, a friendly old man with spectacles and a pointed beard, looking rather like a village school-teacher. The proceedings were rather informal in spite of the cameramen who swarmed around us, their flashlight cables crossing our path, so that old Kalinin stumbled and asked me apologetically, "Are the newsmen just as impudent in Germany?" When our conversation turned to the Baltic States and to Reval, he remarked thoughtfully, "Oh yes, I know Reval. I was in prison there for some months." Kalinin was very kind and sympathetic, but a mere figurehead without any influence whatever. The ceremony was devoid of military display. G.P.U. General Peterson, the commander of the Kremlin and later a victim of the 1936 purge, was the only military man present.

Having returned to the Embassy in the almost prehistoric motor-car of the *Narkomindiel,* accompanied by M. Florinski, the *Chef de Protocole,* I settled down for the evening performance. The Soviet Government had organized a "German Engineering Week," to which a considerable number of leading German engineers and professors from the technical colleges had been invited. As always when they wanted to start something

76

important, the *Narkomindiel* and the Soviet Embassy in Berlin executed a carefully arranged plan with great alacrity and without informing the Foreign Office beforehand. They invited their prospective German guests individually and had gathered quite a representative lot. It was not until after my arrival in Moscow that I realized that this was to be more than a mere congress. The opening session united the scientific *élite* and a considerable number of prominent party men. My speech, skillfully drafted by Herr Hilger, evoked an enthusiasm which surpassed all our expectations. The reception at the Embassy was even attended by Mikoyan and an atmosphere of friendship, appreciation, and eagerness pleased the German guests.

By and by the important motives behind this "German Engineering Week" began to emerge: we had assisted at the inauguration of the first Five-Year Plan and had acceded to the Russian request for German co-operation in the industralization of the Soviet Union. Thus, by a strange chance, my mission to Moscow coincided with a new start in Russo-German relations, while I had also participated in the opening of a new epoch in the history of the Bolshevik revolution and of Russia.

As I cautiously felt my way through the atmosphere which prevailed during those months in the Russian capital I observed a certain uneasiness, a state of transition, something indefinite and unsettled in the functioning of the State and party machine. Stalin had ousted Trotzky. The NEP period had finished for good. The State-planned industralization of Russia was being set in motion. The voluntary collectivization of farms had failed and was to be replaced by a compulsory system. The Russian element within the party was about to initiate an opposition against the ruthless treatment of the peasants. But a definite victory for Stalin did not seem to be secured, and the new strategic aims and methods had not yet been hammered into the brains of the rank-and-file party official.

After a bitter underground struggle which developed into open conflict, Stalin succeeded in dislodging his far more brilliant and versatile rival, Leo Trotzky, from the secure position which he held among the intelligentsia of the party, the students, and the army. The slow, systematic work of organization on the part of the relentlessly stubborn and wily Caucasian had triumphed over the brilliance, the wit, the oratorical genius, and valor of the somewhat unbalanced and fickle leader of the army. The slow-working party machine, manned by carefully selected and reliable henchmen of Stalin, proved superior to the flaming appeals of Trotzky and the enthusiastic cheering of his admirers.

Trotzky was forced into exile: first to Alma-Ata, in Central Asia, then to the Prinkipo Islands after Turkey had agreed to shelter the emigrant upon whom the final ignominy of expatriation was being inflicted. But in those first few months of 1929 there was unrest in the ranks of the Party still. Leaflets in support of Trotzky were distributed and were even smuggled into the Embassy, while the members of the "Trotzky gang"—Kamenev with his wife, Trotzky's sister, Zinoviev and the versatile Radek— were still holding influential positions, to say nothing of the lesser people, the host of admirers and followers who were later to be branded with increasing furore with the deadly epithet of "Trotzkyite." Hardly one of them was spared: Radek was a notable exception, for, in the long run, the Soviet Press could ill dispense with his brilliant pen.

Gradually the hard political core began to emerge from this turmoil in the form of Stalin's doctrine of "Socialism in one country" as opposed to Trotzky's slogan of permanent world revolution. The conclusions which were being drawn in the outer world from Stalin's doctrine, namely that the Soviet Union had settled down to the consciousness and resolve that a Bolshevik Russia was prepared to collaborate peacefully with the capitalist States, was perhaps somewhat premature. It was probably only a change of method, the frontal attack being replaced by a subterranean approach, so that the bomb, as it were, could be exploded under the very headquarters of the enemy whenever the moment seemed propitious.

But scarcely had this policy been decided upon when new enemies had to be defeated, the adherents of an outmoded doctrine which had been prevalent only a short while previously. The economic boom in conjunction with the NEP had brought about the resurrection of a prosperous peasantry. The more industrious among them, the *Kulaks*, had acquired wealth and were consequently less inclined to collectivization in particular and to the blessings of Soviet rule in general. The party felt that it would have to act. This potential open opposition, which might be added to the latent opposition already in existence, had to be destroyed before it became too powerful.

Stalin himself was no passionate adherent of collectivization merely for the sake of the doctrine. He had been attacked for his slackness by the more ardent theoreticians. He now swung round in favor of compulsory collectivization and of the elimination of the *Kulaks*. Forcible methods, such as deportations, were being applied in spite of the catastrophic consequences to agricultural production and to the minds of 80 per cent of Russia's population; but the cataclysm of the 1932–33 period was nowhere attained in those initial years.

The anti-*Kulak* campaign was slowed down in 1930 by Stalin's famous article in *Izvestia* in which he condemned the excessive zeal which arose from great triumphs. This excess of zeal had had a very unfortunate effect on the Red Army, which consisted for the greater part of peasant boys. Moreover, the Russian peasant element within the higher ranks of the party was still too firmly entrenched to be recklessly ousted by Stalin. Its chief representative, Rykov, who was popular among the peasantry in spite of—or on account of—his heavy drinking, was still Prime Minister. He had to be sidetracked cautiously into the unpolitical office of Minister of Posts and Telegraphs before he could be annihilated, first politically and then physically (a few years later the sinister chief of the G.P.U., Jagoda, received his first *memento mori* by his appointment to the same post). Bukharin, the intellectual and scientific protagonist of the Russian element, still wielded unchallenged influence over the minds of the vast majority of the population. The young and sympathetic Syrzov, the newly appointed Prime Minister of the R.S.F.S.R., the Russian Federal State within the Soviet Union, was the only one who revolted too conspicuously against the persecution of the *Kulaks*. He was deposed, never to be heard of again. These were important reasons prompting Stalin to go slow in his campaign against the peasantry.

The end of the NEP made a new economic policy essential. The encouragement of private enterprise had not only failed by bringing about increased wealth and consequently increased independence and hostility on the part of the peasants, the NEP had also disappointed those who had hoped that it would develop industry by granting concessions to foreign capitalists (as already mentioned, the response was rather poor). The swing back to orthodox Marxism produced its effects in the economic field. State planning came to the fore again, and the Five-Year Plan was drafted and published. Its fundamental principle was, of course, autarchy.

The Soviet Union wanted to be independent of foreign countries for heavy machinery and for goods of every other kind. The main reason behind this scheme was the resolve to build up an armament industry. After the first and somewhat turbulent phase of the interventionist wars and Trotzky's leadership, the systematic organization of a regular army commenced. The deep mistrust felt by the Soviets for the aggressiveness of the capitalist countries prompted them to make the Union completely independent of foreign armament industries.

This trend became perceptible among foreign writers, who classified collectivization with industrialization and described this phenomenon as the second phase of the Russian revolution, as the "revolution from above." In my opinion, however, this classification was artificial and in the nature of an afterthought. It was not confirmed by events. Stalin's rule is characterized by expediencies, by the tendency to counter surging difficulties and problems with appropriate measures without adhering too closely to principles. When the NEP had outlived itself, another way of attaining the goal of industrialization had to be found. This was the gradual and planned building up of an industry under the leadership of the State.

Similarly, as the danger of a wealthy anti-Bolshevik peasantry arose as a consequence of the free enterprise under the NEP, this deadly peril to the party had to be eliminated somehow. Enforced collectivization best served these ends and fitted well into the orthodox doctrine.

But however that may be, the task set by the Five-Year Plan was indeed staggering. Practically every essential condition for the execution of this grandiose scheme was lacking. There was no capital available. Skilled workers formed only a negligible percentage of the working population. The engineers and technicians had been decimated by the revolution. The existing industries were inconsiderable and had declined in many years of war, civil strife, and neglect. Foreign help from France and Great Britain was dangerous, whilst the United States preferred other markets which were easier to handle than enigmatic, revolutionary, and distant Russia. Thus the eyes of the men at the Kremlin turned to Germany.

The able and energetic Ordzonikidse, a close friend and fellow countryman of Stalin, was a particular protagonist of this trend towards Germany. She had maintained friendly relations with the Soviet Union. The consequences of her defeat ruled out any military danger, and she had a highly developed industry and a first-class staff of engineers and skilled workers. The "German Engineering Week" served to encourage the German technical and scientific staff in this new venture. Technical aid was most urgently required, whilst the question of financing it would have to be taken up later on.

A state of transition was also discernible in the realm of foreign policy. Tchitcherin had been undergoing a cure at a German sanatorium for several months, and, in addition to his delicate state of health, he was suffering from a kind of nervous breakdown or a deep inner conflict. Well-founded rumors which leaked through to our Embassy maintained that he wanted to stay in Germany for good, whereas the Kremlin insisted with increasing vigor that he should return. At that time the era of the *nievozvrazhenti*—of the "non-returner" who escaped abroad and started trouble for Moscow by divulging the secrets of the inner circle of the Soviet potentates—was just beginning. At last two friends of Tchitcherin—one of them Dr. Levin, the Kremlin physician who was executed in the purge of 1937—were dispatched to Wiesbaden to coax the Foreign Commissar into submission. They were successful. Tchitcherin obeyed and spent his remaining years in a small flat, musing over the vicissitudes of life.

Thus Litvinov became my partner during my five years of office in Moscow. He had at last achieved his ambition of emerging from the shadow of his much-hated rival Tchitcherin. He exchanged the post of the external emissary for that of the independent statesman, at least as far as this was possible in Moscow. But he was still far from happy. Being no more a member of the Politburo than Tchitcherin, he remained of much lower standing in the party hierarchy than his predecessor.

Foreign politics was not a priority subject with the Politburo at that time, and it was not until ten years later that the appointment of Molotov to this post recorded a change of heart on the part of the Kremlin in this respect. Maxim Maximovitch Litvinov was therefore suffering from a certain inferiority complex. But his capacity for work was unlimited and he was not subject to that somewhat erratic way of life which characterized Tchitcherin; the night-working team Rantzau-Tchitcherin was replaced by the daytime team Dirksen-Litvinov. Whilst he lacked the *finesse* and brilliance of Tchitcherin in his writings, his notes were composed with a terse lucidity of style coupled with a blend of impudence. He was indeed a redoubtable antagonist, being quick-witted and well versed in affairs. Our personal relations almost reached the level of friendship during the years spent handling difficult matters in a conciliatory spirit. The farewell letter which he wrote me some months after my departure from Moscow —he was in Turkey when I left my post—bore ,testimony to these friendly relations.

My official association was rendered somewhat more difficult with him than with his predecessor by reason of the fact that he was no dyed-in-the-wool Rapallo man but only rendered lip-service to that policy. Although he passionately denied any wavering of his faith in this respect, his sympathies belonged to Great Britain, where he had spent the years of his exile and had married an English woman. He had to be sternly admonished whenever he showed signs of deviating in any particular direction. On the whole, however, he remained loyal to the true faith until the coming of National Socialism provided him with the welcome pretext to be one of the first to leave the foundering Rapallo-policy. The further course of his career was symptomatic, for, from that time onward, his appearance on the political scene showed the desire of the Kremlin to display a conciliatory attitude towards the Anglo-Saxon Powers.

In these circumstances the appointment of Nikolai Nikolaevitch Krestinski, for nine years Ambassador to Berlin, as deputy chief to the Foreign Commissar constituted a welcome consolidation of the ranks of those holding genuine German sympathies. As to his position within the party, it ranked considerably higher than that of Litvinov. He belonged to the Old Guard, and, what is more, he had fought in the revolutionary war in Russia and had not escaped to the comparative comfort provided by exile in Zürich, Berlin, or Paris. Those Bolsheviks who had stayed in Russia and had suffered imprisonment and exile to Siberia—such as Stalin, Molotov, Voroshilov, Krestinski—were admired as front-line soldiers, whereas the intellectuals who, after a short term of imprisonment in Russia, escaped into exile, as Trotzky, Kamenev, Radek, and Litvinov did, could never quite get rid of the stigma of having had an easy time in the rear while their comrades risked their lives at the front. Lenin was the only exception to this rule.

In spite of his pro-German leanings and his honesty of character, Krestinski was not an easy man to deal with. He had the mind of a lawyer rather than of a politician and, with his goatee, his convex spectacles, and his sharp, high pitched voice, he was more like a small-town advocate than a statesman. He never succeeded in dissociating himself from this legalistic, theorizing side of his nature which had served him well during the revolutionary part of his career, as it had enabled him to tread the road of barren theory to the bitter end. As Finance Minister in the first years of the revolution he was the author of a pamphlet advocating the ruination of currency as a means of clearing the way for orthodox Marxist barter. He did not care to be reminded of this youthful extravagance. His heroic stand during the trial following the purge of 1937 is well known. After having dutifully confessed to all the crimes assigned to him by the prosecutor Vyshinsky, he revoked his confession as false and extorted. But the next day he reiterated his confession, his resistance having been broken down by the third-degree methods applied to him, which probably included threats of torturing his wife and his beloved daughter Natasha.

In addition to Litvinov and Krestinski there were two other men forming the collegium of the *Narkomindiel* (everything in the Soviet Union was organized not on a one-man basis but on the basis of a number of men acting jointly). These two were Stomonyakov and Karakhan. Stomonyakov, a Bulgarian and former trade representative in Berlin, was a clever, loyal, and agreeable man whose mind worked more accurately and on more Western lines than the complicated and sometimes distorted mind of the Russian. Karakhan, an astute and wily Armenian, reigned supreme over the Far Eastern department. He had derived a deep knowledge of the intricacies of East Asiatic politics from his turbulent ambassadorship to China. He could play tennis, drive his own smart cabriolet, and court the ballerinas of the Bolshoi Theater without prejudice to his party standing. He was rumored to have close connections with Stalin through his friend Yenukidse, the Secretary of State in Stalin's office—a fair-haired, blue-eyed, kindly Georgian with definite pro-German leanings. In any case, both Yenukidse and Karakhan frequently went to the theater, even going backstage. They both met their deaths from the same firing-squad during the purge of 1937.

2. POLITICAL DEVELOPMENTS, 1929–1930

My experience in Berlin had taught me that the legacy which I had inherited from Count Brockdorff-Rantzau was heavily mortgaged and would have to be handled with great care. The rupture in the sequence of Russo-German friendship caused by the Locarno-policy had not been repaired and could not be, as it originated from the central European position of Germany, which forbade any exclusive devotion to one partner. The danger that relations between the two countries might be impaired by their diametrically opposed constitutions and the aggressiveness of the Communist creed continued without any abatement. On the other hand, there was a lack of political temptations which might deflect one of the partners from the paths of virtue. Neither France nor Great Britain, nor any other power, made any attempt to attract either Germany or the Soviet Union into its orbit.

A realistic policy in accordance with the interests of both parties had to be pursued and developed. Such a policy also corresponded with the nature of the two men who had succeeded their more glamorous and brilliant predecessors Rantzau and Tchitcherin. Although at the time I did not foresee the full implications of the Five-Year Plan and of the "German Engineering Week," I was firmly convinced that a strengthening of the economic bonds between the two countries would best serve the interests of either and would, at the same time, be the best way of consolidating their political relations. I had learned to appreciate that military co-operation between the armies of the two countries was another important factor providing for the security of the political edifice. So long as confidence prevailed in this delicate matter (the drawbacks of which Count Rantzau had appreciated as well as I did), the political storms caused by Cominterm interference could more easily be weathered.

I arrived in Moscow with some ready political cash. Litvinov and I signed a treaty of conciliation (*Schlichtungsabkommen*) which had been negotiated beforehand in Berlin and was destined to serve as a substitute for the customary treaty of arbitration. The Soviets were firmly opposed to this method of settling controversies, as they maintained that the inherent difficulty of finding a mediator free from prejudice against the Soviet system could not be overcome. But as they were anxious to demonstrate their will to co-operate in this sphere and to display some new form of international intercourse, we agreed to a treaty whereby two commissions

83

were to be formed to discuss existing differences amicably and to reach some solution.

Although we had no illusions with regard to this new scheme, we felt that, being the first subscribers to such a treaty, the Soviet Government would take care that it worked, at least for some time. The Soviets regarded us as a convenient object on which they could try out the new schemes in international politics which sprang from their own fertile brains. These expectations were fulfilled, for the treaty functioned quite satisfactorily on one or two occasions when we reached a political impasse. But then it began to wear thin and some other device had to be invented.

The *beau geste* of signing this treaty of conciliation was somewhat counterbalanced by some stern admonitions which I had to administer to Litvinov. In December, 1928, the Foreign Office was informed that the Soviet Government had proposed treaties of non-aggression to its Western neighbors. Although this move was not necessarily directed against Germany, but was rather intended as a test as to how far the states concerned were involved in the French *cordon sanitaire* policy, we considered this unilateral action taken without previous notification as a contravention, at least of the spirit, of the treaties of Rapallo and Berlin. It was in such ways that Litvinov loved to express his disapproval of the Locarno-policy.

There was, however, a more delicate and disagreeable question which Litvinov addressed to me during those first months, namely whether the German Government was prepared to grant Trotzky a visa to enter Germany. I was all the more baffled by this request as Trotzky had already been expelled from Russia and had found an ideal refuge on the beautiful Prinkipo Islands. Neither his health nor his life was in danger there. But in spite of my insistence, Litvinov refused to explain the deeper reasons for his request, which probably arose as a result of some party intrigues in the highest circles of the Kremlin. The Foreign Office, however, abhorring the very idea of becoming involved in what might develop into a dangerous situation, turned down Litvinov's request.

On the First of May, the Soviet National Holiday, there was a major incident. The Diplomatic Corps had assembled in the Red Square to attend the parade of the Red Army and the march past. Stalin and the other prominent Soviet leaders stood at Lenin's tomb. It was an impressive spectacle and provided us with one of those rare opportunities for ascertaining the progress made by the army in mechanized arms and aviation. In those days considerable social tension prevailed throughout Europe on account of the impending economic crisis, and there was a threat of general strikes in many countries. When Voroshilov, mounted on a magnificent horse, galloped on to the Red square and addressed the troops, I was dumbfounded to hear him deliver an inflammatory propaganda speech. The gist of his speech was that the Red Army was the guarantor of the rights of the oppressed world proletariat. He followed this up with the open threat that the working masses would start a fight for the improvement of their lot on that very day. And that is exactly what they did in Berlin, Vienna, and some other capitals, where riots broke out and had to be suppressed by force. I had never for a moment expected that Voroshilov, a quiet and unassuming man, would be singled out to fling this insult into the faces of the assembled foreign representatives who were the guests of the Soviet Government.

But there was still worse to come. Immediately after the parade there followed the carefully staged demonstrations by the "jubilant" population of Moscow. Hundreds of thousands of people surged past their rulers in endless columns carrying banners with slogans, or caricatures of *bourgeois* statesmen on decorated cars. On leaving the Red Square with the Diplomatic Corps, I almost collided with a car which was leading the joyous demonstration. Looking at it more closely, I discovered that it represented a dummy cruiser which was manned by some ridiculous figures. It took no long scrutiny to find out that the cruiser was intended to portray a German cruiser which had been the subject of a heated debate in the *Reichstag,* whilst the figures manning it were the caricatures of German Ministers.

I was furious at this outrage inflicted on Germany, of all countries, for she had displayed only helpful and friendly feelings towards the Soviet Union. I hastened to the *Narkomindiel,* which was guarded solely by a watchman. After some hours I got hold of Karakhan and unburdened myself to him. But the result was the same as usual: why all the excitement? Some evasive regrets; Voroshilov's speech was not intended as an intervention in German domestic policy, and it was impossible to control the jubilation of the Russian masses. The Foreign Office, which generally displayed anger at every revelation of the work of the Comintern, failed to give me the support that I expected. And so the matter ended.

I have related this incident at somewhat greater length because it clearly illustrates the methods employed by the Comintern and the situations which had to be faced. In this case a "happy ending" was brought about by Krestinski, who arrived somewhat later from Berlin. He invited my wife and myself to one of the week-end houses where the *élite* of the party sought their recreation in the pleasant environs of Moscow. We met Voroshilov and his wife there as well as some other influential men not normally accessible to foreign diplomats. Voroshilov took this opportunity of apologizing and professing his friendship for Germany. He then invited us to the "House of the Red Army," where he showed us around the museum with its relics of the wars of intervention. He also showed us the shooting-range, where he and I competed with miniature rifles. This was followed by a pleasant lunch at which we made the acquaintance of some prominent generals. And so began my personal relations with Voroshilov, which are among the pleasantest memories I have of my term of office in Moscow. On this occasion a photograph was taken of the party, which was largely responsible for saving my life sixteen years later when the Red Army overwhelmed Silesia and Gröditzberg.

Towards the end of the summer I deemed it necessary to go to Berlin to report to Stresemann and the Foreign Office. I had last seen the Foreign Minister during a hurried trip which I had made to Germany at Easter, when he had been taking a rest from his overwork at the Schloss Hotel in Heidelberg. His health had undergone a marked deterioration. Despite his animated interest in politics, it was evident that he had not long to live. He suffered from frequent breakdowns in the course of his hectic duties. The two days which I had spent with him would have been melancholy had they not been brightened by the visit we paid to one of our old *Studentenkneipen,* which he enjoyed immensely. Now, in September, he was again absent from Berlin, and I had to wait some time before a reply came from him. At last, on October 1, I got a telegram from him, summoning me to Berlin. At the same time I received the news of his death.

His wire to me was the last he dispatched—he succumbed to a stroke only a few hours afterwards. When he gave his secretary the order to wire me, he added, "You needn't use the secret code, it doesn't matter if the Russians decipher it." I hastened to Berlin and attended the funeral. Herr Curtius was appointed as his successor. He was a member of the same party and was Minister for Economic Affairs. Curtius was a refined and talented man of moderate views who had shown considerable interest in the development of German trade relations with Russia. But he lacked the authority and vision which had elevated Stresemann to the rank of a European statesman.

From Berlin I went to the *Weisser Hirsch,* a sanatorium near Dresden, to undergo a cure for my heart ailment; but this was soon interrupted by one of those sudden incidents which are so characteristic of Soviet politics. The news was received from Moscow that Mennonite peasants of German and Dutch stock from all parts of Russia were gathering near the capital. These Mennonites had been induced by Catherine the Great to emigrate to Russia, where, by their thrift and their progressive farming methods, they had acquired considerable wealth. As it was these very qualities which rendered them liable to the persecution of the Soviet authorities, they had organized a massed march on Moscow and were camping in thousands in the suburbs of the city.

Within a few days their numbers grew from 6,000 to 13,000. They demanded permission to emigrate to Germany, and the Soviet Govern-

Dr. von Dirksen with his wife and a party, visiting the Kremlin

ment, bewildered and quite at loss as to how to cope with this unexpected situation, was all the more inclined to accede to their demand, as the gatherings of the Mennonites were causing quite a sensation in the Diplomatic Corps and among the representatives of the foreign press.

The German Cabinet, which was composed of a Left-wing majority, could not come to a decision, and so the affair dragged on. Realizing as I did the potential dangers of this incident which, in Germany, touched upon the danger spot of the German colonists in Russia and their antipathy to collectivization, I offered to break off my medical treatment and return to my post.

In Moscow the general situation had deteriorated. The Government, having overcome its initial shock and being desirous of getting the Mennonites away from the spotlight of publicity as soon as possible, started to deport the peasants. At last the Cabinet in Berlin gave its assent to the entry of the Mennonites into the Reich. In the meantime their numbers had declined to 6,000, and even this reduced number was not allowed to settle in Germany. In their lack of understanding for the needs of agriculture and for the kind of German minorities which existed abroad, these Leftist Ministers in the German Cabinet saw to it that the Mennonites were dispatched to Brazil to settle there.

German-Russian relations deteriorated during the winter of 1929–30. There were no major conflicts, but the wear and tear of daily friction with Muscovite methods caused increasing irritation in Germany. For years Moscow had regarded the radio as its favorite means of attacking the outside world. Almost daily it blared into the ether its abuse of German institutions and parties. What infuriated us most was the fact that these broadcasts were in German. The storm of protests which I made, supported by the Foreign Office, was of no avail. We were blandly informed that the Government had no power whatever over the broadcasting station, as it was run by the trade unions!

Another difficulty developed: the great economic and consular treaty concluded in 1925 during the Locarno Conference proved to be not even worth the paper it was written upon. Having lost the charm of being a *primeur,* the Soviets no longer cared much about its clauses. The complaints of German subjects living in the Soviet Union multiplied, as did also those of our Consuls. Something had to be done, and we considered that the most effective way of letting off some of the steam in the overheated cauldron would be to set in motion the machinery of conciliation provided for by the treaty signed in 1929. I was accordingly summoned to Berlin in April, 1930, to talk these matters over.

But I soon realized that quite an elaborate intrigue had been launched against me and that my trip to Berlin had been arranged by Minister

Curtius for other reasons. This intrigue had been started by a colleague who was anxious to secure the post of Ambassador to Moscow and who enjoyed the close co-operation of friends in the *Reichspräsident's* office and of a newspaper with which they had good connections. Some other Nationalist papers followed on their own initiative. The *leitmotif* of their allegations was that although I had done good work as chief of the Eastern Department, I had lacked vigor in pressing our claims with the Soviet Government. It was maintained that a firmer attitude was essential. Curtius wavered and, lacking the authority of Stresemann, seemed inclined to give way to the pressure brought to bear by Wilhelmstrasse 76—namely the office of the President.

He inquired tentatively whether I would be prepared to return to my post as chief of the Eastern Department, which I flatly refused. In conversations with politicians and high-placed functionaries—among them the Socialist deputy Breitscheid and General von Schleicher—I had ascertained that they condemned these intrigues against me and urged me to stay on at my post. At last Curtius made up his mind and did not press his point. He authorized me to negotiate with the Soviet Government for a composition of outstanding differences by means of the terms of the treaty of conciliation. At about that time Schubert was appointed Ambassador to Rome and Bülow succeeded him as Secretary of State.

I had hardly returned to Moscow and started the talks with the *Narkomindiel* when the storm broke loose in the Berlin press. Some of the papers renewed their allegations of my slackness in the performance of my duties, and all of them published the news that a change of Ambassador at Moscow was imminent. Some of the democratic papers such as the *Berliner Tageblatt* exposed these intrigues against me. But the press department of the Foreign Office remained silent. I must say I was rather infuriated at thus being attacked in the rear at a time when I had to start important negotiations with the Soviet Union and at not receiving any backing from my superiors. I therefore decided to force a decision by asking Minister Curtius to publish an official denial that any changes were impending in the Embassy at Moscow, and to do so within forty-eight hours; if he declined, I told him that I should resign. The denial was published, the intrigue was exposed, and from then on I was able to continue my work undisturbed and was favored by more luck than I had hitherto had.

As to the conciliation scheme, the *Narkomindiel* willingly agreed, and a meeting was arranged for June. Herr von Raumer was appointed as chief German delegate; I have already referred to him, in my mention of the Conference of Geneva, as a brilliant and witty man, a leading industrialist, and a member of the *Reichstag* in the same party as Stresemann. The second delegate was my friend Herr von Moltke from the Foreign Office and Secretary-General Herr Hencke, Count Rantzau's former adjutant. They stayed with us at the Embassy and we thoroughly enjoyed the daily contact with these intelligent and amiable friends.

As for their negotiations, they took the inevitable course of all negotiations with the Soviet authorities at that time—a maximum of squabbling and a minimum of satisfactory results.. The conciliation commission, however, worked in accordance with our expectations, inasmuch as it served as a safety valve and resulted in a welcome cooling off after the previous heated discussions. The experiment was repeated the following year with less satisfactory results and then passed into oblivion. It had served its purpose to demonstrate the progressive diplomatic methods indulged in by the Soviet Government, and some new means had now to be devised.

Some more lasting results than these purely legal ones were obtained, however, in the conversations which Herr von Raumer had with some of the leading Soviet functionaries such as Mikoyan. Raumer was far too sharp-witted not to be aware of the potentialities of a whole continent commencing its industrialization on German economy. Although he had always been in favor of developing trade with the Soviet Union, he assented to my ideas and proposals, which I put to him in the course of long conversations, and from then onward became one of the most ardent supporters of credits for the Soviet Union. His aid was of all the more value to me as he was on terms of friendship with the newly appointed Chancellor, Dr. Brüning.

---

3. GERMAN CREDITS TO THE SOVIET UNION

The Five-Year Plan was nearing its peak. Its immediate effect on Russo-German economic relations was chiefly limited to an increasing influx of German experts and technicians, the result of the drive started by the U.S.S.R. with the "German Engineering Week." At least 5,000 of them were distributed among the far-flung industrial enterprises of the vast Soviet Union. Many of them stayed in Moscow working as experts in the Ministries or planning offices, but the majority of them were employed beyond the Urals, in the Don basin, the Caucasus, and in even more remote districts. There were many highly skilled men among them, although most of them were just ordinary men, out of work in consequence of the growing depression in Germany and glad to find a job in far-away Russia.

The more efficient engineers had, of course, not been discharged by their employers. Nevertheless, the minor workers played an important part. They were not paid in roubles but in foreign currency. The top-ranking engineers received "capitalist" salaries of between 60,000 and 80,000 gold marks, whilst the average engineers received 5,000 to 8,000 marks a year. This amount of foreign exchange was an important factor in the German economy. It was particularly welcome, because these men were not idle during the years of depression and had the opportunity of gaining valuable experience in a foreign country. As for the political aspect of the matter, these engineers scattered all over Russia were a most valuable source of information to me. As the more important of them kept in close touch with the Embassy or the Consulates, we were thoroughly informed, not only about economic developments in the country but also on other topics, such as the views of the people and developments within the party.

I do not think any foreign country, either before or since, has had at its disposal so much detailed information of the Soviet Union as Germany had during those years. This knowledge was reinforced by a most competent staff of collaborators at the Embassy and by the Consuls in different parts of the U.S.S.R. As soon as the German experts left the country and political relations deteriorated, the Iron Curtain went down, excluding us just as securely as the rest of the world from developments inside the Soviet Union.

Apart from this inflow of technicians, Russo-German economic relations were not very much affected by the Five-Year Plan. The credit which had been granted to the Soviet Union about 1928 was still under way. It had not been increased, nor were there any negotiations in progress or planned. The more I acquainted myself with developments in the U.S.S.R., and especially with the Five-Year Plan, the more my conviction was strengthened that Germany had a unique opportunity to increase her exports considerably and to gain a foothold in a country of seemingly boundless industrial potentialities.

I had no illusions as to the duration of this state of affairs, for I realized that the Soviets had not turned to Germany for co-operation in the industrialization of their country out of mere sympathy. I was quite aware that an autarchy as complete as could be attained was the driving power behind the Five-Year Plan. The Soviet ideal would have been to import nothing at all. Moreover, I took into consideration the fact that in a totalitarian State buying and selling is a highly political matter. If the Soviet Union were to embark on a policy of closer contact with the United States or Great Britain, the orders for machinery and other goods would at once be switched over to the new friend and we should be left out in the cold.

But in spite of these considerations—or perhaps on account of them—my positive attitude underwent no change. Even if the first Five-Year

Plan were but a passing opportunity for Germany to trade with the Soviet Union on a big scale, it should be seized. It was well worth while opening a new market for German exports, if only for a few years, provided that hundreds or even thousands of millions of marks' worth of goods could be sold at a time of acute world economic crisis. But I was not so sure that the Russians would succeed in dispensing with foreign goods even after the completion of their industrialization. They would be dependent on Germany for spare parts in any case, and there was also the possibility that many factories would prefer the machines to which they had been accustomed instead of those manufactured by inexperienced workers in the new Russian factories.

Above all, I, as a German, was sufficiently proud of the quality of German goods and workmanship to be convinced that Germany, with her inventiveness and technical skill, would always be well in advance of the Russians, who would have to fall back on Germany anyhow if they were to attain the pinnacle of achievement and efficiency in the technical sphere. I had no doubt in my own mind that they would want to acquire the very latest machines. It is a familiar trait of the Russian, and especially of the Soviet Russian, that he always strives to secure the most modern technical inventions even if they do not fit into his comparatively backward economic system.

The problem of competition had also to be examined closely. Germany enjoyed a certain priority on the Russian market as a result of the friendly political relations which had been established between the two countries. She was a highly industrialized country, with first-class technical and industrial brains, but without having the military or political power at her disposal which might at some time become a danger. Above all, there was no serious competitor for the exploitation of the riches of the Soviet Union at that time. Diplomatic relations between the Union and Great Britain having been broken off, the latter was entirely out of the running, while the United States had failed to display any particular interest, although the International Harvester Company, General Electric, and Ford had done, or were planning, some business in the Union, and Colonel Cooper constructed the Dnieprostroi in competition with Siemens *Bau Union*. But there seemed to be no very strong desire on the part of the United States to enter the Russian market. Besides, the terms were rather strict, cash down being demanded and no credits being granted.

The German monopoly in a doubtful and revolutionary Russian market was bound to be temporary. It might come to an end within a very short time. As soon as the situation in Russia had calmed down or the depression in America became so catastrophic that new markets had to be found at any price, the Anglo-Saxon powers might appear as serious competitors on the Russian market. The Soviet Russian has a definite predilection for many aspects of the American way of life. The vastness of the American continent appeals to him and evokes a kindred feeling, whilst the grandiose industrial development in America is a dream which he yearns to see fulfilled in his own country. America, he thinks, is Russia's only equal.

It has never been Germany's ambition to gain a monopoly of the Russian market, for this would have been far too big a proposition for one country to handle. The risk was considered too great. So we tried to attract interest in the Russian market especially in America and France, just as we had endeavored to bring the Soviet Union into political contact with the outside world. The general motive underlying this was the belief that the risk involved in long-term credits should be shared with other countries. Our Consul-General, Herr Schlesinger, was very adept at shaping such plans and having them discussed in Paris and in the United States. But these ideas only developed at a later date, round about 1932, and before they had been grasped by the capitalists, who are slow to embark on anything new when they can make money more easily in other ways, National Socialism came into power and destroyed these schemes together with many others.

Of course, the idea of common risk and joint business could only mature after Germany had firmly established herself in the Russian market. In order to achieve this we had to provide the Russians with some incentive to induce them to give priority to Germany over other competitors. If they had been able to pay cash down, they would probably have bought their machines in America. But they had no gold or other assets—at least, not in any considerable quantity—and they were anxious to pay with their grain surplus or with other goods which they were going to produce.

We could secure their orders if we were willing to grant long-term credits. This was not new to us, as economic relations between Germany and the Soviet Union had been developing along these lines during the past few years. The point at issue which had now to be decided was whether these credits were to be multiplied or not. This was where the important and heart-searching question arose: whether the Soviet Union could be trusted as a debtor.

After long and careful consideration and a thorough examination of the whole situation, I took my courage in both hands and decided that the Soviets were to be trusted and that we should go ahead with our trade plans. The main reason which induced me to take this stand was my recognition of the fact that the Russian economic system was identical with the Soviet State. The credits granted to a certain trust were only nominally a business transaction concluded with a private concern. In reality, the

Soviet State backed the credit. If the Soviet State was solvent, the credit would be safe.

It all boiled down to the question whether the Soviet Union was going to be a sound concern, and I was convinced that it was.

The boundless energy and ruthlessness of the Soviet leaders had made a deep impression on me. Although not yet out of the economic wood, they had surmounted the toughest obstacles and were on safer ground. I felt sure that they would do their utmost to honor their obligations, as every bill of exchange which was not met meant the bankruptcy of the State.

This trend of thought sounds logical and simple enough, but it cost me many a sleepless night. It was in those very years, namely 1930–32, that the Soviet Union seemed to do everything that was apt to undermine its own solvency. It destroyed the very basis of its remaining assets, its agriculture, by forced collectivization; it ran amok with its human resources, peasants, and industrial workers. Instead of softening its language and methods in order to ingratiate itself, at least to a modest extent, with the capitalist world, it continued to antagonize that world. There was conclusive evidence that the hopes of many naïve people all over the world for a normalization of the Soviet Union were doomed to grave disappointment.

My last retort to all those who did not believe in the solvency of the Soviet Union was that if the Union should become insolvent, the credits invested in Russia could at least be regarded as a productive form of unemployment relief. It seemed to me that this answer was effective because it was based on the catastrophic economic crisis which swept Germany in the years 1930–32. With 6,000,000 unemployed and the thousands of millions which were paid out in unemployment relief, there could be no greater folly than to reject the opportunity of keeping hundreds of thousands of German workers and engineers employed on useful work.

Finally, there was the objection that encouragement would be given to a potential rival. Could we bear the responsibility of helping to build up the resources of a country that might become a dangerous competitor, whose aim was to obtain autarchy and to organize an armaments industry? My answer to this was that Russia would be industrialized in any case, and that the sole effect of our refusal to collaborate would be merely to slow down or postpone this process and not to prevent it. Such a refusal would have to be made at the cost of dispensing with important facilities for German exports. The industries of our competitors would seize such an opportunity and the Russian market would be lost to Germany, perhaps for good.

It was these considerations which prompted me to advocate with

increasing vigor a greater initiative on the part of Germany in her economic policy towards Russia. I used the representations advanced by German
industrialists and made appropriate speeches which they arranged for me
during my stay in Berlin. I drafted my reports to the Foreign Office along
these lines and discussed these matters with my colleagues in Berlin both
orally and in private letters. The more the industrial outlook darkened all
the world over, the more enthusiastic became the Federation of German
Industry. Many leading firms dispatched the chiefs of their Eastern departments to Moscow to study the situation in Russia. But the key men in
German industry were still too proud to come to Moscow themselves,
which the Russians—always sensitive on such points—regarded as a snub.

Thus the German industrialists were quite prepared to make the
handsome profits which were awaiting them in Russia so long as there was
no risk involved and the financing was done by others. This was where
the Finance Ministry of the Reich and of the separate Federal States came
in. The great German banks—the *D-Banks*—refused, of course, to finance
these credits. They were busily engaged in granting long-term loans to
quite fantastic enterprises out of the short-term loans which they had
received from the United States. This was one of the major causes of the
crash in 1931.

The method of making money by the big banking concerns is always
the same: when they borrow, they give 2 per cent interest, and when they
lend, they ask for 8 per cent. The bank tycoons have acquired the psychological *habitus* of functionaries, and it serves them right when the State
comes to devour them by introducing socialization. In the case of the Rus-
sion credits, however, most of the *D-Banks* condescended to form a group
which was to handle and administer the sums paid to or borrowed from
the State. One of them, Jakob Goldschmidt, of the *Darmstädter Bank,* was
even too proud to do this much. After long and complicated discussions
and negotiations with the Ministers and bankers of the Reich and of the
Federal States, a scheme was gradually worked out which created the
foundation for credit operations on a large scale.

Thus the situation in general, together with the experience hitherto
gained in the technique of long-term credits and the comparatively calm
political atmosphere, favored a further extension of our trade with Russia. A certain initiative was taken by the Soviet Union and by Ordzonikidse, the originator of the Five-Year Plan, in particular. He invited the
leading German industrialists to the Soviet Union for a sightseeing trip.
As always, the preparations of a plan to which the Soviet Government
attached great importance were executed with extreme thoroughness and
efficiency. Some of the leading Soviet economists—among them Pyatakov,
if I remember rightly—were dispatched to Germany to issue the invitations

personally and to bring gentle pressure to induce the prospective guests to accept. In this they bypassed the Foreign Office, which only reluctantly took notice of what was going on. This time Soviet initiative met with complete success, for all the important firms accepted the invitation and sent their leading men on the trip to Russia.

It was indeed a most representative delegation of German industry which arrived in Moscow in March, 1931: Krupps, A. E. G., Siemens, Demag, Klöckner, Borsig. The most important firms in the iron, steel, electrical, and machine-tool industries had dispatched their most prominent men. Peter Klöckner, owner of foundries, coal mines, and various other factories in the Ruhr, had been chosen to head the delegation.

He was a self-made man of attractive appearance, very skillful in negotiation and in dealing with men. After a lunch at the Embassy I delivered a long speech to them in order to initiate them into the Moscow atmosphere. The delegation followed my advice not to be in a hurry to commence business talks, but to keep up the appearances of a sightseeing trip, which, after all, was what they had been invited for. After a sumptuous dinner as the guests of Ordzonikidse, which was attended by many leading men, our host said to me rather disappointedly, "Your people don't seem to be very keen on doing business." He had obviously imagined the *bourgeois* capitalists to be greedy profiteers all out for business and nothing else.

A deadlock of some days' duration ensued as each party waited for the other to take the initiative; hosts and guests drove round Moscow seeing the sights and toured factories. At a reception held at the Embassy —a *buffet,* as the Russians call it—I succeeded in setting the ball rolling by a deliberate slip of the tongue while talking to Ordzonikidse and Klöckner. As a result a conference was arranged and hard bargaining started. The Russians almost overwhelmed our people with orders for more than a thousand million marks and provoked not a little incredulity by the length of the credit terms which they demanded. But the German industrialists had not full power to conclude a bargain or to concede credit terms. They were only to be used as the spearhead and driving power to break down the walls of bureaucracy and inertia.

In this they were thoroughly successful. The German representatives were impressed by the results already attained in the construction of heavy industry in and near Moscow and Leningrad, by the prospects for the German industry, and above all, by the energy and the indomitable spirit of the Soviet leaders. Consequently they were quite prepared to incur great risks which were to be shouldered by the Government. Accustomed as they were to direct methods, they did not wait for bureaucratic conferences behind closed doors before expressing their views. Almost before the train bringing them back from Russia had stopped at the Schlesischer Bahnhof in Berlin, they started giving their first interview to the press, namely to the B. Z. *am Mittag*, the great Berlin midday newspaper.

They described in glowing terms the possibilities of German export trade in Russia. Those whose function it was to hold in check rather than to impel the motive forces of German export trade were absolutely aghast. But no effective resistance was possible to the concentrated energy of heavy industry, to the growing economic catastrophe, or to the preparatory work which had been done. A further credit of 300,000,000 marks was granted by the *Reichstag* and was enlarged still further. The credits already granted were transformed into recurrent ones.

It was a very complicated apparatus that was being set up. What was most memorable in this maze of technical detail was that during those two to three years German goods to the value of almost 2,000,000,000 marks were sent to Russia, that in this period Germany headed the list of importers from and exporters to the Soviet Union by about 50 per cent of the total sum of both, that Germany did not lose a penny in these transactions, and that, long after Russo-German trade had been interrupted by the accession of National Socialism, the "gold from Russia" continued to flow into the coffers of the *Reichsbank*.

As a result of the visit of the German industrial delegation, I lived on terms of friendship with some of its members. When we were on leave in Germany, my wife and I visited Herr and Frau Klöckner at their hospitable house near Duisburg, and we also called on Geheimrat Reuter of the Demag works near by. It was a source of satisfaction to me on visiting numerous factories in the Ruhr to see huge boxes and crates everywhere destined for Moscow, Leningrad, or Rostov. These orders from Russia kept a considerable part of the Ruhr industries busy. Hundreds of thousands of German workers and engineers were able to make their living and were thus spared the hardship of unemployment during the most violent economic crisis which the world had experienced for decades.

4. ATTEMPTED MURDER

The period which followed the grant of the long-term credits to the U.S.S.R. and the visit of the German industrialists to Moscow was one of the calmest and most agreeable of my five years in the Russian capital. My belief that close economic relations would create harmonious political relations between Germany and Russia proved to be correct. This atmosphere of calm, however, was soon to be shattered by a dramatic incident.

At noon on Saturday, March 5, 1932, I received a hurried telephone call informing me that a number of shots had been fired at Herr von Twardowski, the counsellor of the Embassy, who had been seriously wounded. I immediately drove to the hospital and saw Twardowski, whose hand had just been X-rayed. Two bones of his left hand had been smashed by the bullet and an operation was necessary. Although he was suffering considerable pain and shock, he displayed great fortitude. Krestinski and the chief of the German section in the *Narkomindiel*, Stern, appeared and offered the apologies of the Soviet Government for the attempt on the life of Twardowski and on mine, for it had been ascertained that the murderer had intended to shoot me and that Twardowski was the victim of a mistake on the part of the criminal, who had been caught by the G.P.U. immediately after the attempt. This is what happened:

Twardowski was driving home from the office, and on reaching a busy crossing where his car was held up by the traffic, a young man fired a shot through the rear window aimed at Twardowski's head, but which fortunately only grazed his neck. He had instinctively raised his hand, which was pierced by the second bullet. By quickly ducking, Twardowski had escaped the three following bullets, which were coolly and accurately aimed, having pierced the window only a few inches away. The murderer then rushed to the car and tried to kill Twardowski with his last bullet, but his revolver jammed and he was arrested on the spot by some G.P.U. officials, who, most fortunately, happened to be passing in their car. The would-be murderer was found to be a young student by the name of Stern.

The mere routine work which this incident involved kept me busy until late in the evening. Happily, Twardowski recovered from his wounds comparatively quickly, although several further operations were necessary and it was years before his hand was properly healed. I had an earnest conversation with Krestinski, urging him to press for an inquiry and to keep me informed about further developments. I had no doubt in my own mind that the Soviet Government would not fail in their duty to prosecute and punish the criminal. They would do this, I felt, not so much out of respect for a friendly power but because Stern had committed a crime against the Soviet Union, for it was evident that the attempted assassination had a political motive and not a personal one. I made the most of the occasion by urging Krestinski to settle some outstanding questions immediately in order to placate the German Government. I wired to the Foreign Office to advise a patient attitude before taking any drastic steps. Late that evening I attended a gathering of the German colony, which had become almost panic-stricken by the news and feared a general pogrom of Germans.

It was, however, rather the political implications which provided the really important and interesting aspect of the incident. Political murders are complicated affairs in Russia, where they are almost a time-honored institution. They bring to the surface more than anything else the twisted thinking of the Slav mind. The most obvious mistake usually made by the Western onlooker is to assume that such murders are committed in order to eliminate somebody whom the murderer regards as noxious in some way. The contrary is often the case. The plotter and his gang frequently intend that the murder they commit shall bring about certain reactions, the ultimate effect of which is their real goal.

When Stolypin was murdered at the Opera in Kiev he was not killed by a desperado who wanted to free Russia of a criminal, but by a secret service agent of the police who wanted to provoke certain repressive measures by the Government against revolutionary movements. When Count Mirbach, one of my predecessors in Moscow, was murdered in 1918, the act was committed not by an ardent Bolshevik who loathed the representative of reactionary, militarist Germany, but by a bitter enemy of the Bolshevik Government, a Social Revolutionary, whose aim was the overthrow of the Soviet system, for he calculated that the German Government would react to the murder of its representative by declaring war on Moscow.

The idea of a plot against my life was quite familiar to me, for I often received menacing letters, frequently, strangely enough, after the conclusion of a credit agreement. The anonymous writer would then declare that the machines to be imported from Germany would have to be paid for with Russian grain and that as a result there would be more starvation in Russia. Thus when this man Stern made his attempt on Twardowski, my first guess was that he was probably some discontented citizen who intended making trouble for his government. I was all the more convinced of this when it became known that he had been ejected from the *Komsomol*, the Communist Youth Organization, and that he was an embittered character who had been difficult to handle ever since childhood.

The G.P.U. inquiry was conducted along these lines. There was, at the same time, quite a significant side-tracking by the competent authorities. They discovered that a second man named Vassiliev was also involved in the affair. Both Stern and Vassiliev had made careful preparations for their plot, and for weeks they had been keeping watch on all visitors to the Embassy from the window of a building opposite our premises in Leontiewski Periulok, and they had especially observed my habits—the hours of my arrival and departure. It was only because on that fateful Saturday I had left the Embassy ten minutes earlier than usual that I was spared.

But the G.P.U. maintained that the Polish Embassy had also been involved. It had been ascertained, so we were told, that both Stern and

Vassiliev had been in touch with the Polish Embassy and with violently anti-German Polish circles. It was further alleged that the intermediary had been the driver of Twardowski's car, a Pole who had been in the employ of the Embassy for ten years. Thus the motive of the two culprits was clearly established: they wanted to embroil the Soviet Union in a conflict with Germany by murdering the Ambassador and had been supported in their act by an anti-German Polish underground movement. I vigorously protested against the attempt to involve our Polish driver in this evidently cooked-up scheme, since I knew him to be a reliable fellow of decent character. I saw to it that further allegations were dropped. Furthermore, I did not believe the story about the Polish plot, and I was quick to pay a return visit to my Polish colleague Patek, who had called on me in this connection.

An entirely different story about the background of this attempt has been told in a book by a German Communist named Albrecht, an idealist who had spent many years in Russia in the service of the Soviet Union in a non-political post as supervisor of forests. Disgusted and disillusioned, like many other German Communists, he returned to his old Fatherland and wrote an interesting and revealing book of some 600 pages *Der Verratene Sozialismus* (The Betrayal of Socialism).

Albrecht claims to have received first-hand information concerning the Stern-Vassiliev plot from a fellow prisoner of both. According to this version, the Comintern considered that the situation in Germany was ripe for a revolutionary outbreak and it regarded the murder of the German Ambassador in Moscow as the best way of bringing things to a head. Overestimating the importance attached to Ambassadors in Germany, they thought that this crime would be immediately answered by the German Government breaking off diplomatic relations with the Soviet Union. They believed that the German proletariat, exasperated by such an outrage, would rise to a man and free itself from the shackles of the Weimar Republic.

Although this version sounds rather fantastic, it certainly is characteristic of the twisted thinking of these people. An acquaintance of mine who was well versed in the practices of the G.P.U. even became suspicious when I told him that a G.P.U. car had by chance been close to the scene of the shooting. He was not quite sure whether this was part of the plot or not!

The climax of the whole episode, namely the trial of Stern and Vassiliev, also raised some difficult questions. The *Narkomindiel* was very anxious for me to be present. But I was not prepared to legalize it by my presence. And yet it was my duty to stress the importance which the German Government attached to the proper conduct of the trial by not ignoring it altogether. I therefore decided to attend that part of it at which the foreign aspect was to be dealt with *in camera*. The show—for only thus could it be described—was produced in an ideal setting, Ulrich being the president of the court, while the notorious Krylenko acted as prosecutor. At that time Vyshinsky had not yet come to the fore. Everything went according to plan—the Soviet plan. The questions put were answered without hesitation, and it was obvious that the various parts had been taught and learned efficiently. But one hitch did occur, and that was when a certain question was put to Stern which he answered in a halting manner. Then he stopped altogether, and thereupon blurted out the following sentence: "I must say here that I was not treated in a European manner during the preliminary interrogation." What he meant was that he had been subjected to torture.

The court and the prosecutor were dumbfounded, and Ulrich ordered an adjournment of twenty minutes. When Stern returned to the witness-box he answered all the questions addressed to him without any further delay and according to plan. They had obviously settled the matter somehow during the adjournment. Both defendants were sentenced to death and, as Albrecht relates in his book, were executed.

But even after the trial, menacing letters to me did not cease. A few days later I received one which warned me, evidently with good intention, that a new plot was being hatched. As the attempt to kill me by shooting had failed, the writer hinted that the next time they would use a bomb. But nothing happened.

The effect which the whole affair had on our daily life was that the G.P.U. kept an even stricter watch on every step I took. The secret police gladly seized this opportunity of abandoning the surreptitious shadowing of the movements of the diplomatic representatives and they now made no attempt to conceal their activities. Under the pretext that after the attempt on Twardowski's life more efficient protection was essential, the Ambassadors were followed by plain-clothes police agents in a Ford car as soon as they left their houses. Whenever I stopped to go for a walk, the occupants of the Ford did likewise and surrounded me, more or less inconspicuously. They accompanied me on my travels, and when I was on a shooting expedition in the Northern Caucasus, they insisted on occupying the next stand. When I shot a hare from some distance they enthusiastically exclaimed, *"Isklyuchitelno udachno!"* (Marvelous indeed!) And when, in 1933, Russo-German relations became strained, the G.P.U. brought home to me the alleged enmity and exasperation of Russian public opinion by employing *two* Ford cars with G.P.U. men to follow me.

---
5. THE SECOND PERIOD

The second period of my mission to Moscow lasted from the autumn of 1930 until January 30, 1933. It started with the negotiations of the conciliation commission which had revived the rather downcast relations between the two countries. It reached its climax with the visit of the German industrialists and the political and economic after-effects of that visit. But even while these after-effects still lasted, the political edifice was showing the first signs of collapse. It was difficult to fix a date or a definite cause for this feeling of uneasiness in the political sphere.

In Germany some important changes had occurred in high places. The Foreign Minister, Curtius, had been a victim of the attempt to conclude a customs union with Austria. Both he and the Austrian Chancellor Schober had acted in all sincerity, but there had been an immediate and sharp reaction on the part of the French Government. So the post of Foreign Minister remained vacant until 1932, when Herr von Neurath was appointed a member of the Papen Cabinet. Until his appointment, Chancellor Brüning acted as Foreign Minister. He gained renown throughout the world for his statesmanship, his courage and loyalty, and, above all, for his moral integrity, his human understanding, and the deep religious faith which governed all his actions. But the times were too troubled, the political situation at home too confused, and his own modesty too pronounced, for him to give more than perfunctory attention to foreign affairs.

Thus the dominant figure, so far as the shaping of German foreign policy was concerned in those years, was the Secretary of State, who collaborated in perfect harmony with the Chancellor. There was one respect, however, in which Brüning had a definite conviction of his own, and that was on the subject of the Soviet Union. His religion was too profound for him to have anything but feelings of repugnance for that anti-religious State and its methods. He was always willing to listen to arguments put forward in support of co-operation with the Soviet Union, if only for the economic benefit to his country, which was prostrated by the effects of a terrible crisis. But he avoided any initiative in that direction, and any support which he did give was confined to a bare minimum.

Thus my opposite number during this period was chiefly Bülow. Although we were good friends, we came to realize more and more, in our handling of routine matters and political questions, how fundamentally different our characters were. His personality has been ably and sympathetically described in the book by the former French Ambassador in Berlin, M. François-Poncet. Bülow's high intellectual standard, his flair for politics, and his wide knowledge of international affairs in their most varied aspects were somewhat handicapped by a critical and analytical mind which prevented a positive and creative approach to political problems. His analysis of every situation was so thorough that he always found weighty reasons for a policy of "wait and see." Furthermore, everything connected with Soviet affairs was almost physically repugnant to him. Thus in Russo-German affairs he was somewhat bypassed by events, but on other occasions he did not fail to assert himself.

It was a source of sincere regret to me that there had also been some sweeping changes among the top men in the department of Eastern affairs. My successor, Trautmann, had been appointed Ambassador to Nanking, and my friend Moltke to Warsaw. He was succeeded by Herr Richard Meyer, whose boisterous and dynamic personality had earned for him the nickname of *Raketen-Richard* (Rocket-Richard). He handled Russian affairs more according to the fluctuation in the different moods prevailing in Berlin than by the maintenance of any steady long-term policy. He often had to be reminded of the policy which ought to be pursued.

The following example may serve to illustrate the atmosphere I want to describe. In 1931 the Berlin Treaty of 1926 had been renewed for a similar period on its expiration. To celebrate this event Krestinski had invited me and the leading members of the Embassy staff to a luncheon at which, we were told, Molotov (who, in the meantime, had succeeded Rykov as Prime Minister) would act as host. This was quite exceptional, as Molotov generally loathed any intercourse with foreigners. But as we spoke Russian pretty fluently—Hilger speaking it as well as a Russian—we had an agreeable lunch with interesting conversation.

In the middle of the meal I was called to the telephone to speak to Meyer, who frantically asked me whether the press had been informed of the treaty of prolongation. When I replied that this very likely was so, he urged me to do everything in my power to stop publication. I returned to the luncheon party with an uncomfortable feeling, for it was obvious that some unfavorable development was in the making. When I replied some hours later that the Press Bureau of the *Narkomindiel* had informed the press, Meyer became almost desperate and again urged me to do my utmost to effect the suppression of the news. Meyer insisted that the Chancellor attached the greatest importance to this suppression. It was, of course, quite impossible to revoke news which had already been issued to the press for publication; and the net result of "Rocket-Richard's" activity was inevitably that he invoked the deep distrust and disappointment of the Soviet authorities who had tapped our telephone conversation. Thus the salutary effect of the signing of the treaty had been nullified and the treaty itself was dogged by ill luck. As a result of the incredible domestic muddle in Germany of changing Cabinets and of disagreements between the thirty-two or more political parties, the ratification of the treaty was protracted for nearly two years. Indeed, it was not ratified until after the Nazis had come to power.

It is characteristic of the whole atmosphere and of the persons holding office at that time that Chancellor Brüning desired to withhold the news of the signing of the treaty because the German Government intended to make a *démarche* in Paris on one of the urgent economic questions which was then pending. The Chancellor feared that on hearing the news of some Russo-German accord, the French Government would not feel so disposed to give favorable consideration to the proposals which we intended to put forward. Never have the Allied Powers had to deal with German Governments of such honest purpose and so eager to please them than those which held office in the fourteen years of the Weimar period, and never have opportunities been wasted in such an incomprehensible way.

The men at the Kremlin, however, were far too hardened politicians to be influenced by such minor social incidents. They were more influenced by the general situation in Germany. The financial breakdown of the banks, followed by a moratorium and the disastrous economic crisis with 6,000,000 unemployed, had reduced Germany's international standing to nil. The efforts made in the twenties to restore her economic and political prestige had been futile. Social unrest was increasing almost to the point of revolution. The rise of Left- and Right-wing radicalism presaged civil war. Scarcely a day passed without some act of violence between these antagonists. The Communists seized power in Leipzig and maintained their hold on the city for several days until the *Reichswehr* intervened and restored order. In Berlin police officers were attacked and killed in broad daylight, and in November, 1932, the Communists and the National Socialists joined in a widespread strike.

The Papen Cabinet, which had been installed by the *Reichspräsident*, only had the support of the *Reichswehr* and the police, whilst in the *Reichstag* it had the backing of the moderate Right, the followers of which diminished alarmingly at every election. The Soviet Government might will have gloated over the rise of Left-wing radicalism. But the scale was evidently tipping towards the Right. The Soviets viewed the Papen Cabinet with little favor, as Papen was rabidly anti-Bolshevik. The fact that General von Schleicher, who was popular with the Russians, also belonged to the Cabinet as War Minister offered them little consolation.

Hitler was looming in the background, and the *Narkomindiel* became almost panic-stricken when, in August, rumors were current concerning negotiations between Marshal von Hindenburg and Hitler. But this time the danger passed, and the reshuffle of the Cabinet, as a result of which Papen was ousted and replaced by Schleicher, gave them some respite, although this was to be of only short duration.

While the Soviet Union observed the situation in Germany with some uncertainty and misgiving, pressure was brought to bear upon her from another quarter in order to induce her to loosen her bonds with her Rapallo partner. The Russian policy of France grew more positive than it had been during the last few years. The open hostility which had characterized the relations between the two countries for several years was replaced by an attempt on the part of the Quai d'Orsay to gain the friendship of the Soviet Union and to reconcile her with her ally Poland. The period of Franco-German reconciliation, as advocated by Briand and characterized by Locarno, Geneva, and Thoiry, came to an end with the resignation of that statesman. His successors, and in particular Barthou, looked with suspicion at the growing tide of nationalism in Germany and resolved to strengthen the coalition of the allies who were to keep Germany at bay on her Eastern frontier.

To ease the tension with the Kremlin proved a comparatively easy task. The influence of the Westerners in Moscow, which was never to be underestimated, increased in proportion to the feeling of uneasiness towards Germany. Litvinov had no difficulty in persuading the Politburo that the French offer to conclude a non-aggression pact involved no risk and might be useful in any case. No pertinent objections were to be expected from Berlin, although such a pact might cause feelings of jealousy there comparable to the corresponding state of mind in Moscow during the negotiations which led to the conclusion of the Locarno Pact. Such misgivings, it was thought, might even be quite helpful to those German politicians having definitely Western views. Thus Franco-Russian negotiations were opened, and in due course the treaty was concluded.

To achieve the ulterior end which they desired, namely a Polish-Russian reconciliation, proved to be a much more difficult task for the French, for these two States had never been on really friendly terms with each other. The Soviet Union still bore resentment against the Poles on account of Pilsudski's attack and the strongly anti-Russian attitude of his followers. It had watched with apprehension and distrust the rôle of Poland as France's watchdog in Eastern Europe, directed as much against Russia as against Germany.

This common attitude towards Poland on the part of Russia and Germany was an important link in the friendship of the two countries. Moscow was fully aware of Germany's susceptibility to anything which might strengthen or legalize the possession of the East German territories ceded to Poland under the dictate of Versailles. Article 19 of the Covenant of the League of Nations, which provided for the revision of frontiers and which, incidentally, proved to be unworkable, had been one of the strongest inducements to the German Government to join the League.

On the other hand, the Soviet Union did not want to display an aggressive attitude by declining the Polish proposal, backed by France, to resume negotiations for the conclusion of a non-aggression pact which had been broken off some years before. And so the preliminary talks commenced and took a slow and difficult course.

The Foreign Office was deeply alarmed at the news. Above all, it was particularly those who had never displayed any keen interest in keeping the temperature of our relations with Russia above freezing-point, namely Bülow and, even more so, Meyer, who were highly indignant at the infidelity of our Russian friends. I was summoned to Berlin several times in order to explain the intentions of the Soviet Government and to be exhorted to bring the utmost pressure to bear on the *Narkomindiel*. But my state of mind was much calmer, for I felt pretty sure that the Russians did not intend making any dramatic change of policy, provided they were confronted with frankness and determination. The conclusion of a Russo-Polish treaty only constituted a political danger in so far as it meant that a bridge would be constructed by which the Russians could withdraw to another political combination should they feel constrained to sever the bonds which linked them with Germany. I was even able to reassure the Foreign Office by drawing attention to an interview which had just been granted by Stalin to Emil Ludwig. It was quite unusual for the actual ruler of Russia to emerge from his anonymity in such a definite manner to assert that the negotiations with Poland were in no way intended to alter the relations with Germany. But even this medicine failed to produce any soothing effect.

When Litvinov passed through Berlin on his way to Geneva in the summer of 1932, he was closely questioned as to the ulterior motives behind the negotiations conducted by the Soviet Union with Poland. He gave an assurance of the unchanged loyalty of the Union in her attitude towards Germany. After returning to Moscow from my leave, which I had to interrupt in order to settle a strike of the crews of German ships in Russian ports, I remained in close touch with Litvinov in the ensuing autumn months of that year. He loyally kept me informed about the course of the negotiations and even showed me me the drafts of the clauses under consideration. I was thus able to raise objections and to suggest counter-proposals which, to some extent, were accepted.

Of course, the extravagant demands with which Richard Meyer

bombarded me from Berlin could not be entirely satisfied, for after all it was a Russo-Polish treaty which was being negotiated and not a Russo-German treaty. But our main demand was satisfied unequivocally, namely, that the Soviet Union should refrain from guaranteeing, even in the remotest sense of the word, the actual frontiers between Germany and Poland. Then the inevitable happened—the treaty was signed. The event passed without creating any great stir in German public opinion, which was engrossed by the successive crises during the months that led up to January 30, 1933.

As far as the treaty was concerned, I felt inclined to believe Litvinov's assurance that it did not constitute a change of heart and that, for obvious political reasons, the Soviet Government could not decline the conclusion of a treaty which professed such peaceful intentions. But all non-aggression pacts can be compared to a bowl which can either be filled with the milk of peaceful intention or with the virulent brew of menace. One fact of paramount importance was that, so far as Moscow was concerned, Russo-German relations were undoubtedly beginning to totter. One could not but reach this conclusion from an utterance made by Marshal Yegorov, the Chief of Staff of the Red Army and one of the staunchest supporters of Russo-German friendship. Yegorov, an officer of high character who was later to be executed in the 1936–37 purge, implored our military attaché, General Köstring, to impress upon the German Government that Germany would have to make up her mind whether she wanted to align her policy with the East or the West. If she preferred to waver between the two or to take sides with the West, a fundamental change in Soviet policy would be inevitable.

Thus the accession to power of the National Socialists coincided with a crisis in Russo-German relations, but did not cause it. The end of the positive policy of collaboration pursued by both countries which came about in the year 1933 under Hitler's rule was not unavoidable. At least it might have been postponed.

It was into this highly complicated situation that the long-foreseen and dreaded bombshell burst. During a reception at the Japanese Embassy the news reached Moscow that the Schleicher Cabinet had resigned and that President von Hindenburg had requested Hitler to form a new Cabinet. The National Socialists had come to power.

6. THE THIRD PERIOD, 1933

Such a momentous event as the beginning of the National-Socialist era was bound to leave its mark on the life of the individual. Prevention is better than cure, and it is easy to pass judgment, after the catastrophe, on those who believed that the collaboration of moderate and sensible men with this new mass movement might direct the forces unleashed by Hitler into normal and productive channels. We, the permanent officials, had endured fifteen years of crises, upheavals bordering on revolution, changes of Cabinet, and economic catastrophes. It was evident to us that the foundations of the parliamentary régime of the Weimar Revolution were crumbling, and that Germany was facing the alternative of Communist or National-Socialist rule. We all loathed Communism, but National Socialism did not appeal to us either, and we were highly skeptical of its leaders. Hitler seemed to be a successful and highly efficient demagogue, his doctrines as revealed in *Mein Kampf* dangerous and lacking in originality, whilst the programme of the party was nebulous.

Nevertheless, the impression prevailed that enormous energies had been released by this movement, that an enthusiasm had been set in motion which justified the hope that this new state of mind might develop into a new and creative period following fifteen years of unrest, uncertainty, and growing economic and social chaos. After all, history had taught us that the first leaders of the revolution were selected by fate, not for their conservative and productive qualities, but for their demagogic skill and their restless energy. It was generally believed and hoped that the incurable revolutionaries would be eliminated in time and that their successors, after having tasted the wine of power and the comforts which it brought, would turn to productive work and to a more conservative mentality.

And so we felt it to be our duty to assist in this process of normalization. We had been successful so far in our endeavors to train the newcomers in political leadership and to keep the ship of state on a straight course in spite of the storms which it had encountered. Thus, almost all the career diplomats as well as the other permanent officials remained in office. It was not until years later that I heard of the earnest and insistent requests which had been made to this effect by Chancellor Brüning to Bülow. As to the constitutional and juridical implications of the new situation, the permanent officials were perfectly justified in placing their services at the disposal of the party which had gained power by constitutional and democratic elections.

The Foreign Office in particular remained unaffected by the new rule in Germany. The Nazis did not press for changes in key positions as they did in other Ministries, and all the leading officials remained at their posts, including one Jew and one who was married to a Jewess. Although they planted one rather harmless man in the personnel department, he had no executive function, was smothered with files, received no information, and retired in disgust after a few months. Then Ribbentrop was brought into the Foreign Office in a minor position. But his boundless ambition was not satisfied. He only attended social functions arranged by the Foreign Office when it was found impossible to exclude him. One such occasion was the luncheon given in honor of Mr. Eden. But instead of being placed next to the British statesman, Ribbentrop had to be content with a seat among the junior officials.

He thereupon displayed his anger by leaving the Foreign Office and starting a competitive enterprise of his own.

It is doubtful whether this almost provocative and negative attitude on the part of Bülow and Neurath was altogether wise. Perhaps a more conciliatory tendency might have prevented the Hitler-Ribbentrop counter-move to bypass entirely the official channels to other countries which had the result that really important problems were dealt with solely by Ribbentrop and his office of amateurs. But looking bock on those happenings now, one realizes that the ultimate result would not have been any different, for sooner or later it was inevitable that Ribbentrop would assume office as Minister of Foreign Affairs.

Of the countries likely to be affected by Nazi foreign policy, Russia was foremost. In his book *Mein Kampf,* Hitler, who was himself a rabid anti-Bolshevik, had divulged his intention to partition Russia and to annex the Ukraine. The all-important question both as regards our policy in general and for me personally was whether Hitler, as the responsible leader of Germany, would carry out this intention or whether his book was merely the unconsidered outburst of a youthful hothead who had since abandoned such principles in favor of more statesmanlike reasoning.

If Hitler was planning deliberately to incur the hostility of the Soviet Union, my work in Moscow would be finished. If, on the other hand, he confined himself to a suppression of German Communism, I deemed it possible to maintain mutual relations with Russia on a satisfactory level. We had for so many years endured provocation and difficulty on the part of the Soviets that it was now their turn to accept our assurances that the suppression of German Communism did not represent any hostile feelings towards the Soviet Union and was to be regarded as a purely domestic measure. The Two-Track Policy (*Zweigleisigkeit*), so characteristic of our relations, which had so far worked unilaterally, would have to be balanced.

In my eager desire to clarify the fundamental question of Hitler's attitude towards Russia I was somewhat thwarted by Neurath and Bülow. They advised me to postpone my intended visit to Berlin until things had become more settled. So I had to wait. On the Soviet side complete silence prevailed during those first few months. The press refrained from all diatribe and confined itself to reporting mere facts. The anxiety and skepticism which was felt in the inner circle, however, became apparent in all my conversations with leading Soviet politicians. They willingly accepted the thesis that the treatment of the German Communists would not affect our relations. But they were extremely skeptical of Hitler's intentions and eagerly awaited the new dictator's first official speech. But Hitler postponed this for almost two months.

In the meantime the first decisive setbacks were being administered to the friendly policy towards Russia which had been pursued hitherto. These took the form of a long series of incidents provoked by the rowdy gangster methods of individual S. A. men and minor party officials, who, in their determination to bait Communists, committed outrages on Soviet citizens. They beat up a Jew in a railway train who turned out to be an important representative of some trust. They would, on their own initiative, attack some Soviet consulate or arrest the Soviet members of a trade representation. The increasing irritation which this caused in Moscow was evident, and it was obvious that an explosion might occur at any moment.

Gradually a clearer line of policy with regard to Russia seemed to crystallize in Berlin. On March 23 Hitler made his famous speech on the foreign policy of the Third Reich, which was comparatively moderate in tone and, so far as Russia was concerned, positive. He desired, he said, to establish friendly relations with Germany's great Eastern neighbor provided that there was no interference from that quarter with German internal affairs. Hitler gave proof of this intention by an act which, although it was kept strictly secret, rendered an important service to the Soviet Union on the delicate question of the payments due by her under the long-term credit agreement which had been negotiated two years previously. Up to that time the Soviet Union had always met these obligations promptly. But now, for the first time, we were being informed in confidence that a postponement for some months of the drafts due in March and April would be extremely welcome in Moscow. The banks and the Ministries concerned were prepared to agree to this, but, of course, the matter had to be brought before Hitler for final approval. Contrary to our expectations, he declared his consent.

Now at last Neurath and Bülow considered the time propitious for my trip to Berlin for an interview with Hitler. I had not to wait long for an appointment, but when I arrived to keep it, I was kept waiting almost

an hour. Precision and punctuality were not among the outstanding qualities of Hitler and his staff. While Marshal Hindenburg received his visitors
punctually at the fixed hour and the Chancellors tried their best to do so,
an interview with Hitler and the other leading Nazis was usually something of a gamble. It was quite likely to be postponed at the last minute to
another day, or one was kept waiting indefinitely. At last these nuisances
came to an end, so far as I was concerned, when he declined to receive me
at all after my appointment as Ambassador to Great Britain.

No question has been addressed to me so frequently as that about
my impressions of Hitler and my conversations with him. In all truth,
I must confess that he failed to impress me at all, and as to the interviews I
had with him, only a few highlights remain impressed upon my memory,
and these are not backed by notes or diaries. Whilst I was keenly aware of
the demonic spell which he was able to cast over his audiences by his gifted
oratory when addressing gatherings at Nüremberg or in the *Reichstag*, he
failed to introduce this hypnotism into intimate conversation, at least so
far as I was concerned. He lacked the self-assurance and dignity of a truly
strong character—qualities which are entirely independent of social standing. Ebert had impressed me by his unassuming dignity: Otto Braun, the
Prussian Prime Minister, by his forceful character; Noske by his gruff
frankness; and Brüning by the modesty of a noble mind. But greeting me
as he did with almost exaggerated courtesy, addressing me as "Your Excellency," Hitler failed to hypnotize, particularly as his cold blue eyes averted
my glance.

Our conversation, however, took a favorable turn. He listened to my
report, asked some questions, and reiterated his desire, which he had expressed in his *Reichstag* speech, for the maintenance of friendly relations
with the Soviet Union, provided that she did not interfere with the internal
affairs of Germany.

Then an episode occurred which I have never forgotten. Hitler rose,
went across to the window, and, gazing into the park of the *Reichskanzlei*
remarked dreamily: "If only we could come to an agreement with Poland!
But Pilsudski is the only man with whom that would be possible." I replied
that this would be possible only if Germany were to renounce her claim to
the "Corridor," and that this claim, upheld by the entire German nation,
had united the German people in the years of internal strife. But Hitler
refrained from taking the subject any farther.

At that time I also had the opportunity of acquainting myself with
President Hindenburg's state of mind. When he received me for my customary interview, I addressed a personal question to him, for he had always
been very kind to me. I asked after his health. He replied with a sigh, "It
is all very difficult. Look here," and he pointed to a pile of papers on his

desk; "here are the files of a Jewish lawyer, an honorable man who has always paid his taxes punctually, and has now committed suicide." The President of the Reich had demanded that the Jews be treated in a decent manner. He had obtained a promise from Hitler that those Jews who had done active service in the war should be allowed to retain their positions as officials and lawyers. But, of course, Hitler broke this promise within a very short time.

After having called on Göring, Gœbbels, and Frick, to whom I reiterated my exhortations and warnings as to the Soviet Union and the consequences which a continuation of the outrages on the part of individual S.A. men might produce, I left the capital quite satisfied with the result of my conversations. I had gained the impression that the authorities had asserted themselves in the face of the unruly elements of the party, that no rash acts directed against the Soviet Union were intended, and that it might be possible, after all, to get the Russo-German apparatus into working order again.

But it was too late for appeasement. Litvinov listened attentively but incredulously to the description of my Berlin visit. The incidents did not cease altogether, and one day in April the Soviet press exploded with a series of furious articles which were followed up by a sharp note from the *Narkomindiel*. The waiting attitude had been abandoned and the offensive had commenced. The most favorable psychological moment for a restoration of normal relations had been allowed to pass. But even then things did not deteriorate to the extreme. We sent a comparatively courteous reply to the Soviet Note, admitted most of the outrages, and gave an assurance that steps were being taken to prevent the continuation of such lawlessness. A new impetus was given to the conciliatory trend on both sides by the ratification of the treaty of prolongation under the "Berlin Treaty."

As I have mentioned in a previous chapter, this treaty had been drawn up in 1931, but the German Government had so far failed to secure its ratification by the competent authorities and by the *Reichstag* owing to the uninterrupted series of Cabinet crises and new elections. Nothing illustrates more effectively the decay of the latter years of the Weimar period than the inability to fulfil the purely routine function of ratifying an insignificant treaty to which no essential objection existed among the parties and the government. The Russians, who, throughout these two years, had been incapable of grasping the fact that these delays were simply due to the deficiencies in the German constitutional apparatus, could only be soothed with difficulty and were always suspicious that there was some dark plot looming in the background. Now the ratification was completed within a few days, and the documents were exchanged on May

5, 1933. The supporters of Russo-German understanding, such as Krestinski, were frankly delighted, while Litvinov could not suppress his moroseness and incredulity. He had evidently broken with the Rapallo-policy for good.

Although things settled down somewhat and the press bombardment subsided into spasmodic sniping, the situation was still far from normal. The destruction of an edifice which had been constructed in the course of many years with infinite pains was now being continued from both sides in a more scientific way. In Germany the *Derop,* the powerful Soviet organization for the distribution of Soviet oil throughout the Reich, which was doubtless also used for the dissemination of Soviet propaganda (or at least to provide well-paid jobs to favored Communists and Fellow Travellers), was searched, scrutinized, and undermined by the German authorities. This was done partly to extirpate Communist cells and partly to replace Soviet favorites by Nazis. The Soviet Government in its turn gave notice of its intention to liquidate the so-called *Drusag,* the great agricultural concession which the Reich had taken over from private owners in the Northern Caucasus almost a decade previously. The aim of the *Drusag* had been to propagate German farming methods, livestock, seeds, and agricultural machines. Under the able and energetic leadership of Dr. Dittloff, who was assisted by sixty qualified German agriculturists, some important work had been performed during those years. But following the unambiguous advice of the *Narkomindiel* we preferred to close the concession and to hand it over to the Soviet authorities rather than wait for compulsory liquidation.

On the initiative of the Soviet Union, military relations were now also terminated. They had weathered the first storm quite successfully, and I had taken advantage of an occasion which arose to invite Voroshilov, Budenny, and other leading generals to a dinner at the Embassy. They accepted after some hesitation, and after dinner we entertained them with a film show which included some Russian scenes, which my wife had filmed, and one of the so-called "Day of Potsdam," on which Hindenburg and Hitler had paid their respects to Frederick the Great and to the traditions of Potsdam. But in May or June our military authorities were given to understand that the Red Army desired to sever its bonds with the *Reichswehr.* A *Reichswehr* delegation headed by General von Bockelberg arrived in Moscow and everything was settled in an amicable spirit. The military representatives of both countries took leave of each other in a somewhat melancholy atmosphere, rather like good friends who part not of their own free will but under the pressure of adverse events.

Another negative factor which had its roots in pre-Nazi days now began to mature, contributing to the general deterioration in mutual relations.

The First Five-Year Plan was coming to an end. Its results had been impressive and had been duly magnified by Soviet propaganda. As were to be foreseen, the achievements under the Plan greatly increased Communist self-assurance. That common trait of backward nations of depending on foreign helpers for their development, only to expel them as soon as they had served their purpose, now came to the fore again. The Russians wanted to get rid of the German technicians and engineers. This desire had become apparent in 1932 by the unmistakable sign that difficulties were cropping up everywhere. The competence of some of the men began to be questioned, and contracts were broken on some flimsy pretext or other.

Then the Russians arbitrarily began to pay them in roubles instead of *hard* currency, whilst many of them were discharged for no apparent reason. These tactics continued on a large scale in 1933, so that considerable resentment was created among the German engineers, who returned to their home country in thousands. By publishing their experiences, they created further ill-feeling against the Soviet Union in Germany.

The general economic situation in the Soviet Union had a similar effect. The process of forced collectivization introduced by Stalin in 1928–29 was entering upon its final phase. The Soviets were determined to break the passive resistance of the peasants at all costs. Those who refused to surrender their private property and join the *Kolkhoz* were deported or starved to death.

According to conservative estimates, between six and seven million people died of starvation. Whilst the outward signs of this tragedy were not evident in Moscow itself, the situation in the provincial towns, where the dead had to be collected from the streets and loaded on to carts, was so horrifying that the families of our Consuls had to leave Russia. Starving men flocked together from hundreds of miles away in order to reach the German agricultural concession known as *Drusag*, to which reference has already been made, where they hoped to get some food. Hundreds of them were found dead in the vicinity.

In spite of all secretive counter-measures, it was impossible to conceal this catastrophe from Germany, as the bonds established between the two countries by the old German "colonies" and the thousands of engineers were too deep-rooted. The German public was genuinely shocked by these reports, and steps were immediately taken to organize some relief for the German settlers. Standard parcels were to be sent to the Ukraine and to the Volga colonies. But the Soviet authorities raised objections and sabotaged the scheme. This gave rise to a campaign of indignation and criticism in the German press, whereas the Soviets were furious at being exposed to the condemnation of the world for their extermination methods.

Yet another crop of difficulties arose in an entirely unexpected quarter. The call of National Socialism was directed to a considerable extent to the extreme Left, and many former Communists began to join Hitler's ranks. These also included numerous stalwart and honest German Communists who had emigrated to Russia during the Weimar period in order to play a part in the establishment of the "workers' paradise." Most of them had been deeply disillusioned by their experiences in their new fatherland and they now wanted to return to Germany. For those of them who had accepted Soviet citizenship there was no hope. If they had remained German subjects, their return was granted by the German Government, but long and arduous work had to be done before the Soviet authorities could be induced to loosen their grip on them.

By delivering lectures on their experiences in Soviet Russia, these repatriates did not exactly contribute to the re-establishment of mutual friendly relations between the two countries. The book by Albrecht, *The Betrayal of Socialism,* to which I have already referred and which was a work of 600 pages, created quite a sensation. Some 60,000 copies were sold before it was banned, following the Hitler-Stalin pact in 1939. But it reappeared in the bookshops after Hitler's attack on Russia in June, 1941.

The most notable and pathetic example of the would-be repatriates was the notorious bandit chief Max Hölz. He succeeded in making contact after dark with a member of the Embassy staff and requested him to secure permission for his return to Germany. He offered to deliver public lectures on his experiences with the Bolsheviks. He also feared that his comrades were planning to get rid of him and that somehow he would be liquidated. In spite of the propaganda value of a reformed leading Bolshevik and "Hero of the Red Flag" delivering anti-Bolshevik speeches, the Embassy lacked the authority to take the matter up as Hölz was a Soviet citizen. But the foreboding which he had felt proved to be justified, for he was drowned in the Volga near Nijni-Novgorod during a boat trip. This is at least what persistent rumors alleged, and it is confirmed in Albrecht's book.

While these various cross-currents undermined Russo-German relations, which were already in an advanced state of deterioration, a crushing blow was administered from quite an unexpected quarter. It was the leader of the Conservative party, Hugenberg, who crowned a career of political bungling by the mischievous and colossal blunder which he committed by his attack on Russia at the World Economic Conference in London in 1933. A shrewd businessman and a wily politician, Hugenberg had been responsible for the frustration of the hopes of the moderate Right wing during the Weimar period that a great Rightist movement under progressive leadership might prevent the growth of the radical ultra-Nationalist party of the Nazis. By his reactionary stubbornness he had brought about the split of the Right at the elections in 1931, and he had then turned to

Hitler and staged the so-called *Harzburger Front,* named after a great rally of the Nazis and the Nationalists in that charming resort in the Harz mountains.

This alliance was far from sincere, as both partners were determined to cheat each other somehow. Self-assured and vain as he was, Hugenberg had not yet realized that in such practices he had found his master in Hitler. To the great relief of President Hindenburg, Hugenberg and some of his followers became members of the first Hitler Cabinet. They served the new dictator as stool pigeons as long as he wanted the collaboration of the industrialists and the old Conservatives. Then, in June, 1933, Hugenberg as Minister for Economic Affairs was sent to London as the German representative at the World Economic Conference. For some unknown reason Hugenberg deemed it appropriate to present to the Conference a memorandum without even asking Hitler's consent. I do not remember the details of his proposals, but the *pièce de résistance* was a diatribe against the Soviet Union which could not have struck that country at a more vulnerable spot, namely the partition of the Union, the exploitation of the wealth of the Ukraine, which, although he may not have actually said so, he certainly implied.

This, of course, was the last straw for Moscow and constituted the final inducement, to all those who had hitherto adopted a patient attitude, finally to abandon their pro-German policy and step over into the safer atmosphere of Anglo-French collaboration. It now seemed that the concern felt by Hitler's intentions as announced in his book was justified. To the Russians it seemed doubly invidious of the Nazis to have chosen the platform of a world conference of capitalism from which to make such a pronouncement. Nobody would believe that in an authoritarian State a responsible Minister would dare to present such a memorandum without the cognizance of his leader.

The matter produced a howl of indignation in the Moscow press. Radek, who had hitherto been a bitter enemy of Versailles, now began to support the *Diktat.* Litvinov, the head of the Soviet delegation in London, lost no time in opening negotiations, especially with France, and official visits to Moscow were arranged for Herriot and Pierre Cot. The fact that Hugenberg resigned did not affect the situation, for the storm continued to rage for quite a while before it gradually subsided. But even so its repercussions continued to be felt.

In spite of everything, I still had hopes of being able to straighten things out. I perceived that two factions were about to form: on the one hand there were those who had abandoned any policy which might lead to a friendly understanding with Germany, whilst on the other hand there were those who might be prepared to make another attempt at conciliation.

Two representatives of the latter body of opinion spent their leave in Germany in spite of National-Socialist rule, namely Krestinski, undergoing his customary cure at Bad Kissingen, and Yenukidse, staying for some weeks at Königstein in the Taunus mountains. On his return to Russia, Yenukidse seemed to have been visibly and favorably impressed. He had observed a new spirit of activity and energy, whilst no untoward incidents had occurred to cloud his stay. Yenukidse invited my wife and me together with the Twardowskis to his *datcha* near Moscow, where we were also joined by Krestinski. I talked matters over with them and tried to persuade them that it might be possible to find a *modus vivendi* with the new régime. I suggested that an influential representative of the Soviet Government should have a conversation with Hitler. They seemed to agree in principle, and the plan crystallized that, following his cure at Kissingen, Krestinski should try to secure an interview with Hitler.

It was on these lines that Twardowski worked when I left Moscow for my summer vacation. I formed the idea that, in the event of the Hitler-Krestinski conversation proving a success, a new political and economic basis might be worked out with a political protocol defining the attitude of both States towards each other. In this way it might then be possible for a new long-term credit to be arranged for the restoration of the Russian railway system, which was badly in need of engines and carriages. As German industry was at that time just emerging from the throes of the economic crisis and was not yet working to capacity on rearmament, one felt justified in hoping that this deal might prove advantageous for Germany, too. After my departure from Moscow, Twardowski was informed by Hitler that he would be prepared to receive Krestinski.

On my arrival in Berlin I received confirmation of the rumors which had been circulating for some time concerning my future. Friends had told me that I should probably be assigned to another post. It is a time-honored tradition in our foreign service that notice of such moves never reached the official concerned by the direct route of a private letter from the Minister or by an official *ukase,* but somehow only in a roundabout and unofficial way. Intimation of such an impending move would generally be given by the offer of the removal contractor to transport your furniture from the old post to the new one. This practice is easily explicable by the fact that most of these contractors had secured the services of one of the minor officials in the Foreign Office, who, by their contacts with their former colleagues in the personnel department, were immediately informed of any change of office before the move took place.

When I received such confirmation of the rumors that had been circulating about me, I asked Herr von Neurath whether there was any foundation for them. The Foreign Minister confirmed them and added that my new post would be Tokyo, provided that the Japanese Government would give its approval.

I have never succeeded in discovering the real reasons for this transfer. Seen from an objective point of view, it did not seem wise to change the German representative in Moscow at such a critical time. The assumption that a change of policy was intended was without foundation, since my prospective successor was an even more outspoken adherent of a *rapprochement* with Moscow than I was and had coveted this post for years. Neurath, whom I questioned on the subject, explained that after five years a change was due and that after the strain which my term of office in Moscow had imposed upon me, I was to be given a more agreeable post. Bülow confirmed this version by saying that I had been exposed to direct personal danger for so long that it was now the turn of another to face the risk. It seemed likely that from the point of view of the party this was meant to be a promotion, since they deemed Moscow such a terrible place to live in that any other city would be preferable. After surveying the whole problem, I came to the conclusion that the transfer was purely a matter of routine and had no connection with political considerations.

I refrained from urging Neurath to allow me to remain in Moscow. The question as to whether I had succeeded in my efforts to re-establish satisfactory relations between the two countries would, in any case, be decided before my departure for Japan. Moreover, it was a principle of mine never to interfere in matters connected with my career. Japan greatly appealed both to my wife and to me, and it did not matter to me that Japan was of less political and economic importance to Germany than Russia was. Neither did I feel at all concerned at the fact that the Tokyo Embassy had only a counsellor, four secretaries, and two typists, while Moscow had the biggest staff of all our Embassies. The most attractive features of the new post were, firstly, the distance of Tokyo from Berlin (and the long journey to a beautiful and interesting country); secondly, the opportunity which I should have of revisiting the Far East, which had deeply impressed me on my first visit twenty-five years earlier; and thirdly, I should be able to indulge in my passion for Eastern art and ceramics.

I returned to Berlin in October to prepare for the final act of my term of office in Moscow, namely for Krestinski's visit to Hitler. But this scheme was frustrated; a wire was received from Twardowski to the effect that he had been informed by Litvinov that Krestinski was returning to Moscow *via* Vienna. I was angry and disappointed that this plan for reconciliation which augured so well for a successful outcome had been foiled by some Moscow intrigue. I immediately resolved to point out to Litvinov the political consequences of this refusal, whilst I, personally, gave Moscow the cold shoulder for having disavowed me.

So I wired Twardowski telling him to inform Litvinov of my disappointment and that I should be returning to Moscow for only a few days without my wife just to pay the official farewell visits. Litvinov replied in an apologetic tone stating that Krestinski's change of route had not been based on any political considerations, but that he was urgently wanted in Moscow as Litvinov was about to leave for a state visit to Turkey together with Marshal Voroshilov. I later discovered that the cancellation of Krestinski's Berlin visit had been arranged by Litvinov in a personal intrigue against his colleague. Litvinov was quite jealous of other officials of the *Narkomindiel* appearing in the limelight. He might also have regarded with disfavor and misgiving any attempt to interfere with his efforts to align Soviet foreign policy with that of the Western Powers.

I had interviews with both Marshal Hindenburg and Hitler. The latter confined himself to some general phases without revealing his designs as to his policy towards Japan. This was the last time I saw the old *Reichspräsident.*

The few days in Moscow were crowded with dinners, receptions, and arduous work. I had the satisfaction of knowing that the Russians as well as the Germans testified to their sincere regret at my departure and expressed their gratitude for the efforts I had made during my five years' term of office. The Soviet Government gave me a great farewell dinner which was attended by many of those dignitaries who normally avoided any contact with foreigners. As a farewell gift I was given a beautiful onyx bowl. Voroshilov ordered one of his generals to hand me his gift of a writing-set in lacquer with a modern design but executed in the famous old technique.

Months later I learned that the *Narkomindiel* had intended conferring upon me the highest of all distinctions, namely an interview with Stalin. But as I left Moscow before the dictator had returned to the capital from his summer resort at Sochi, this plan did not materialize. As Stalin at that time had no official function and was entirely inaccessible to foreigners, it would have been most exceptional had I been allowed to meet him. Litvinov wrote me a very warm and friendly letter, in which he praised my loyalty and untiring efforts directed at the establishment of friendly relations between our two countries.

Thus I left Moscow quite satisfied, at least so far as my personal relationships were concerned. That my work remained an "Unfinished Symphony," so to speak, is a fact which is usually the lot of those officially engaged in the promotion of friendly relations between nations.

On Parade in the Red Square
Left to right: Kork, Shaposhnikov, Voroshilov, Tuchatshevsky

7. MY PRIVATE LIFE IN MOSCOW

An account of my five years in Russia would be most incomplete indeed without a few remarks about my personal experiences. Russia, and especially Soviet Russia, is much too impressive a country not to put every semi-permanent visitor—and it is to this category that diplomats belong —before the alternative of feeling utterly unhappy or of being strangely attracted. My wife and I belonged to the latter category. We tried hard all the time to come into intimate contact with the Russian people, with Russian art and music, with the landscape and architecture of the country. As the Russians are very sensitive to the imponderables in the attitude of their visitors, they soon became aware of our unspoken wish to learn and understand them without any prejudice, and they rewarded us by giving us their confidence and introducing us to the spiritual life of their country. On the whole, human contacts are very difficult to establish in Soviet Russia. But the friendly atmosphere which then prevailed between the two Governments made the problem easier for us. Thus my wife and I were enriched by impressions and experiences which were bound to leave their marks upon our lives.

To our great regret we had no possibility of indulging unrestrictedly in our passion for travelling and sightseeing. It was not only that we were tied to Moscow by the routine work that had to be done, but each time we started for a trip, say, to Kiev or Leningrad, something untoward happened which prevented us from going: a political incident or an important visitor or some other unexpected event. I cannot now remember how many times I had to postpone such trips or the departure for my holidays, and once on leave I was hardly able to enjoy it undisturbed. More than once I had to interrupt it either to rush to Berlin for a conference or to hurry back to Moscow.

But, of course, the work in which I was engaged was the principal impediment for travelling, study, and relaxation. Never in my life was I under such a strain for pressure of work as during those years in Moscow. It goes without saying that my official duties were very exacting. The staff of the Embassy was the largest, or at least second largest, of all German diplomatic representations abroad—the most convincing proof of the scope of work to be done. In addition to my official duties I had to handle my private affairs connected with the execution of my father's will. This task proved to be a heavy strain on my nerves, all the more so since it was in the nature of things that the job was not one of construction but of liquidation.

In addition to my official duties and my private worries, there was another task that took away much of my leisure hours, but which was almost a pleasure: learning Russian. When I was appointed to my post in Moscow, I was firmly resolved to do my best to acquire at least a working knowledge of the Russian language. It was my ambition to read the newspapers, understand conversations and theatrical performances, and use at least a few elementary phrases in the spoken language. As all the politically influential circles in Russia were not in command of any but their mother tongue (and rather indifferently at that, if they hailed from Georgia or Armenia), and as people generally are highly appreciative of a foreigner's effort to learn their language, I deemed it well worth while making the attempt. Thus three times a week a little professor, a learned and cultured man with the thoroughly Russian name of Alexander Carlovitch Schneider, came to initiate me into the intricacies of the beautiful, but extremely complicated, Russian language. The other three working days of the week were devoted to cramming words and grammatical rules into my tired and harassed brain. Gradually I succeeded in attaining my goal, the top mark being reached when I was able to have conversations with responsible persons in Russian. On occasions my usual procedure was to rehearse my initial statement in the morning with my teacher. Having delivered it, I would listen intently to my partner's reply and then continue as best I could, using the stock phrases of which I was in command and additional phrases snatched up in the course of the conversation.

We felt quite at home in Moscow, chiefly because our surroundings and the atmosphere of our daily life suited our taste. On our arrival we decided to take the house that had been occupied by Count Rantzau and to decline the offer of the *Narkomindiel* to put at our disposal one of the gorgeous palaces of a former Moscow sugar magnate. The unassuming little one-storied villa in the quiet *Christy Periulok* satisfied our requirements: five living-rooms, most of them small but well furnished (partly with our own furniture), a dining-room capable of seating twenty-five persons, a few tiny guest-rooms, and, on the upper floor, our bedrooms and dressing-room, an excellent kitchen, garage, and servants' quarters. There was no necessity for huge State dinners in Moscow, and the number of guests that gathered for the customary evening receptions could easily be accommodated in the available rooms which allowed of easy circulation. The garden adjoining the house proved to be spacious enough for a tennis court. The orders for its establishment were among the first *ukases* which I issued in Moscow.

One of the main reasons why our life in Moscow was so harmonious and agreeable was the fact that my colleagues and their wives formed a homogeneous body. Throughout those five years Herr von Twardowski acted as Counsellor of the Embassy. On his efficiency and diligence, political tact, and adroit handling of men and matters I could unfailingly rely. His wife, who had a keen sense of humor and a fine poetic gift, excelled in the arrangement of New Year's Eve parties and amateur theatrical performances carried out by the younger members of the Diplomatic Corps. Herr Hilger, the Commercial Counsellor, has won an international reputation as one of the foremost experts on Russia, so that his faculties need not be described in detail. His own and his wife's kindness and helpfulness made life much easier for all those who were less familiar with Russian conditions than they were. The bonds of friendship which tied me to Twardowski and Hilger remained unbroken even after our common period of service in Moscow.

An important member of the Embassy's staff was the Agricultural Attaché. After the holder of this post, Professor Auhagen, an excellent man, had been recalled at the request of the Soviet Government, who resented the courageous support he had given to the German Mennonite colonists, I secured the services of a young scientist and practical agriculturist. He was Dr. Schiller, and had spent some years on one of the German agricultural concessions in the Northern Caucasus. He came to be the foremost authority on Russian agriculture. His annual report, published in one of the technical periodicals, became, as it were, the bible for agriculturists of all nations interested in Russian affairs. With a full command of the language and motoring about the country some five or six thousand miles every year, he acquired an unrivalled knowledge of the highly complicated problem.

Dr. Schiller's reputation as an agriculturist was paralleled by that of General Köstring as a military expert. Born of German parents who owned an estate in Russia, he had spent his youth in that country and had acquired, quite apart from a perfect command of the language, a deep and almost instinctive understanding for the Russian mentality. As the Russians are the most difficult people to handle, psychological insight is a far greater asset in dealing with them than a piercing intellect or crafty tactics. General Köstring, the model of an old-type Prussian cavalry officer, straight, chivalrous, intelligent, and courageous, enjoyed the unlimited confidence of the Red Army commanders as well as his colleagues.

His unofficial predecessor, Herr von Niedermayer, was fond of being nicknamed "the German Lawrence." During the First World War on a military mission in Afghanistan, he had returned singlehanded *via* the Persian desert across the Russian and British lines, disguised as a Persian pilgrim. On his return from Moscow he rejoined the German Army and became Professor of Geography at Berlin University. During the Second World War he commanded a division composed of units of Russian prisoners-of-war and men from Georgia, Azerbaidjan, and Turkestan, who had volunteered for service with the German Army. After July 20, 1944, Niedermayer was denounced for criticizing the Nazis and ultimately condemned to death. His execution was averted by the capitulation. He fell into Russian hands and is now in jail in Moscow. He was one of the most colorful and energetic persons I have ever met. A thoroughbred Bavarian, mellowed by intercourse with foreigners, he had an ascetic and stubborn mind. He was intelligent, amusing, and a good sportsman. Although vastly my superior, he often condescended to play tennis with me.

Herr Baum, thoroughly experienced and competent press attaché, and Herren Pfeiffer, Bräutigam, Pfleiderer, Brunhoff, and Herwarth as able and loyal members of the junior staff of the Embassy—not to forget the untiring *chef de bureau,* Herr Lamla—complete the list of my most important staff members. Their numbers were rounded off by our Consuls and Consuls-General, who were spread all over the vast Russian territory. They rendered most valuable services under extremely exacting living conditions. The way in which Consul and Frau Grosskopf spent ten years in Novosibirsk was almost heroic. None but a giant of six feet four, sturdy, with a faculty for hard drinking, a predilection for shooting bears, and a full command of the Russian language could possibly have stood the strain. He became the leading expert on Siberia. His colleagues, Zechlin in Leningrad, Dienstmann in Tiflis, Sommer and Hencke in Kiev, Balser in Vladivostok, rendered equally valuable services, but under far more agreeable living conditions.

Ever since I had been appointed to the Eastern Department I had been striving to build up a Russian service for the Foreign Office. I am no great supporter of the system of training different schools of foreign service officials for different spheres such as Europe, the Middle East, and the Far East. But this system certainly is extremely useful when a specialized experience and a long period of training are required. A capable young man, transferred to Moscow or Nanking without any preparatory training, particularly in the language of the country, is no good for efficient work. He will mingle only with other foreigners and draw up reports from translated bits of local newspapers. During my nine years of work devoted to Russian affairs—and later on in Japan—I made a systematic effort to train a set of officials with special knowledge on the subject and a special pride in their work. I think I succeeded. The least I can say is that bonds of friendship have continued to unite us, even after the German catastrophe.

That in those years the German Embassy was thoroughly acquainted with all developments in the political field was not only due to the efficiency of its staff. It was also a result of the atmosphere of economic and political collaboration between Germany and Russia which characterized the post-Rapallo period. As I have already mentioned, thousands of German experts and technicians were engaged in the construction of new factories, and the relations between the two armies were very friendly. The circle of well-informed men was enlarged by the eminent German journalists resident in Moscow, Paul Scheffer and Artur W. Just. Also casual visitors, such as explorers or scientists with a special mission to a univerity or a research institute somewhere in the provinces, greatly contributed to our knowledge of things.

The members of the Embassy formed the core of the German community in Moscow, whose numbers were considerably increased by the influx of German experts. It was a somewhat motley crowd that assembled for the monthly dances and social gatherings in the Grand Hotel: some leading intellectual figures, some reliable foremen and minor engineers, and quite a number of adventurous young men. Of the once rich and numerous pre-war German colony nobody had survived except a few old, impoverished couples.

Visitors were constantly arriving in Moscow from Germany or stopped there on their return journey: industrialists who had to negotiate some important affairs; scientists invited to give a course of lectures; artists, engineers, officials—in a word, men from all walks of life—would gather two or three times a week at the Embassy for lunch, and they kept us in touch with the outer world. They were all compelled to get in touch with the Embassy. Whereas in other countries foreigners tend to approach their diplomatic representatives only in case they are in trouble, all Germans arriving in Moscow had to fall back on the services of the Embassy. We had to provide transport for them and their luggage to be taken from the station to the hotel where we had booked accommodation for them. We had to advise them as to which of the innumerable offices they were to make contact with, and we had to make the necessary arrangements for their return journey. Thus we got acquainted with all our fellow countrymen visiting Russia and had an excellent opportunity of collecting valuable information about conditions in Russia as well as in Germany, quite apart from the privilege of making friends with interesting and important personages. Frequently we had friends and relatives visiting us; they sometimes spent several weeks as our guests.

Social life had to adapt itself to the peculiarities of the Soviet capital. The sharp distinction that was made between Russians and foreigners was bound to have its effect on social intercourse. The result was that the members of the Diplomatic Corps were welded together into one large family.

The intimacy of our social relations was further accentuated by the fact that there was a comparatively small number of diplomatic representations in Moscow. The diplomatic relations between the United States and the Soviet Union had not yet been established. Nevertheless many American citizens came on a visit to Russia, and quite a number of them called upon me. Great Britain had severed diplomatic relations with the Soviet Union on account of the Arcos incident and the famous Sinoviev letter. She did not appear on the scene until late in 1929 or early in 1930. The South American States and numerous smaller European nations such as Switzerland, Belgium, and The Netherlands were not represented in Moscow either. But all the missions in Moscow did not put in an appearance. My colleagues from the eastern satellite states of the Union such as Tannu-Tuva and Outer Mongolia came only on great Soviet festivals, dressed in their picturesque costumes.

Thus the remaining Embassies and Legations came to form a community whose members maintained an intimate social intercourse, particularly if they were keen on playing bridge and tennis. We had our regular tennis matches alternately at the Italian, British, and German Embassies, the chief event of the season being a tournament in July. The distribution of the prizes, followed by a dance, would always take place at our Embassy. Another set of devotees indulged in bridge, either in small parties arranged for the purpose or after official dinners—in that case to the dismay of the uninitiated partner of some married couple or other, who was condemned to wait until the last rubber was finished. This was frequently the lot of my wife.

I was on very friendly terms with my Italian colleagues Cerruti and Attolico and their charming wives. After leaving Moscow, they succeeded each other as Ambassadors to Berlin. With my British colleague, Sir Edmond Ovey, I got on well. We both had a predilection for tennis and bridge. He and Lady Ovey transplanted the English week-end to the palatial premises of the British Embassy and the adjoining spacious park. Arriving in the morning, one started with a game of tennis. After lunch we would have a rest and then go on playing tennis in the afternoon until it was time to dress for dinner. A game of bridge concluded the day. Ovey was witty and of quick repartee, but did not like music. Nevertheless I had to invite him from time to time to evening parties with music. So, when a well-known singer gave a concert in the Embassy, I consoled Ovey, greeting him at the entrance, and added, "But the singer is a very beautiful woman." Whereupon he remarked, "Then why the noise?"

As to my colleagues from the Scandinavian States, I remember gratefully the hospitality shown to us by the Norwegian Minister, Urbye, and the Danish Minister, Engel. My three French colleagues, Herbette, Comte

Dejean, and Alphand, who succeeded each other in the course of those five years, were three entirely different types, but each of them very intelligent, courteous, and highly cultured, although having no interest in bridge and tennis. Of the three Japanese colleagues I had, Tanaka, Hirota, and Ota, it was with Hirota that my wife and I came to be on most friendly terms. It was with him also that I collaborated for most of the time during my mission to Japan.

My contacts with the Diplomatic Corps became particularly close owing to the fact that after a comparatively short stay in Moscow I was promoted to the honorary post of doyen. My functions were by no means limited to those of serving as a figurehead on festive occasions. The intricacies of conditions in Soviet Russia necessitated a constant exchange of opinions and advice among the heads of the diplomatic missions, and sometimes even full-scale action. A recurrent subject of our conversations was the indirect intrusion of the G.P.U. into the love affairs of staff members, particularly the military attachés and their staffs. Usually these gentlemen had made the acquaintance of a seductive Russian lady, who infallibly pretended to belong to the uppermost circles of the former aristocracy. They were invited to tea and then their *tête-à-tête* would be rudely disturbed by the police or the G.P.U., who would accuse the lady of counter-revolutionary activities or the gentleman of attempting espionage. The only possible solution of the embarrassing problem was, of course, the speedy departure of the frustrated lover.

One day my Italian colleague, bewildered and upset, complained of a strange observation he had made: the mail of the Italian Consulates in the Soviet Union was dispatched to the Embassy in sealed envelopes. He had noticed that the mail of the Consulate in Odessa had been closed with the seal of the Consulate in Kharkov. I had no difficulty in explaining this phenomenon by pointing out that the G.P.U. had committed a similar error while searching the mail of the German Consulates. There had also been some muddle with the seals. On the other hand, the same authorities had proved to be very helpful in appending a Russian translation to letters from Germany to Moscow—the censor's *quid pro quo*, so to speak.

Of course, rumors about the tapping of telephone conversations, and devices concealed in electric lamps, for example, for transmitting conversations to the "authorities concerned," were common talk in Moscow. But I do not know whether there is any truth in the allegation that the telephone services with such small States as Lithuania or Estonia were interrupted altogether during mealtimes (12–2 P. M.), as there was only one interpreter capable of understanding these languages—and he had to have his lunch and a little rest.

It is only when its own petty interests are impaired that a Diplomatic

Corps as a body rises to the height of genuine passion and eloquence—that at least is my experience. The constant trouble we had in this respect in Moscow concerned the currency. The gold value of the paper rouble was a myth to which the Soviet Government clung with great obstinacy. The theoretical rate of exchange was one rouble equal to two marks and two roubles equal to one dollar. Thus one pound of butter available for ten roubles would have cost five dollars. Obviously it was impossible to live decently in Moscow on such a basis. Special shops for diplomats could not solve the problem. I cannot remember all the details now. At any rate, some other interference with what we believed to be our diplomatic privileges was the straw that broke the camel's back. A wave of indignation swept the Diplomatic Corps. There was a fervent demand for a common *démarche* and it was suggested that the matter should be discussed in a conference of the *chefs de mission*. The conference was held and I tried my best to pour oil on the troubled waters. I was convinced that a common *démarche* would be prevented by dissident opinions and that the legal situation—with the inevitable buying of roubles on some European black market—would provide the *Narkomindiel* with sufficient ammunition to shatter even a united front.

On the other hand, I was aware that the Soviet authorities resented being talked about in phrases like "Eastern methods," "infringement of international courtesy," and so on. I therefore resisted all attempts to force the issue by an official protest or a common *démarche* and gradually settled the matter in private talks with Litvinov. I was greatly amused while writing these lines to read an account of a similar incident which happened in Moscow only very recently: again interference with diplomatic privileges (this time on the occasion of the monetary reform), again a wave of exasperation, again a conference of the *chefs de mission,* in which, however, the Yugoslav Minister upset the united front. *Plus ça change, plus c'est la même chose. . . .*

The gap between the foreign diplomats and the Russians was bridged by a few members of the *Narkomindiel* who had been granted the *privilegium odiosum* of mingling with foreigners and of wearing evening dress. But they only attended diplomatic dinners, those arranged by the countries assigned to their departments. A general permit was issued only to two persons. One of them was M. Florinski, the *Chef de Protocole*, a former member of the Tsarist foreign service, by nature and by training a wily and astute person who successfully evaded all efforts to induce him to plead the wishes and requests of the Diplomatic Corps with his superiors. But he played an excellent game of bridge. The other was his colleague, Boris Sergeyevitch Steiger, a former officer, who arranged theater parties for the diplomats and was helpful in a general way.

Among the initiated it was understood that he was the chief agent of the G.P.U., planted for the observation of the foreign representatives. But this fact being known, his connections could be utilized for passing on remarks or warnings to those men who were definitely more influential than the Ministry of Foreign Affairs. And, *vice versa,* his opinions and remarks were sometimes inspired by the views of really important people. After my departure from the Soviet Union both Florinski and Steiger suddenly disappeared from the international scene in Moscow. Florinski was deported to Siberia, and the dramatic arrest of Steiger during a dinner-party at one of the two "elegant" hotels has been described by the former United States Ambassador, Davies, in his book *Mission to Moscow.* Later on it was publicly announced that Steiger belonged to a gang of eight men who had been shot during the purge. Other members who shared his fate were such prominent people as Yenukidse and Karakhan.

While it is easily understandable that Steiger's rope-walking activities would one day lead to an abrupt and tragic end, I have never been able to find out what might have aroused the dictator's suspicion against the other two victims. Yenukidse, a fellow countryman of Stalin and one of his most faithful henchmen, certainly did not belong to any oppositional group. Karakhan, who sailed in the wake of Yenukidse and, as an Armenian, somehow belonged to the Georgian clan, seemed to me to be safe, but his worldly life was, of course, apt to arouse envy and to foster intrigues.

I remember an episode with Karakhan which may be regarded as characteristic of certain sides of Moscow life. Every now and then Karakhan used to come to the German Embassy to play tennis, on the tacit understanding that no other foreigners should be present. When he heard that I was fond of riding, he invited me to go riding with him. He came to fetch me in his elegant cabriolet and drove me to a comfortable rest-house on the outskirts of Moscow. A very good horse, Irish hunter type, from Red Army stock, and a Red Army captain were waiting for us. We had a lovely ride in the lonely forest and meadows that were still untouched by industrialization. On our return a *déjeuner à la fourchette* awaited us. None of the inhabitants of the house was visible except Ordzonikidse, whom I watched walking about in the garden. Driving home, we overtook a couple; the corpulence of the man reminded me of Bela Kun, top Bolshevik leader during the sanguinary period of the Bolshevik rule in Hungary after the First World War. Shortly afterwards Karakhan asked me quite casually whether I could grant a visa to Bela Kun's wife, who wanted to undergo medical treatment in Germany. As Bela Kun was a *bête noir* in Germany, I had to give an evasive reply. It was the first and last riding party with Karakhan.

An invitation to a bear-hunting party did not come off either. One day when we were discussing our common passion for shooting, Marshal Yegorov, the Chief of Staff, invited me to take part in a bear hunt. He bluntly asked Krestinski, who was sitting at the same table, whether there was any objection to my being invited to this hunting party. Krestinski reflected aloud, "The British Ambassador is not fond of shooting, nor are the French and the Italian Ambassadors—you have my blessing." No precedent being established, there could be no harm in having me as one of the party. But nothing happened. Evidently my hosts got cold feet and on second thought they had decided that they would rather not allow me to become too closely acquainted with their private lives.

These episodes answer to a certain extent the question which has been put to me almost as frequently as that other one: did I ever meet Stalin personally? It is the question: what was our social intercourse with the Russians like? The answer is that that depended on two conditions: on the political situation and on the personal qualities of the diplomat concerned. If prolonged tension between a certain country and the U.S.S.R. developed, the social intercourse with the representatives of that particular country gradually ceased and no Russian was allowed to frequent the mission's premises any longer. If, on the other hand, mutual relations were friendly, the receptions, concerts, and other social gatherings of the Embassy in question were attended by numerous Russian intellectuals, who turned up not individually, but in groups specially selected for the purpose. Thus, at a reception given in honor of some German scientist, his opposite numbers on the Russian side would make their appearance, or a delegation of German economists was met by the prominent economic representatives of Soviet Russia. Should you, however, try to invite one of your guests individually to a lunch, he would certainly stutter, with extreme confusion, that he probably would be ill that day. The party bigwigs, of course, were not bound by these rules, but they generally felt uneasy in the company of foreigners. They did, however, visit Embassies and invited the Ambassador if they liked him personally and appreciated the atmosphere of the place.

The customary form of these social functions was a reception late in the evening with a *buffet*. This appealed more to the taste of the Russian, who loathes the strict formality of an official dinner with evening dress and prefers to turn up and leave when he likes, to make his choice from a variety of food and drinks, and above all, to smoke and talk. Apart from these set groups of people—the party men and the members of the intelligentzia turning up for special occasions—there was quite a number of individual Russians with whom we became acquainted and even friendly—artists, scientists, singers, actors, who just took the risk of coming to see us or were not afraid. Some younger members of the Embassy staff succeeded in starting some kind of bohemian life in their flats where actors and artists gathered and displayed their talents.

Visits to our Consulates as well as to industrial plants such as the motor works at Nijni Novgorod, the tractor works at Kharkov, or the Dniepostroi Dam contributed a great deal to increasing my knowledge, not only of the country itself and its potentialities, but also of the human element. In Leningrad, Kharkov, Kiev, and Tiflis the restrictions on social intercourse were not so strict as in the capital. The leading men in the provincial towns could not help making an appearance when the representatives of a friendly power paid a visit. My command of the Russian language, however poor it was, enormously facilitated these contacts. Conversations with factory hands and officials were more revealing than scores of articles in *Izvestia* and *Pravda*.

Looking back on my five years in Moscow, which gave me an opportunity of meeting people from practically all walks of life, I may say without any presumption that I acquired a pretty thorough knowledge of the Russian people in general and of the Soviet Russians in particular. I got on extremely well with them and I harbor a definite sympathy for them on account of their human kindness, their intimacy with nature, their simplicity, frugality, and endurance. I was deeply impressed by their faculty of suffering and making sacrifices, of doing hard work and being enthusiastic about it. I was equally impressed by the passionate fanaticism of the rank and file of the party members, whose ambition it was to develop their backward country so as to bring it into line with the most advanced nations—an almost pathetic attempt. I closely observed the types of party men from the lower ranks right up to the highest level, and I could not help wondering whence came the grandiose richness of their schemes and the ruthless power of their decisions which involved the sacrifice of the well-being—nay, of the very lives—of millions in favor of a goal which, they knew, was looming at a far distance and which most foreigners deemed altogether unattainable.

From their outward appearance, these party members were simple and unassuming men who did not impress one by a forceful, dominating personality. There were brilliant intellects among them, mostly of Jewish origin, with whom—as, for instance, Radek—it was a genuine pleasure to converse. But behind this seeming simplicity of mind there was hidden a fervent and unshakable, almost religious, faith in their doctrines which rendered any deep discussion utterly senseless. I remember a conversation with Voroshilov in 1932, in the course of which I expressed serious doubt as to whether the forced collectivization was not going to endanger, or even destroy, Russia's agriculture. This was the most solid foundation of her economy, and the result might be that the exports of grain and, consequently, the means of repaying our credits would be reduced to nil. Voroshilov listened attentively and endeavored to dispel my doubts, but later on, deeply disappointed and disconsolate, he said to a member of my staff, "The Ambassador has no faith in us." He simply could not understand that a friend of his country should harbor even a shadow of doubt concerning the principles and plans of the Soviet State.

Imposing as the determination may be with which the industrialization of Russia was accomplished, I cannot help reaching the conclusion that a minimum net effect has been achieved with a maximum of expenditure—and human suffering.

Those among the Soviet representatives that appealed to me most were officers of the Red Army. Here a new class had been created that corresponded—at least so far as the generals and staff officers were concerned—to approximately the same standard as had been exacted by the old German Army from its leaders. These Red Army officers were entirely devoted to their task, earnest, reticent, efficient. The educational work carried out by the Red Army in combating illiteracy and backwardness must be regarded as the most prominent achievement of the whole Soviet system.

Generals such as Uborevitch, Yegorov, Kork, Heidemann, Putna, Alksnis may be classified at the same level with the best types of German generals. These men can safely be praised as they all became victims of the purge, together with such doubtful and adventurous types as Tukhachevsky. It is, however, a remarkable feat that the Red Army succeeded, within a couple of years, in creating a new set of leaders capable of conducting such campaigns as they did in the war against Germany. Considering the fact that nearly 70 to 80 per cent of the Red Army officers from the rank of colonel upwards had been liquidated, this result is almost inexplicable.

The term "inexplicable" applies to the Russian mind and mentality in general. Underneath a surface of kindliness, wholehearted understanding, and unassuming helpfulness there is a layer which offers an impenetrable resistance to the searching Western mind. It would surpass the scope of this chapter to give an analysis of the Russian soul in all its aspects. I need only mention the name of Dostoievsky to suggest the trend of my thoughts. Kipling's resigned statement concerning the gulf that separated the Western from the Far Eastern mentality, "and never the twain shall meet," may be applied, to a still higher degree, to the gap dividing the Western from the Russian mind. This gap is outwardly marked by the Cyrillic script. It is widened by the Bolshevik creed and is altogether unbridgeable.

There were many other angles from which to view this problem. I was confronted with it while attending theatrical performances, listening to Russian music, admiring old Russian architecture, or even while enjoying the vastness of the Russian landscape. The representation of historic personages such as Peter the Great or Rasputin, the endless soul-searching discussions in the masterly performances of dramatized Tolstoyan novels by the classical Stanislavsky Theater, the psychological intricacies of contemporary plays, the peculiar rendering of *Boris Godunov*—all these things opened up for me new approaches to the mystery of the Russian mentality, which proved to be just as inexplicable as the fanaticism of self-castigation and self-accusation that constitutes a continuous trend from Dostoievsky down to the mock trials of the Bolshevik era.

Waiting for an express train in the middle of the night on our return journey from Dnieperpetrovsk, our Kharkov Consul-General, Walther, who was thoroughly acquainted with Russian ways, inquired about the railway schedule and received the following information from the stationmaster, *"Nikto nichevo nie snaet"* (Nobody doesn't know nothing)! The Consul-General commented, "How thoroughly Russian—this triple negation!" But then, quite unexpectedly, the train arrived in spite of the schedule, berths were available, and the journey back to Moscow was quite comfortable. This is Russia in a nutshell.

Whilst in the early stages of my ambassadorship we were under the spell of the new impressions provided by the Russian scene and the Soviet rule, which was then performing experiments that have since become commonplace and are now being imitated by many other countries, life in Moscow began to weigh pretty heavily on us as time went on. Moscow was not a gay place to live in even if there had been no Soviet rule. The somber pompousness of the Kremlin, and the graceful elegance which Italian architects had managed to transplant to Russia when constructing the Novo-Devichy Monastery in the Baroque style, failed to elate us in view of the dreary monotony of dilapidated houses, the drabness of shabbily dressed crowds milling along the streets, and the pathetic emptiness of the shop windows decorated only with busts of Lenin and Stalin. There were no parks to relieve the monotony of this desert of stones which is Moscow. In order to be able to take a walk and get a breath of fresh air, you had to drive to some place in the environs of the city and start for a stroll round the unimposing woods and hills, with their quiet charm and the glowing colors lent to them during the short weeks of the transcontinental summer. During the winter season I made some attempts at skiing, being dragged across the hills and slopes by Twardowski's sons.

As the excitement caused by the novel surroundings began to subside, the older residents belonging to the foreign communities in Moscow became increasingly subject to moods of depression, particularly when a glimpse behind the stage revealed to them the numerous individual tragedies under the rule of a police State. Some of our acquaintances disappeared, whilst their wives committed suicide; news leaked through about tortures in Butirki and other prisons.

Our life in Russia offered two kinds of relaxation: music and the theater, and travelling. Russian music was a revelation to my wife and me. The difference between a performance of Tchaikovsky's *Pique Dame* or Mussorgsky's *Boris Godunov* in Western Europe and a performance of the same operas in Moscow was similar to that between drinking a glass of water and enjoying a bottle of Burgundy. The Russian ballet can only be compared to a bottle of champagne. As regards the ballet, we were neither so crazy nor so competent as the Moscow and Leningrad fans, who would have heated arguments as to whether the Leningrad or Moscow technique of moving the hands had a more graceful effect, let alone pirouettes and paces which elicited almost scientific dissertations. In addition to the above-mentioned standard operas, we became acquainted with many thoroughly Russian masterpieces that are little known on European stages, such as *Pskovitianka* and *Khovanchina*. Whilst the elaborate art of Stanislavsky's classical theater was apt to satisfy even an old-fashioned taste, the Vakhtangov would use *Hamlet* for a bold and almost sacrilegious experiment, and Taïrov would embark upon extreme surrealism.

Of course, current events and achievements, the civil war with its partisan activities, and the Five-Year Plan with the brave *Comsomol* engineer and the bad old saboteur (who, happily, met his fate in the fourth act), provided the subject-matter for innumerable plays along the party line. Patriotic sentiments were not yet allowed to be stirred up, but a slight predilection for Peter the Great became discernible. However, even the audiences in the theaters were not exempt from party propaganda. I remember once seeing a play by O'Neill, in which a Negro character had to act a part. During the interval the spectators were addressed by a man who referred to the impending execution of two American Negroes who had been condemned to death and urged a unanimous vote of sympathy in favor of them. Twardowski and I chose to oppose the motion by lifting our arms in protest.

In concerts the orthodox way of conducting prevailed, the experiment of the orchestra without conductor having been abandoned. In the programmes classical symphonies took first place, and no Shostakovitch had to be rebuked for atonal Western leanings.

We were particularly interested in the numerous specimens of classical Russian architecture ranging from the old churches of the Grand Dukes' period in the 12th and 13th centuries to the buildings in the Russian Empire style as represented by the palace of Prince Yussupov Arkhangelskoe and including the Russian variants of Renaissance and Baroque architecture as well as the beautiful architectural achievements of the period of Alexander I. We went on sightseeing excursions which extended to distances of more than 125 miles from Moscow, sometimes spending the night in a small provincial town, which was, however, only possible after elaborate preparations by the German department of the *Narkomindiel*. A trip to beautiful old Vladimir, with its golden cupolas and a lovely steeple far away in a meadow, is an unforgettable memory. Equally impressive were the fortress-like monasteries of Sergeievskaia Lavra and Yerozolimskoe. Parallel to this admiration for old Russian churches, I developed a growing appreciation of icons and a slight tendency to collecting them.

As a welcome relaxation from everyday life in Moscow, we used to make frequent trips to Leningrad. The "window to the West," constructed by Peter the Great, had retained some of its European atmosphere. The hospitality which Consul-General Zechlin offered us in the former German Embassy contributed a great deal to making those days of relaxation really restful and comfortable. The treasures of the Eremitage seemed inexhaustible. We particularly enjoyed the unique collection of Scythian gold coins and trinkets. The excursions to the Tsarist palaces in the vicinity of Leningrad—Gatchina, Pavlovsk, Czarskoye Selo—were always an interesting diversion. I also renewed my acquaintance with the Ukraine by paying several visits to Kharkov and Kiev.

On one occasion we managed to fit in an extensive sightseeing trip to Odessa, where the Maritime Youth Organization invited us to a cruise to the Crimea in a beautiful yacht, which we exchanged for a comfortable passenger boat that took us along the east coast of the Black Sea down to semi-tropical Batum. We liked Tiflis and the Georgians, who combined the manners of gentlemen with the drinking habits of Heidelberg students, and we drove along the famous mountain road, not quite as far as Vladikavkas, but well within the orbit of the snow-covered ridges. Proceeding to Baku, we found that the scene had changed overnight, Baku being a typical Asiatic place, with its arid, sandy plains, its caravans of camels, its devotion to Persian rites of sun-worship, and above all, with its wells and cracking plants. A dinner party on the windswept roof garden of our hotel with a grand view of the Caspian Sea, the glittering lights of the city, and a band playing Russian and Asiatic folk songs—all this combined to make an unforgettable impression.

What we liked most, however, was our annual trip to the German agricultural concession at Drusag, near Kavkaskaia, in the rich farming district of the Northern Caucasus, to attend a shooting party. With Dr. Dittloff at the wheel, we slithered down the slippery slopes to the bank of the Kuban River to enjoy, for some days, the atmosphere of German country life, together with Herr and Frau Dittloff and his colleagues. The sporting side of our visit—the shooting—was performed in accordance with good old German tradition. There were no bears or wolves (I saw only one at a great distance), but hares, pheasants, and rabbits, with an occasional fox or snipe. It was only the beaters that gave the scene an exotic touch, most of them being members of one of the neighboring *stanitsas* of the proud Kuban cossacks, wearing fur caps and colored silk sashes. I was greatly impressed when, on my first visit in the summer, Dr. Dittloff took me to a hill which was surrounded by a veritable ocean of wheat covering an area with a radius of about two miles and a half. This sight is probably common enough in the United States and in Argentina, but it was amazing to German eyes.

In the last days of October I left Moscow for good. From Moscow I proceeded *via* Vienna to Rome, where I met my wife and spent a few days of rest at the Villa Bonaparte with my sister and brother-in-law, the German Ambassador to the Holy See, Herr von Bergen. I also picked up my niece, Elka Wedel, who was to accompany us to Japan. In Naples we went on board the Japanese boat S. S. *Hakusan Maru*. We had decided in favor of the sea route as on the way to my new post I wanted to acquaint myself with the problems of the Far East by paying at least a short visit to some of the important places, such as Singapore, Hong Kong, and Shanghai. Only a few days before Christmas the *Hakusan Maru* moored at the pier in Kobe. For me the Eurasian crisis was now replaced by the Far Eastern crisis.

IV

Ambassador to Tokyo

1933–1938

---

1. JAPAN IN FERMENT, 1933–1936

At the time of my arrival in Tokyo the task of the German Ambassador to Japan was an ideal, almost idyllic, one. It is very nearly the most distant place from the homeland, and this, in itself, is an invaluable asset in my profession. No other post offered greater amenities in the daily life of the diplomat and of foreigners in general: a beautiful, hospitable, and interesting country with a blend of Far Eastern culture and Western civilization. We had an inexpensive household with an efficient and friendly Japanese staff; there were comfortable travelling facilities to the coast and mountain resorts with their European hotels and to historic temples and castles with their valuable art collections. In fact there was every opportunity for a study of Far Eastern art, history, and culture, whilst every facility was offered for maintaining fairly close contact with the Western way of life and thought through frequent visitors from Europe and by concerts and cinemas.

The official duties of the German Ambassador to Japan were not hampered by any clash of interests or innate conflicts between the two countries. For sixty years Germany and Japan had been linked by friendly relations which had been cemented as a result of co-operation in the sphere of science and through the presence of Germany military advisers to the Japanese Army. It was well understood in Germany that the interruption of this friendship by Japan's participation in the First World War had been due to a political blunder of the first order during the reign of Emperor William II, namely Germany's support of the Russo-French protest against the Sino-Japanese Peace Treaty of Shimonoseki in 1895. After the Japanese conquest of Germany's foothold in China, Tsingtao, and of her groups of islands in the Pacific, Japan had been a half-hearted partner in the First World War and had soon become alienated from her allies by the post-war regrouping of the great powers. Then she had resumed the old relations with her former adversary. Economic relations, which had proved profitable to both partners throughout the post-war period, had been extended by the inclusion of Manchuria into the Japanese sphere. Thus Japan's passive trade balance with Germany was now being balanced by German purchases of Manchuria's chief product, soya beans, the most important buyers of which were German firms.

These friendly relations were deepened by political developments in the post-war period. Although she was one of the victorious nations, Japan felt that she had been slighted and humiliated by her war-time allies, whilst her numerous ambitions had not been satisfied. She had been forced by the pressure of the Anglo-Saxon powers to loosen her grip on China, and this had been openly, though prematurely, declared in 1915 by the notorious Twenty-One Demands. Tsingtao was no longer a Japanese stronghold. She had to withdraw from the Russian Maritime Provinces, and the keen resentment which she felt as a proud nation over racial discrimination in the United States had been further deepened by the rejection of a race-equality clause proposed at the Versailles Conference by President Wilson and by further discriminatory laws passed in America. Japan considered that the Four-Power Pact, as well as the Nine-Power Pact, was directed against her, and this belief was strengthened by the 2:1 ratio to which she had to agree at the Washington Naval Conference as compared with the Anglo-American navies.

It is here that the affinity between Germany's post-war development and that of Japan becomes apparent. Like Germany, Japan had made an honest effort to reach a real and fundamental agreement with the Western Powers. During the years 1920–31, known as the Shidehara period after the outstanding statesman who advocated this policy, Liberal Cabinets had ruled Japan in accordance with the principles of democratic parliamentarism and had followed a Western trend in the policy of their country. In Germany as well as in Japan—although for different reasons—this effort was doomed to failure.

I have already mentioned the causes of Japanese resentment. In Germany as well as in Japan a catastrophic economic crisis intensified the feeling of frustration and political radicalism. The conviction that Japan's future well-being could only be assured by complete independence of world markets and political undercurrents became firmly implanted in the minds of Japanese politicians and strengthened the hands of the ultra-nationalist diehards. It became almost the gospel of these expansionists that this independence could only be secured by the inclusion of the Chinese, or at least of the Manchurian and North Chinese, markets. These dreams were realized by the conquest of Manchuria and, later on, of North China. Interference by the League of Nations and by the Lytton Commission, which was dispatched to the Far East, aroused antipathy towards international co-operation in Japan and in Nazi Germany with equal intensity. Within a year Germany followed the Japanese example and also left the League.

In both countries the period of Liberalism had come to an end and had to make way for totalitarian rule. But whereas the transition period in Germany lasted only one year (1932), the struggle between the two systems was protracted in Nippon for almost ten years and developed with the application of purely Japanese methods. The sources from which this revolutionary and subversive dynamism sprang were also different in the two countries. In Germany the original adherents of National Socialism consisted of those sections of the population which had been the victims of the inflation and the economic crisis. Their ranks were swelled by disgruntled men from the most varied walks of life and by honest patriots who resented the "ignominy of Versailles." They were men who despaired of a resurrection of their Fatherland by a parliamentary system which split the nation into thirty-two parties and which proved incapable of coping with the mounting difficulties. When, as a result of increasing Left- and Right-wing radicalism the alternative had to be faced as to whether Germany should be ruled by Communism or National Socialism, the nation voted for what it believed to be the lesser evil.

In Japan the ferment developed within a more restricted sphere. Junior officers from the army and, to a lesser extent, from the navy, students, and other hotheads, animated by an exaggerated and boundless nationalism which was rooted in the plight of the peasants, formed conspiratorial societies such as the "Black Dragon." These societies were under the spiritual guidance of philosophical ascetics such as Toyama or pseudo-philosophical military men of more advanced years like General Araki. The methods and aim of these revolutionaries were directed not towards the formation of a mass movement ultimately to seize power by a majority vote at the elections, but to the elimination of the chief representatives of the parliamentary and capitalist régime by acts of terrorism. A series of ghastly murders, the victims of which were outstanding statesmen and leading industrialists, had failed to yield any political results. But the conquest of Manchuria acted as a temporary safety valve, focusing the energies of these activist circles on the new field of action offered to them on the mainland of Asia. Inner political developments followed along the same lines at a slower rate. While the really Liberal statesmen were being discarded, the formation of an outright nationalist Cabinet was delayed by the counter-pressure of the elder statesmen. It became abundantly evident in the following years that the ultra-nationalists were not inclined to tolerate this delay.

Thus, at the time of my arrival in Tokyo, Germany and Japan were "on the march"—as that state of potential aggression was termed. Whereas Japan's nationalist movement had scored its first foreign triumph by the conquest of Manchuria before it had gained control of the Government, National Socialism reigned supreme inside Germany, while awaiting an opportunity for expansion. The fact that Germany and Japan had been tied by the same shackles, had attained their freedom by identical means, and were pursuing similar aims strengthened a feeling of sympathy and friendship between the two countries which had developed since Japan had been forced to abandon her medieval seclusion.

But the two nations were linked, almost unconsciously, by an even stronger bond. Their history and the fundamental facts of national existence pressed both nations into an alliance which rested on a more solid foundation than merely the common desire to expand. The identity of their fundamental ideas with regard to the State and the relations between the State and the individual was attained in spite of obvious differences which counterbalanced the analogous traits.

Germany and Japan have been singled out by Fate for a tragic destiny emanating from different, almost contradictory, sources. Whereas the geographical position in the center of Europe without definite frontiers governed the development of the German Reich and prevented the attainment of national unity until 1871, Nippon's history was shaped by her geographical seclusion as an island kingdom, reinforced by a definite policy of isolation. Never in history has a country been known to pursue a policy of seclusion from the outside world for 250 years as its sole and paramount goal, as has been the case with Japan.

Throughout these centuries Japanese statesmen concentrated the efforts of a highly efficient bureaucratic and military machine on the task of severing their country from any connection whatsoever with the outside world. They believed that in this way Japan would avoid foreign entanglements and the greed of other nations which were casting a menacing eye at the Far East during the first half of the 19th century. But the island kingdom was not permitted to continue this defensive and negative policy. The "Black Ships" of Admiral Perry's squadron forced Japan to throw open her gates to the impact of the Western nations and their competition for new markets and new spheres of influence. She now had to face the alternative of being reduced to a semi-colonial and dependent State like Turkey or China, or to accept the challenge and force her way uphill to the status of a sovereign, modern State capable of standing up to foreign interference.

In spite of her truly medieval backwardness, her feudal army equipped merely with swords and arrows, Japan decided to take up the challenge. Conquering the disadvantages of a poor soil and denied the help of natural riches, she succeeded by untiring efforts throughout decades of heavy sacrifice in building up a State on Western lines, with a powerful army and a modern industry. But as a result of this very success Japan became entangled in world affairs. In order to provide her growing population with food and other vital necessities she had to buy raw materials for her industries from foreign countries. As a payment for these raw materials she had to export her finished products. Her very existence being dependent on the willingness of the rest of the world to sell raw materials to her and to buy her finished products, she became highly susceptible to the least disturbance and was doomed to a precarious existence. Any interruption in the regular flow of imports and exports was bound to threaten the very foundations of the State.

Similar causes had led the German Reich on the road to industrialization and increased exports. Being newcomers to the world market, both countries had to struggle for their export trade with the methods of the upstart: efficiency, dumping, longer working hours, both achieving the same result, namely of arousing the hostility of the "have" nations towards the "have-nots." So long as free trade and unhampered competition dominated world economy, the newcomers were able to earn their living. But as soon as customs barriers were erected to protect the home markets, difficulties were bound to arise. As a result of the restriction of world markets these nations acquired a craving to create economic spheres of influence in which they could purchase raw materials and sell their finished products unhampered.

It was in this way that a tendency to expand developed which threatened the peace of the world, and this danger was heightened by the existence in the characters of both nations of identical traits. In the fundamental problem governing the attitude of the individual towards the State, both the Germans and the Japanese had, for different reasons, reached the same conclusion. According to their philosophy, the State was the paramount and primary institution to which all the personal needs and desires of the individual had to be subordinated. By devoting his services to the concentrated community of citizens incorporated in and personified by the State, the individual could fulfill the highest duty incumbent upon him, namely to further the well-being of his fellow countrymen. This Spartan line of thought had been adopted in Prussia as well as in Japan, and had led to the growth of an authoritarian State with a highly efficient executive administered by a hierarchy of soldiers and officials.

This austere and strict frame of mind combined with the hardships of a poor and barren country had created types of men who compensated themselves for their self-abnegation and hard work by an imperative and autocratic method of ruling. The Germans, like the Japanese, became accustomed to being unpopular. The fact that the methods employed by this unpopular rule achieved results which did it great credit—such as in Korea, Formosa, and the Eastern provinces of Prussia—was overlooked by the rest of the world and did not earn any appreciation until after their destruction.

Neither Germany nor Japan succeded in finding a solution to the problem as to how they should adapt themselves to that community of States which had developed on different lines—that is to say, to the Western democracies. When they felt that their very existence was being threatened by the increasing barriers erected to obstruct economic expansion or the emigration of surplus population, the dangerous *Lebenstraum* philosophy evolved which, when put into practice by force, led to the catastrophe.

This resort to force was also a characteristic common to both nations. They are both disciplined; indeed, intelligent obedience to a strong and efficient leadership is one of their outstanding qualities. If they become aware that they are being guided by inefficient government, this willingness to obey gives way to a sudden and violent explosion, and the same attitude characterizes their conduct in international relations. (Germany and Japan went a long way on the road of co-operation—the Germans during the period of the Weimar Republic and the Japanese during the liberal Shidehara epoch.) But when they feel frustrated in their endeavors, they stop abruptly and resort to peaceful efforts.

The great intimacy which developed between the German and Japanese nations after they had chosen the totalitarian way, and which led to the conclusion of an alliance in 1940, was thus particularly deep-rooted on both sides. Yet while the friendly feeling towards Germany was widespread throughout Japan, sympathy for the Japanese in Germany was very limited. In Japan particular friendship and admiration for Germany was felt by men of science, especially medical science, and by the army. These men had received their training from German instructors, and the lifelong gratitude shown to his teacher is one of the noblest traits in the Japanese character. One German professor or military instructor attracted hundreds or even thousands of pupils, whereas the number of German sympathizers for Japan was limited to the former German residents in the country and those who, by their studies or for other reasons, had developed an interest in and knowledge of Japan.

German sympathies in the Far East went out to China rather than to Japan. China appealed to the German mind as the home of Confucianism. Lao-Tse was a philosopher whose writings and teachings appeared in numerous popular editions. The novels of Pearl Buck and other American authors added to this popularity. Chinese art was highly appreciated by a growing number of German collectors. There were those who regarded themselves as the real orthodox connoisseurs—the enthusiasts for early Chinese pottery such as Sung and Tang—or the Ming collectors and those who merely appreciated and understood the 18th-century porcelain. Some eclecticists even specialized in picture scrolls. In comparison with this vast number of admirers of Chinese art there were few enthusiasts for Japanese woodcuts and lacquer, whereas the market was inundated by the awful baubles produced by Japanese dealers for foreign consumption. The really refined and what one might call the reticent classical art of Japan had to be studied intensely and with devotion in the country itself.

In Germany, as in other countries, the Chinese enjoyed greater popularity than the Japanese. Their easy-going manner, their sense of humor, and their command of European languages secured for them a favored position as compared with the studied formality of the Japanese, whose exaggerated politeness, even though it may be only a cover for shyness and the lack of any gift for learning foreign tongues, borders on the arrogant. Even German residents in Japan who have been there many years failed to find their way to the heart of their Japanese hosts, although no more reliable and loyal friend exists than a Japanese once the outer crust of distrust and formality has been pierced and his confidence has been won. The Japanese is, indeed, the most complicated and difficult human being to handle.

Even the traditional German friendship for the Japanese Army had shifted to China. While the German military circles rendered lip-service to Japan, they were at heart more attracted to China, since Marshal Chiang Kai-shek had secured the services of a strong delegation of German officers for the training of Chinese divisions. Under the able leadership of General von Falkenhausen they rendered valuable service to the Chinese Government. These officers enjoyed a great measure of popularity, and became deeply imbued with that alluring atmosphere of China which sometimes gains the devotion of passionate acolytes with an astonishing swiftness. Examples of this type are to be found in Pekin—such as, for example, the case of the German lawyer who, when already in his fifties, came over to Pekin on business which was to have kept him there for some weeks but who never returned home. He succumbed to the spell cast upon him by that beautiful and mysterious town, acquired a full command of the language, translated Chinese poems into German with a masterly touch, and led a happy life of seclusion near Pekin.

Such complete absorption into Far Eastern life on the part of foreigners is never found in Japan. Such absorption as there is is confined to intermarriage. But although these marriages generally turn out harmoniously, their number is restricted by pressure brought to bear by both races.

The temperature of German friendship for Japan naturally rose when the centralized Third Reich aimed at establishing closer relations with the Far Eastern island kingdom. A wave of sympathy was set up and duly deepened by all the machinery of the party.

I personally favored the policy of friendship with Japan. I was too much of a Prussian myself not to feel sympathy for other nations who, like ourselves, "had hungered themselves to greatness." Furthermore, I realized the necessity of applying some kind of brake to the Russian machine, after the relations between Germany and the Soviet Union became more strained. I had never believed in the possibility of a Russo-Japanese war on Japanese initiative. Moreover, I had always adhered to Joseph Chamberlain's plan of an understanding between Britain, Germany, and Japan, a scheme which had been frustrated by that psychopathic leader of German foreign policy, Holstein. But I thought that this combination might occur again. The belief was to be strengthened by the conclusion of the Anglo-German naval agreement in 1935 which put an end to naval rivalry between the two countries. This proved to be an error of judgment on my part, but it was perhaps excusable.

As usual the Foreign Office gave me no specific instructions when I took my leave of Berlin. But from a hint dropped by General von Blomberg, the War Minister, I gathered that it was Hitler's intention to establish closer relations with Japan.

The rôle of the German Ambassador to Japan was at first that of a spectator of the general political scene. This was an interesting task and one not difficult to fulfil, thanks to the presence of two factors: an efficient staff and favorable political circumstances. Herr Noebel, who had been a colleague of mine during my Berlin period in the Eastern Department, had been appointed Counsellor of the Embassy. We worked together in perfect harmony and our destinies were to be linked even more closely by the vicissitudes of the Second World War. Two senior secretaries of the Embassy, Herr Kolb and Herr Knoll, were particularly valuable colleagues owing to their complete command of the Japanese language. The former was in charge of cultural affairs and the latter was employed as commercial secretary. The civilian staff was rounded off by Herr von Etzdorff, who was my personal secretary. Noebel and Kolb remained with me throughout my term of office in Tokyo.

In a country where the army and navy played such an important part, the qualities of the military and naval attachés were especially important. I was fortunate in having as my military attaché one of the most prominent officers in the German Army—both as regards his character and his ability —in the person of General Ott. As political right-hand man to General von Schleicher at the War Ministry for five years he had played a leading part in the negotiations with the Nazis. Although Hitler decided not to subject him to the same fate as that of Schleicher and General von Bredow, who were murdered on June 30, 1934, the War Ministry deemed it advisable to keep Ott out of the dictator's sight for a few years. In spite of his desperate efforts to secure the command of a division or an army corps—for he was a passionate soldier—Ott had to remain at his semi-diplomatic post. By his character and ability he won the esteem of the Japanese General Staff as well as that of the Diplomatic Corps.

The naval attaché, Captain Wenneker, a frank and outspoken sailor, a cheerful and reliable comrade, was also well suited for his post. As captain and commander of the cruiser *Deutschland* during the first stage of the Second World War, he won fame by one of his raids in the Caribbean. He then returned to Tokyo for a second term of office and remained there until the capitulation.

I was also fortunate in having agreeable contacts in the Japanese Foreign Office, outstanding among which throughout my four years in Japan was my friendship with Koki Hirota and my collaboration with him during my term. During those four years he was in office either as Prime Minister or Foreign Minister almost all the time. He was, indeed, the most "Japanese" of all the statesmen with whom I had to deal. The decades which he had spent in foreign countries had scarcely altered his way of thinking. He himself was of humble origin, his father having been a stone-cutter at Fukuoka, Kyushu; but his abilities had been discovered by Count Kato, one of the leading statesmen at the turn of the century. He had sponsored him and trained him for the foreign service as his secretary in London. Having only a moderate command of the English language, Hirota's contacts with the West were limited: his wife never accompanied him to his diplomatic posts, and such sympathies as he had for foreign countries were limited to Great Britain.

He was an active nationalist, a faithful disciple of Toyama, the high priest of nationalism, and a member of the "Black Dragon" nationalist society. I have often wondered how this outlook could be reconciled with the kind, moderate, and almost slow behavior of Hirota, whom I learned to appreciate so highly as a quiet and sensible man. But it is impossible for the European to form an accurate impression of the Oriental mind, and so I thought he was probably one of the philosophical nationalists who adhered to principles in theory, whilst in practice following a more moderate policy.

The difficulties of gaining an insight into the working of the Japanese mind are increased—quite apart from the obstacles imposed by the language—by the fact that in explaining their way of thinking, the Japanese indulge in endless explanations of what they believe to be exceptional achievements of Far Eastern enlightenment which strike the Western mind as rather commonplace. Be this as it may, there is no doubt that Hirota opposed with considerable courage the hazardous policy of the nationalist diehards and worked to the utmost of his strength and influence for peace and reconciliation. I am glad that my eminent American colleague, Mr. Joseph Grew, has arrived at the same conclusion in his diaries published under the title *Ten Years in Japan,* the German translation of which reached me recently.

The other high officials in the *Gaimusho*—the Ministry of Foreign Affairs—were equally capable and agreeable to deal with. The Deputy Minister, Shigemitsu, who later became my colleague in London and was Japanese Foreign Minister at the time of the capitulation in 1945, was a capable official with strong pro-British sympathies and a very Japanese mentality. The most important official so far as the German Embassy was concerned was Togo, the head of the political department. Togo spoke perfect German, having spent several years in Berlin and married a German woman. Being sympathetic towards Germany and more European-minded than his superiors, he was always helpful and agreeable to deal with. As Ambassador to Berlin and later to Moscow, and as Foreign Minister at the time of Japan's entry into the war, he is, at the time of writing, together with Hirota, and Shigemitsu, facing a trial for crimes, the entire responsibility for which, morally speaking, rests with the war party.

My associations with Kurusu, the chief of the economic affairs department, were equally agreeable. He was also a permanent official of great experience, spoke fluent English (his wife was American), and was well versed in international affairs. He, too, as Ambassador to Berlin and as a member of the mission to Washington on the eve of the attack on Pearl Harbor, was to play an important part in the foreign policy of his country.

Thus it did not take me long to establish personal contacts. Upon returning my visit, Hirota in a private and confidential talk immediately broached a question to which he evidently attached great importance. He wanted to bring the puppet State of Manchukuo within the comity of nations by obtaining some kind of diplomatic recognition from a friendly power. Although he did not say as much, he certainly implied it. He invited me to take part in an unofficial, so-called sightseeing trip to Manchukuo. I wired to Berlin for instructions advising the acceptance of this invitation; but the first telegram which I received from the Foreign Office in January, 1934, was a negative answer. A somewhat lively exchange of letters ensued when I pointed out to Bülow that a more co-operative policy towards Japan was in the making on the part of Germany, and that this would have been an inconspicuous but nevertheless effective way of displaying our more friendly attitude.

As was to be expected, the party took up the matter, to the exclusion of the Foreign Office, and a few weeks later a young man by the name of Heye arrived at the Embassy. Herr Heye had called on me in Berlin before I left for Tokyo and had told me that keen interest was felt in high party circles in the commercial potentialities of Manchukuo. He told me at that time that as he had spent several years in the Far East as a merchant, he would probably be entrusted with the task of representing these interests on the spot.

This combination of party, business, and Manchukuo did not appeal to me, and it soon became evident from Heye's remarks that he and the men behind him had embarked upon an enterprise of a much wider and hazardous scope. This ring of profit-hungry party men consisted among others of Göring's brother-in-law, Riegele; Keppler, who later became "Under-Secretary of State" for odd jobs at the Foreign Office; and of Heye. He was a scion of a wealthy and respected family of industrialists from Düsseldorf with artistic leanings and commercial ambitions, who was reluctant to divulge any details of his business career in the Far East. What was worse, this group had secured Hitler's blessing for their venture and had extracted from him the appointment of Heye as something in the nature of "German High Commissioner for Manchukuo." This was to be communicated to the Japanese in a semi-official manner. Heye was to start his business in the highly complicated soya bean trade but also in a semi-official capacity. The whole affair was so amateurish and carried such a strong flavor of reckless profiteering on a political basis that harm was bound to come.

Indeed it was not long before it did. Rumors spread that Germany was about to grant diplomatic recognition to Manchukuo. Heye was regarded as the first prospective ambassador, and the air was thick with commercial combinations. Heye honored Tokyo with frequent visits, whilst ambitious and speculative Japanese swarmed around him. Together with such people, he proceeded at high pressure to urge the official recognition of Manchukuo. Situations like this were the despair of the official representative of a country.

Whilst pointing out the harm which this reckless policy was liable to cause to the authorities concerned, I proceeded to collect data about the persons engaged in this racket. Our Consul at Harbin unearthed some unsavory facts about Heye's activities in that town a few years previously. He had engaged in shady and fraudulent transactions and had defrauded one of his partners, who committed suicide and, in a farewell letter put all the blame for his death on Heye. Although party circles in Berlin endeavored stubbornly to continue support of their emissary in spite of these revelations, they were ultimately forced to withdraw their backing.

So Heye faded out of the picture, and with him the unofficial ambassador to Manchukuo passed into oblivion.

From that time onward Manchurian affairs were dealt with in the regular way. The next step towards the establishment of official relations between Germany and Manchukuo was the dispatch of a delegation to Tokyo and Hsinking to conclude commercial agreements with both Governments—this was in the autumn of 1935. Under the able leadership of Herr Kiep, formerly Consul-General in New York (he was subsequently executed by the Nazis as a member of the German resistance), the delegation accomplished some useful work.

After Heye's mission the Nazis sent only one more unofficial emissary and observer to Tokyo. Since Ribbentrop had established his competitive office, he pestered the Embassies and Legations by sending his young hopefuls abroad to spy on the official representatives of the Reich by establishing contacts without communicating with the Embassies. It was on such a mission that Ribbentrop dispatched Professor Albrecht Haushofer to Tokyo. He was the son of the famous founder of the *Geopolitik,* and an ardent friend of Japan, where he had spent many years as a military instructor. But Albrecht Haushofer was far too clever and too loyal to perform the duties which his mission entailed in a clandestine manner. He maintained close contact with General Ott and me. Some years later he visited me in London. When the gulf of antagonism which developed between him and Ribbentrop became unbridgeable, he left the Ribbentrop Bureau and joined the Resistance. Gaoled and tortured by the Gestapo, he was surreptitiously shot as one of the last victims of the Nazi terror in April, 1945, while being transported from the Moabit prison to another gaol. The poems which he had written in prison were found clutched in the dead man's hand. They have been published under the title *Moabiter Sonette,* and should be outstanding not only for their poetical but also for their documentary value.

The flow of political events in Japan during the first two years of my mission there was characterized by an all-round uncertainty as to the ultimate policy to be followed. There was, indeed, a struggle between the rival factions for power. The nationalist revolutionary element represented by the army had not yet assumed full control of the Government machine, whilst the moderate and Liberal elements had not yet relinquished their hold. This uncertainty was reflected in the gallant but inconclusive efforts to choose a middle course made by the various Cabinets that came to power. And so some permanent changes came about in the triple problem of Russia, China, and the United States in accordance with the ebb and flow of these conflicting elements.

Constancy in foreign affairs could hardly result from this internal struggle. Hirota made frantic efforts to improve Japan's relations with the United States, which had been badly shaken by the occupation of Manchuria and by the exodus from the League of Nations. On the other hand, the nationalist elements wanted to free the country from the restrictions imposed upon the navy by the 2 : 1 ratio agreed upon under the Washington Treaty. This desire, which ultimately led to the denouncing of the treaty, naturally had the effect of a veiled threat to the Government of the United States and administered a chill to the relations between the two countries just as they seemed to be improving as a result of the efforts of M. Hirota and Mr. Grew.

The temperature of Russo-Japanese relations oscillated between the ice-cold and the lukewarm. During 1933, with General Araki as War Minister, the outbreak of a war seemed more likely than the maintenance of peace. Araki, together with Toyama, who was an idol of the Nationalists, indulged in warmongering speeches and preached a somewhat hazy philosophy which, when stripped of its mysterious wrappings, proved to consist of little more than rather commonplace truisms. Such at least was my impression when I was invited to a private and confidential talk with Araki after he had resigned.

He handed in his resignation about the time I arrived in Japan. The *détente* which resulted from his disappearance from the political scene provided Hirota with the opening enabling him to attempt a disentanglement of the overlapping and conflicting interests of both countries in the danger spot of Manchuria. His efforts were successful, as the Soviet Union, which still lacked any military preparedness, regarded its hold on that country as too insecure. In a long-drawn-out bargaining, conducted along the classical line of this art as practiced in Oriental countries, an agreement was reached concerning the purchase of the "Eastern Chinese Railways" by Japan for a comparatively low sum. After having deprived the Soviet Union of this last remnant of Tsarist imperialism, Japanese imperialism gained full control over Manchuria. Now that the danger spots of potential friction had been removed, Russo-Japanese relations improved, and it was only the annual negotiations concerning the lease of the fishing-grounds off Vladivostock that provided an opportunity for heated bargaining or speedy agreement, as the case might be. These negotiations were as a thermometer to the outer world for ascertaining the temperature prevailing in the relations between the two countries.

While Hirota was writing friendly notes to the Nanking Government and a lull in the Japanese advance in Northern China had restored mutual relations to something approaching normal, the same Hirota published a sensational declaration on April 17, 1934, which was bound to have the effect of a challenge to the world and a new humiliation for China. As this declaration was made by Amau, the chief of the press department, it became known as the "Amau Declaration." But it would be more correct and more in accordance with the momentous character of its aspirations to call it the "Hirota Doctrine." By this proclamation the Japanese Government claimed a sort of overlordship over China and shouted a menacing "Hands off China!" to the world, and especially to the powers which advocated "Open door and equal opportunity."

The United States was the protagonist of this policy. Japan's action was the stepping-stone towards the proclamation of a Pan-Asiatic Doctrine embodied in the slogan of the "East Asiatic Co-prosperity Sphere." But while "Co-prosperity" served as the ideological war-cry in the war with the Western Powers, the "Hirota Doctrine" was proclaimed with some timidity and signs of bad conscience.

The Nanking Government cannot be acquitted of the charge of having handled relations with Japan clumsily. It may have been that the intellectual and sentimental sacrifice would have been too great for an effort to be made at improving relations with Japan with an ultimate reconciliation between the two great Eastern nations. Being a realist, however, Marshal Chiang Kai-shek had to face the fact that, owing to the general situation in China, which was rent by war and revolution, she lacked the strength to resist Japanese aggression. He realized, moreover, that he needed one or two decades of normal development in order to gain strength and build up an army, and that he would have to make sacrifices in order to secure this period of peaceful reconstruction.

During those years of comparatively moderate Japanese Government, before the authoritarian State had been fully formed, he might have gained this breathing-space by granting some sort of autonomy to the Japanese in Northern China. He might have loosened the ties with these provinces without detaching them altogether from the mother country and without too great a loss of prestige; in so doing the appetite of the hungry wolf would have been satisfied. But in China, as elsewhere, moral courage is much rarer than military courage and, from the domestic point of view, it was much safer to continue a policy of intransigence towards Japan than to risk becoming the victim of internal feuds and of competitors who might exploit the "treason of China's most sacred rights" for their own egotistical ends. Thus the conciliatory period in Tokyo passed without being exploited by Nanking, and the stage was set for the conflict.

In her economic relations with Great Britain and the British Empire during the Hirota period, Japan was rather on the defensive. It goes without saying that the Cabinet tried to establish close friendship with Great Britain. This was an aim that was pursued with enthusiasm by nearly all those concerned with the conduct of Japanese foreign policy. Enthusiasm for the Anglo-Japanese alliance was more real in Tokyo than it was in London. At that time the Cabinet, the elder statesmen "behind the throne," economic circles and—last but not least—the navy supported this alliance, only the army standing apart. But for reasons which were not quite discernible—perhaps out of anti-totalitarian motives or for purely economic considerations—Great Britain and the Dominions acted to the prejudice of Japanese interests, especially her flow of imports and exports. Economic treaties were denounced, customs barriers increased, and other obstacles placed in the way of commercial exchange with Australia, India, Egypt, and also, if I am not mistaken, with South Africa. The purchase of Australian wool was interrupted, Egyptian cotton was difficult to procure, and the export of cotton cloth to India was throttled. In protracted negotiations these difficulties, it is true, were settled to some extent. But these disturbances in the vital circulation of goods by an unhampered import of raw materials and export of finished goods made it increasingly clear to the average Japanese that only an economic sphere independent of the outside world and subject to his domination would do away with these constant threats to his life-line.

Germany's rôle during this active period of Japanese politics was that of an interested and watchful observer. Whatever attention Germany did attract by reason of her internal political situation was caused by sinister events. The purge of June 30, 1934, which led to the annihilation of Roehm and his faction, and to the murder of scores of other men believed to be potentially dangerous enemies—such as General von Schleicher—caused considerable excitement and some doubts as to the stability of the Hitler régime. But the scanty information divulged by the press and the irresponsible rumors which circulated did not afford one an insight into the inner workings of the Nazi party machine. And so everyone, the German colony included, supposed that in due course the radical revolutionary element in Germany would be ousted. Now that the S.A., with its ambition to gain full control of the armed forces, had been crushed, it was assumed that the regular army would assert itself and that Hitler would lean more on the support of the conservative forces in the country. The abortive *putsch* in Vienna and the murder of Chancellor Dollfuss gave rise to renewed concern, but there seemed to be an early return to normal conditions in Vienna.

Whilst the disgust and disapproval with which these gangsters' methods were regarded continued, the death of Field-Marshal von Hindenburg deflected the attention of public opinion from these misdeeds and concentrated it on the venerable person of one of the true representatives of Germany. Thus, even by his death, the old President had rendered a last service to his country. The German community in Tokyo was all the more deeply moved by this loss, as it was instinctively felt that with the passing of Hindenburg the last remnant of a Germany dear to them had vanished. This foreboding was confirmed when Hitler usurped the office of President of the Reich and vested himself with the unrestricted power of the executive.

The only event of international importance in Japan during the autumn of 1934 was the international conference of the Red Cross in Tokyo. A delegation headed by the Duke of Saxe Coburg-Gotha arrived in Tokyo to represent the German Red Cross. I was unfortunately prevented from attending the conference and its various social functions by a severe attack of bronchitis, which laid me up for several weeks and forced me to go on sick leave to my favorite resort of Nara. This time my health was completely restored, but the next attack, which I had just a year later, left me with the scourge of asthma, which compelled me to relinquish my post sooner than I had intended.

So far as Japan was concerned, the year 1935 was uneventful. The Saito Cabinet was replaced by the Okada Government; the new Premier, a retired admiral, being merely a figurehead for a set of ministers who bore the mark of transition, with Hirota the only firm and outstanding personality. There came a new outburst of militarist terror which was an evil foreboding of events yet to come. A colonel who felt that he had been slighted when a certain new appointment was made called on the head of the personnel department at the War Ministry, and when the General declined to accede to the colonel's wishes, he shot him dead on the spot. This outrage was the most blatant sign of the revolutionary disintegration within the Japanese Army.

2. THE MUTINY OF FEBRUARY, 1936

Towards the end of February I had left Tokyo for Nagasaki, where I was to meet the German cruiser *Karlsruhe,* which, in the course of a world cruise, was to pay visits to Yokohama and the capital. The Commander, Captain Siemens, who later became naval attaché to the Embassy in London, invited me aboard his ship for the cruise through the Inland Sea to Yokohama. But at Moji, when I was boarding the ferry to Shimonoseki, one of the police officials whispered to me that some political murders had been committed in Tokyo during the night.

At Nagasaki I succeeded in getting a telephone call through to Tokyo

Dr. von Dirksen with Japanese in traditional costume, watching an ancient ball game

and so received some more detailed information. A gang of rabidly nation-alist young officers had perpetrated a series of ghastly murders. The victims —ex-Prime Minister Marquis Saito, the Finance Minister Takahashi (who was eighty-six years old), and General Watanabe—had been killed in spite of the heroic efforts of their wives to protect them. Other officials had been wounded. Prime Minister Okada had managed to escape, thanks to the self-sacrifice of his brother-in-law, who had been murdered in his stead. Count Makino, the most important of the Elder Statesmen, had been fore-warned and saved by the courage of his young granddaughter, whose father, M. Yoshida, later Ambassador to Rome and London, is rendering valuable service to his country as Prime Minister since the capitulation.

But that was not all. The Third Infantry Division stationed in Tokyo mutinied under the command of a group of junior officers and assumed control of vital parts of the capital. So my cruise through the Inland Sea had to be cancelled, and, as no air transport was available, I had to endure a wearisome eighteen hours' train journey to reach Tokyo. But my train was stopped at the station before Tokyo and I was requested by members of the Embassy staff not to proceed, as the main station in the capital was in the hands of the insurgents. We motored to the house of the naval attaché to which my wife and the other ladies had been evacuated. As the telephone was still functioning. I had a long talk with General Ott, who, together with the rest of the staff, was besieged in the Embassy, which was only a hundred yards away from the War Ministry. As the stately parlia-ment building was situated just opposite the Embassy and the General Staff headquarters were not far away, we were in an area of the highest strategic importance.

The insurgents had occupied all these government offices and were busily entrenching themselves and preparing their defense against any attempts which might be made by loyal troops to dislodge them from their strongholds. General Ott agreed to attempt a break-through of the cordon and thus enable me eventually to reach the Embassy. He arrived safely within an hour accompanied by a "loyal" gendarme, and we started immediately on our return to the Embassy.

It was dark and it was raining; the broad streets with their montonous little houses looked even more desolate than on ordinary days. As we drove through the parts occupied by the mutineers, the general aspect became unpleasantly ominous. The streets were deserted; at different points small crowds of civilians and soldiers gathered round some military orator who was addressing them with revolutionary fervor. We decided to leave the main streets and try a break-through along one of the narrow and winding side streets, and in this we were successful. One of the mutineers lying on his stomach with a machine-gun in front of him raised no objection after being sternly addressed by the "loyal' gendarme. So we arrived at the Embassy unmolested.

The mutiny was mounting to its climax. The leaders had refused to obey the orders of their superiors to lay down their arms, so that they were now to be forced into surrender by a combined "loyalist" attack with heavy artillery. The bombardment was due to begin next morning at eight-thirty, and so we made preparations for this emergency. Food and some furniture were assembled in the cellar. The confidential files were piled up in front of the boiler fires in case of any immediate danger, and Herr Kolb, one of the secretaries, was quite enthusiastic about the possibility of having to burn them, saying that he was experienced at the job, having done so at the outbreak of war in 1914. In a number of urgent telephone calls from the Ministry of Foreign Affairs we were summoned to evacuate the Embassy as the staffs of the other Embassies and Legations had done. This we refused to do, however, pointing out that we were entitled to the protection of the Japanese Government and it was for them to see that no harm came to us.

After a somewhat hectic night we were prepared for the worst, and from 8 A. M. onwards we awaited the first detonation. But at eight-thirty everything was still quiet and remained so, and at nine o'clock we cautiously went up on to the roof to survey the situation. From that vantage point we were able to observe small figures climbing down from the cupola of the parliament building in single file. Evidently the insurgents were surrendering. This observation of ours was soon confirmed when we saw "loyalist" tanks driving past. One of the officers told us the Emperor had ordered the mutineers to submit, in leaflets which had been dropped from aircraft, and they dared not disobey a royal order. Thereafter everything returned to normal within a few hours with all the precision and discipline which had hitherto been customary in the Japanese Army. The mutineers were assembled in small squads and led away by armed "loyalists." The leaders surrendered and were imprisoned.

The unbelievable breach of loyalty and discipline which the mutiny constituted shook the structure of the Japanese State to its foundations. The country was accustomed to political murders and might not have reacted vigorously to the butchery of some prominent old men of honorable character. But the disobedience of whole units of the Imperial Army to the orders of their superiors, and the restoration of discipline only by the emergency measure of an Imperial order, had the effect of a thunderstorm clearing the overheated and unhealthy atmosphere. To their great astonishment the ringleaders did not escape with merely a few years' imprisonment. Thirteen captains and lieutenants were sentenced to death and executed, while minor offenders suffered long terms of imprisonment.

Attendance at the court-martial and the executions imposed a terrible mental strain on the officers concerned. One of the judges went insane and another committed suicide. However, generally speaking, the crisis was overcome and there were no further acts of terrorism. The outbreak of the China "incident" one year later was, it is true, in accordance with nationalist wishes, and the ensuing eight years of war absorbed the entire physical and mental strength of the army.

I had been particularly anxious for a speedy end of the mutiny as I had booked a passage to Vancouver on a boat sailing from Yokohama on April 9. The winter months had been rather strenuous for me and I struggled in vain to overcome my insidious asthma, an after-effect of my attack of bronchitis, which was probably due to some unknown irritant in the air. Together with other sufferers, I was subjected to torments of semi-suffocation just from October to February and only so long as I was on Japanese soil. After a few hours on board ship I was all right again. The principal current affairs had been settled. Trade relations between Japan and Manchukuo had been regulated by the agreements mentioned above, while in another sphere closer co-operation between Germany and Japan was commencing. A mission of German naval technicians had paid a visit to the Japanese Navy and had asked to be furnished with the experience and technical details of the construction of aircraft carriers. The German Navy had, until then, lacked an opportunity to gather information on a subject which had hitherto been unknown to it. The Japanese Navy had been helpful to an extent which was in direct contradiction to her customary secretiveness. This was all the more remarkable as, in spite of the age-old ties which linked the Japanese Army to its former German instructors, relations between the two navies had not been particularly close.

But there were also other reasons which necessitated an urgent visit to Berlin on my part. Since December, 1935, we had received confidential information from the Japanese General Staff that Ribbentrop and the Military Attaché at the Japanese Embassy in Berlin, Colonel Oshima, had started conversations in the German capital with a view to establishing closer political understanding between the two governments. No details were yet obtainable. Both the Foreign Office and, as was to be expected in view of the undeclared state of war prevailing between the two rivals, Ribbentrop's office maintained an impenetrable silence. As I still clung to the old-fashioned belief that in such cases the advice of the Ambassador on the spot might be of some value, I resolved to go a little more closely into the matter.

Thus the first part of my mission to Japan concluded on April 9, 1936, when the S.S. *Empress of Canada* left Yokohama for Vancouver. The first half of my four and a half years in Japan constituted the more agreeable and varied part of my term of office there. Social duties and routine work were frequently interrupted by various short journeys which had to be made, whilst I also had occasion, of course, to visit the more distant parts of the Japanese Empire. Even ordinary daily life was enlivened by games of tennis and visits to the many curio shops. As my hopes of finding a cure for my asthma in Germany were not fulfilled, the second half of my stay in Japan was dominated by increasing illness and, of course, by the Sino-Japanese conflict. I therefore propose at this juncture to insert a survey of my travels and more personal experiences in Japan.

3. ART, TRAVEL, AND SOCIAL LIFE

Tokyo with Yokohama and Kobe-Osaka with Kyoto being the two centers of cultural and economic life in Japan, my official duties made it necessary for me to make frequent journeys to the province of Kobe-Osaka, or Kwansai as it was called, and I must confess that these trips gave me great pleasure. We spent many pleasant times at the hospitable house of Consul-General Wagner at Kobe. The German community, which was as numerous as that of Tokyo and Yokohama, was flourishing, well-to-do, and responsive to all appeals for charitable or cultural institutions. There were two Japanese societies with hundreds of members who devoted their activities to the development of friendship and understanding between Germany and Japan. The enormous industrial activity of these cities, which combined the concentration of heavy industry comparable to the Ruhr with the port facilities of Hamburg, was interesting as an object of study and important for the development of mutual trade relations.

But what attracted me more was Kyoto, the cultural center of Japan, and, to an even greater extent, the religious sanctuary at Nara, where I spent some of the happiest days of my whole stay in Nippon. Kyoto, it is true, had lost much of its charm during the thirty years since I had visited it on my trip round the world. It had grown into a thriving industrial city with a million inhabitants, and in this process the dignified old temples and palaces had been almost obliterated in a sea of modern traffic and noise. But they still existed; the old-fashioned Miyako Hotel was still there, and, under its proprietor, Dr. Nishi, who had acquired his degree in Leipzig, it was more a home for friends than a shelter for strangers. And then, within an hour's motor drive, there was Lake Biwa, which was almost an ocean compared with the minuteness of most other Japanese lakes; and one could escape from the noise of the city by a walk to the quiet hill where the vagrant poet Bassho, the Omar Kháyyám of Japan, had lived and conceived his fragile seventeen- or thirty-two-syllable poems.

Professor Trautz, the President of the German-Japanese *Kultur-Institut,* was an understanding and devoted interpreter of the spiritual atmosphere of Kyoto. It was during those years that the new building of the *Kultur-Institut,* to which Japanese friends of Germany had largely contributed, was started, thus symbolizing the growing interest which both nations felt in each other's cultural achievements.

Old Japanese and Chinese art appealed to me to an even greater extent. As the Japanese are devoid of any nationalist feeling with regard to Chinese art, which they collect almost as passionately as their own, Japan was a happy hunting-ground for the collector and admirer of Chinese art. And the same curio dealers still existed, among them Yamanaka, famed the world over for his beautiful curios and low prices, who greeted me with enthusiasm. As even bargaining is performed in Japan with a certain amount of grace, visits to the curio dealers are a means of studying Japan in her most lovable aspects: her refined taste and the consummate skill of her handicrafts, concealed almost to the point of disappearance by an intense desire to avoid ostentation.

The less glamorous an object of art or an edifice is, the higher its value in Japan. The pottery masters, above all the Raku family—the pottery dynasty in Kyoto—may be mentioned as an example of this out-look. I visited this artisan artist who belongs to the twelfth generation of his family and profession. As their masterpiece and the incarnation of their artistic ideal, and of their handicraft, each generation had created a tea-bowl, concentrating in this humble object of everyday life their ideal of beauty and their experience of lifelong work. Considerable self-discipline is required to express one's artistic ideal and longing in the treatment of a tiny earthenware object only a few inches high. And even the master's son, a lad of sixteen, had tried to create a bowl to his own taste and had succeeded. It goes without saying that the collection of the complete series of Raku bowls is one of the greatest treasures of every collector. Apart from Master Raku's, I have found them only at the Metropolitan Museum in New York and some of them at the home of an American lady living in London.

Although in a more concentrated form, the art and history of Japan made a big appeal to the visitor to Nara. This place had been spared the debasement of modern industrialization, and the visitor is impressed and overawed by a cultural and historical tradition dating back 1,200 years. The combination of the dignified wooden temples with the soft curve of their roofs and a forest of huge old cryptomerias, the stone lanterns which lined the paths to the temple and the gentle fallow deer roaming between the gothic pillars of the trees made one aware of the spirit which had created this sanctuary: these temples were not erected merely for their own sake nor in order to impress the visitor by their splendor and magnificence. The harmony and simplicity of their proportions, the perfect combination of nature and art, were intended to exalt the faithful.

In the neighborhood of Nara some of the oldest monasteries, such as Horiuji, enshrined the most ancient, beautiful, and revered Japanese works of art, having been saved from destruction by the island isolation of Nippon, on whose soil no enemy had ever set foot. Frescoes more than a thousand years old adorned the walls of the temple, being only slightly damaged by the effects of the climate. They were only on show, however, for a few short weeks in November, as for the rest of the year they had to be protected from the destructive effects of heat and damp. In the adjoining building and temples the incomparable statue of the *kwannon* of Horiuji and the wooden portraits of priests impressed the visitor with the fact that in those centuries Japanese art had reached the height of perfection. It is a strange fact, and contrary to that innate sense of proportion which the Japanese possess, that these statues were frequently displayed in rows like soldiers lined up on parade, in a vast low shed which was as harmful to their dignity as it was to their artistic effect.

One of the rarest and most interesting sights, even though it had little attraction in the way of beauty and harmony, was the *Shosoin,* or Imperial Treasury. Visitors were admitted only on special recommendation and, as in the case of the Hoiuji Temple, only in November. Even then, admission was dependent on the humidity of the air. You had to run the risk of being turned out if rain influenced the hygrometer beyond the ordinary level. As the treasures preserved there for the past 1,200 years could not stand being exposed to daylight, the visitor had to be equipped with a strong torch. The *Shosoin* contained objects of applied art such as saddles, tapestries, arrows, and household objects, and it was more the sensation of having seen something unique than any sense of beauty which one felt by visiting the treasury.

I was fortunate in having already travelled through the greater part of Japan before my illness forced me to avoid any kind of exertion. So far as travel was concerned, 1935 stands out in my memory. Together with Consul-General Wagner, I visited Kyushu, the southern island of Japan, which in its vegetation and culture differs little from the main island. It is the marked individuality of its inhabitants which strikes the visitor. By reason of their isolation and the separate tribe which they constitute, they might be called the Bavarians of Japan, although their minds are more alert and their intelligence quicker than that of the corresponding tribe in Germany. Kyushu is a beautiful island, with its volcanoes, tropical vegetation, and hot springs, but its landscape is more like that of Honshu. The rocks of Shimabara are an impressive reminder of the tragedy which befell medieval Japanese Christians who, in a feud between Christian and Buddhist *daimyos*, were beleaguered at this place and hurled down from the rocks by the thousands. And it is moving to recall that after 250 years of suppression of the Christian faith during the Shogunate, thousands of Japanese turned up again who had preserved their faith, although in a strangely different form, when the armor of isolation had been pierced by the Black Ships of Admiral Perry.

Whereas Kyushu forms a part of Japan separated from the mainland as if by chance, the Shimonoseki-Fusan channel between Japan and Korea is a boundary between two continents. Although surrounded by the sea and connected with the continent only by a narrow neck of land, the clean, dry, sub-continental climate extends to Korea and is a relief to the visitor after the oppressive humidity of the Japanese climate. Korea is almost as mountainous as Japan, where less than 20 per cent of the terrain is arable land, although it lacks the almost sinister beauty of the Japanese volcanoes. Cuckoos and other birds enliven the forests, which, after centuries of devastation through neglect, have been cultivated by the Japanese and their German experts. Although the Koreans stress their reluctance to overwork by wearing white gowns, the quiet dignity of the men and the grace of the women fit the harmony of the landscape. Korea has become known by the name of "the land of morning calm," and this seems to me to be an appropriate characterization of this charming country.

I made the most of the few weeks at my disposal and hurried through the country which stretches like a thin finger pointing to the south; a number of long railway journeys were therefore unavoidable. Seoul, the capital, appealed to me rather by reason of the treasures of its museum than by the charm of its architecture. I climbed to the top of the Diamond Mountains, where one is greeted by giant sculptures of Buddha and his disciples carved in the rocks by pious medieval priests. I spent some interesting days with the German Benedictine monks at Genzan, who, with Bishop Sauer, had done most valuable work in educating the population and teaching them handicrafts; I travelled to Heijo in North Korea, where the digging of the millionth ton of anthracite was being celebrated, and, in strange contrast, Chinese tombs a thousand years old were being explored by Japanese archeologists. My travels also took me to Kaishu, the southernmost point of the country, and I looked down on the Straits of Tsujima, where, exactly thirty years previously, the fate of Russia as a great power in East Asia had been sealed for a generation, and I paid my respects to the famous Bukokuji temple and the beautiful statue of Buddha surrounded by his twelve disciples.

My study of the country, however perfunctory as it may have been, and my conversations with many Japanese officials, especially with the open-minded and capable Governor-General Ugaki, confirmed the opinion I had formed with regard to the colonizing ability of the Japanese. They had undoubtedly done some splendid work in developing, within a few decades, a backward country disrupted for centuries of internal strife and attack from without, and inhabited by an intelligent and critical, although not very industrious, population. A network of excellent roads and railways had opened up the country. Industry and agriculture were developed and adapted to modern standards. The mountains had been reforested. There was an obvious tendency on the part of the Japanese to further the education of the Koreans so that they might be entrusted with administrative posts. Seven Korean governors had been appointed out of a total of twelve.

But the Koreans loathed their masters, whom they regarded as foreign invaders. The world at large never condoned the enforced occupation and the cruelties committed during the first few years. The Japanese shared the lot of the Prussians, who lacked the grace to win the sympathy of the outside world, although they raised the populations of the countries they occupied from medieval squalor to the standards of the 20th century. This applied as much to Prussia and German rule in Poznania and in the colonies as it did to the Japanese administration of Korea, Manchuria, and Formosa. This has been confirmed by the course of events in Formosa after the withdrawal of the Japanese, where two years of Chinese mismanagement sufficed to transform a flourishing and quiet island into a country seething with rebellion and unrest.

These impressions were further confirmed by a visit to Japan's northern island, Hokkaido, on which my wife and I set out some two months later. Here again we found ourselves in a country which was entirely different from the motherland and which gave the visitor the impression that he was on colonial soil. Hokkaido seemed to me to be a kind of halfway house between the Japanese islands and the Asiatic continent. The numerous active volcanoes revealed landscape like that of Honshu and Kyushu, but the Gulf Stream having turned away from the shores of Northern Japan, the climate is a continental one with long, cold winters and huge masses of snow.

Hokkaido was the Eldorado for the increasing winter number of sport enthusiasts. The cold climate had proved an insurmountable obstacle to any Japanese plans for settling the country with the surplus population of the overcrowded southern provinces. So Hokkaido remained colonial by nature and had a population of only 3,000,000 Japanese in spite of its size —it is equal in area to Bavaria and Württemberg together. These 3,000,000 people led a rather miserable existence, living in thin wooden houses which they did not feel able to replace with stone buildings. They exchanged the potatoes they had to grow for rice, in spite of the loss incurred by the transaction. Cattle breeding, grain production, and general agriculture in Hokkaido were adapted to European methods.

There was evidence everywhere that the Japanese administrators were doing their utmost for the development of Hokkaido. There was a comparatively narrow network of roads and railways and there were model farms; the principal towns of Hakodate and Sapporo were clean and modern with stately buildings. Hakodate had been ravaged by fire a year previously, half the city being destroyed and 2,000 lives being lost, and was now being rebuilt in feverish haste. The strange charm of this northern island consists of the contrast of a northern climate and landscape with the ever-present danger of volcanic eruptions. The active volcanoes and the numerous hot springs testify to its insecurity. Dozens of such springs, varying in color and temperature and containing sulphur, iodine, and alum interspersed with boiling hot blue water lakes are concentrated at Noboribetsu, the famous health resort.

Those, then, were the most important journeys which we undertook within the "Great Asiatic Co-prosperity Sphere." To my lasting regret, it was not possible to include a trip to Pekin and China. Just when I was ready to start on such a trip the *incident* with China—which is the way the Japanese referred to their eight years' war with their great continental neighbor—started. But we availed ourselves of every opportunity of increasing our knowledge of Japan by several smaller expeditions to its innumerable beauty spots: to the scores of tiny islands at Matsujima, to the venerable shrine of Ise, to Toba Bay, where that charming and talented old craftsman M. Mikimoto raises his cultured pearls, and, of course, to such world-famous places as Hakone, the red-lacquer Baroque temples in Nikko buried in a forest of old Japanese cedars, to the pleasant Kamagori Hotel near Nagoya, and to Atami.

During the hot and rainy season we rented a small house at Karuizawa, where the majority of the European and Japanese "Upper Ten" took refuge from the oppressive heat and humidity of Tokyo. Alas, my golf was not good enough for me to take full advantage of the truly ideal golf courses which were to be found all over Japan. Herr Noebel, our Embassy Counsellor, and Mrs. Ross, the German-born wife of the British assistant naval attaché, tried with unrelenting ardor to initiate me into the secrets of this sport. But somehow the balls generally seemed to have a preference for taking a sharp turn to the right from the training stand, thence to disappear among the trees. It was only furtively and with some cheating that I dared to go over the course with one of my instructors. The Japanese caddies were more reverent than their European colleagues, it is true; but in spite of these humiliations I enjoyed the splendid views of the sea and the mountains.

Only once in my life have I ever scored a triumph as far as golf is concerned. This was in London when I was interviewed by the press on my arrival and asked whether I liked being appointed Ambassador to London. I replied in the affirmative and added that I hoped to improve my golf. This answer was highly appreciated by my colleagues as a fine specimen of that love of understatement which is so ingrained in the British character. If only they had known that my reply was far from being a clever trick designed to make a favorable impression on public opinion. It was a simple, undeniable truth to state that my golf was only capable of improvement, but not of deterioration.

My most pleasant recollections of Tokyo are the hours and sometimes even days which I was able to spend studying or collecting Eastern Asiatic art. Quite apart from my own passion for old Chinese ceramics and my love of Oriental art generally, an official touch was added to this hobby of mine, for, after the death of my eminent predecessor in Tokyo, Ambassador Solf, I was elected to be his successor as President of the German "Society of Eastern Asiatic Art," the leading German society representing widespread interests in Germany for Oriental, and especially for Chinese, art. The Japanese are great connoisseurs and, being fanatical in everything they undertake, they are particularly fanatical collectors. Their appreciation of what Europeans admire is exceeded to a certain extent only by their own sense of beauty. They pay high prices for Chinese ceramics, scrolls, sculpture, and bronzes, but it is less ostentatious objects which find their most refined appreciation. They are just as abstract, as unostentatious in their love of works of art as they are in their evaluation of architecture, nature, or furniture. The inner circle of collectors will reserve its most exalted admiration for a scroll bearing the ideographs of a great scholar, painted with a bold brush on the silk. A minute teaspoon made of bamboo, provided a few Chinese ideographs by a well-known statesman or poet are imprinted on it, will fetch thousands of yen.

The real abstractionist among Japanese collectors will concentrate on swords; not the gorgeous swords with gilded handles and scabbards, but on the blade and the quality of the steel. From the shadings which have been created by forging the different layers of steel he will be able to ascribe the blade to the master blacksmith who created it. Of course, the great masters among them are known individually and esteemed according to their merits. Tens of thousands of yen are paid for such blades forged by a master from Gifu, or for a tea-bowl made by a prominent potter.

Behind the secretiveness with which the Japanese art collector conceals his treasures there is a certain disdain for those uninitiated who would only desecrate them by their foolish remarks, and are considered unworthy to set eyes upon them. It goes without saying, of course, that this reserve is also due to a lack of space. The structure of the Japanese house forbids the display of many objects of art. Besides it would be considered barbaric to display them, as the human intellect and feelings are only able to absorb the spirit of the object when seen one at a time. Thus we find the decorative corner in Japanese houses with just one bowl or vase adorned with a carefully arranged sprig of cherry blossom.

There were some very wealthy collectors such as Baron Iwasaki, the head of the Mitsubishi firm, and the Marquis Hosokawa, who, in their European houses, displayed their beautiful collections of ceramics in cases such as are found in European museums. But most of them store their treasures away in their *Kura,* the little stone-built tower adjoining their wooden houses to protect the most valuable objects against fire and earthquakes. It is, therefore, cumbersome to these collectors to show visitors their collections. They generally hire a dealer to come the day before an expected visit, to unpack the scrolls and ceramics from their wooden boxes in which they are skilfully wrapped with strings of silk. If they suspect that the visitor is a connoisseur, they rise to the occasion and produce much more than originally intended.

I was in a very enviable position when Professor Reidemeister, one of the foremost experts on East Asiatic art, visited us with his wife in Tokyo. The combination of savant and Ambassador opened to us the doors to the most reserved collectors. It was very amusing to observe their astonishment when Reidemeister, after admiring the objects displayed to us, politely but firmly inquired for other specified objects in their collections. They were simply aghast when they noticed that this European "barbarian" knew of every item in their collection. Once this stage had been reached, there was no end to the treasures which were revealed and discussed.

One of the most pleasant episodes I remember in this connection was the visit which Reidemeister and I paid to the house of Baron Matsuda, former manager of Mitsui, eighty years old, and owner of one of the most renowned collections. After we admired the priceless treasures for hours, lunch was served in the courtyard of the house with a view of the carefully designed Japanese garden with its rocks and old bent firs. On the horizon there was a glimpse of the deep blue sea. Our host displayed all the amiability and intelligent manner characteristic of the older generation in Japan, and his granddaughter in her kimono of gay spring colors enchanted us with that charm so characteristic of young Japanese women.

But even everyday life provided me with some opportunity of increasing my knowledge of East Asiatic art. Every Saturday auction sales of curios are held in some part of Tokyo. They offer excellent opportunities for the collector to discover and buy some hidden treasure or, as was often the case, to experience bitter disappointment at having acquired a forgery. Although it was safer to visit the shops of the curio dealers in the Kama-dori Street, one did not learn so much that way. I gratefully recall many such excursions in the company of M. le Gallais, representative of a Luxem-bourg steel works, later representing his country as Minister to Washing-ton. He shared my love for East Asiatic art and again and again discovered new hunting-grounds where we were able to indulge in our passion.

From time to time an exhibition of works of art from the vast and priceless collection of the Imperial Household or from other collectors enabled one to admire otherwise inaccessible treasures. Perhaps the most impressive and, for the European, the most understandable form of Jap-anese art is the screen. A gold screen with a few branches of an old snow-covered fir painted by Korin, or bamboo scrub faintly visible in the foggy autumnal air by Hasegawa, who is perhaps the most eminent Japanese painter, should appeal to the sense of beauty of everyone regardless of national boundaries, and the same may be said of the scrolls with paintings by Sessho. I felt a certain degree of pride when my appreciation of Eastern Asiatic art was acknowledged by a gift which was presented to me by Hirota on my departure from Japan. It was not the glamorous vase customary on such occasions, but quite an inconspicuous bowl, a piece of 16th-century Japanese pottery work; it was of particular value, as the Japanese have not the same ancient tradition in pottery as have the Chinese.

Social life in Tokyo was more strenuous than the casual observer might assume who believed that the great distance from Germany would keep visitors from the home country away. It is indeed a fact that, with the exception of some of the more wealthy families, the Japanese do not entertain guests in their homes. Instead they do so in a restaurant, where they invite their friends to a geisha party. But we did, nevertheless, have many visitors from abroad, especially since the German merchant navy had commissioned three new first-class passenger ships—the *Gneisenau, Scharnhorst* and *Potsdam*—all of which in turn paid visits to Japan. During the spring and summer there was always a steady flow of German visitors from the prosperous German communities in China and Man-chukuo, whilst the German residents of Tokyo and Yokohama took up much of our time. Most of them were wealthy and of high social standing who expected to be invited individually, quite apart from the general gatherings at the Embassy and the German Club, and they returned these invitations.

The majority of our guests were, of course, Japanese. Former diplo-mats and such families as had connections abroad willingly accepted invitations to dinners and lunches. There was none of the inhibition against intercourse with foreigners such as prevailed in Moscow, whilst the language barrier was overcome with comparative ease, thanks to our guests' having some knowledge of foreign tongues. The scientists and the officers had a full command of German, whilst the diplomats and industrialists spoke English. I did not make any attempt to learn Japanese, as at my time of life the brain is not sufficiently receptive to master that extremely complicated language, the rendering of which differs according to the social standing of the person to whom one is speaking. In conversation with members of the Imperial Court, for example, quite different forms are used from those employed when addressing an equal or one of lower caste.

As only a complete command of the language would have been of any use to me for conversation with those of high intellectual standing— the boys and ordinary people all spoke some "pidgin" English—I had to fall back on the services of our Embassy interpreters when talking to those Japanese who did not speak any foreign language; and these men were generally much more influential than those of their countrymen who were tainted with foreign influence. Only my niece, Elka Wedel, with her more youthful brain, was able to pick up enough Japanese to converse freely with her friends.

Like everything else in Japan, social life was somehow dominated or influenced by the Imperial Court. The Emperor and the Empress always invited a newly appointed Ambassador to lunch. The Emperor presided at State banquets held on the traditional festival days. Prominent guests were presented to him in special audience. He also met the foreign representatives at the cherry blossom and the chrysanthemum garden parties in the spring and autumn. The Emperor's brother, Prince Chichibu, married to the charming daughter of the chief Imperial Household official, Viscount Matsudaira, and Prince Takamatsu, both well acquainted with foreign countries through extensive travelling, were fond of mixing with the diplomats and sometimes honored them by accepting invitations to dinner.

Amiable old-fashioned Prince Kanin, Field Marshal and Commander-in-Chief of the army, invited me several times with German and Japanese officers. The high officials of the Imperial Court, the chamberlains and gentlemen-in-waiting, ever present at social functions, observed with watchful eyes and ears what was going on in the Diplomatic Corps and kept the Court exceedingly well informed. There were two other customary invitations, for duck-hunting in February and cormorant-fishing in July, which offered additional opportunities for intercourse with the princes and Court society. The "Court" on New Year's Day united the whole *Corps Diplomatique* for the customary congratulation ceremony.

The burden of these Court functions was far outweighed by their enjoyment and interest. The quiet dignity, the strict formalism, and the excellent organization of the Imperial Household were imposing and almost awe-inspiring. The Emperor was ever conscious of being not only the hereditary head of the Japanese State, but also the impersonation of the deity. He was not merely the first among his peers, as in a constitutional monarchy, and endowed with certain privileges by common consent. There was a distance between him and his people, and even Europeans, which could not be bridged.

In these circumstances it was natural that even diplomats should have to submit to the ritual of this cult. For instance, when the Emperor drove along the streets, the windows of the upper stories of the Embassies had to be closed, as it would not have been the proper thing for the staffs to look down on the sacred being from above. Even when Imperial princes attended some function, there were intricate problems that had to be solved. At the memorial service held in the German church on the occasion of the death of President von Hindenburg I had first to ascertain whether the galleries might be occupied in the presence of Prince Chichibu, who had his seat below opposite the altar. It was always a most impressive scene when a crowd showed their veneration for the Emperor by observing deep silence in his presence, doubly impressive considering the lively temperament of the Japanese people.

At times the strict ceremonial of the Japanese Court proved somewhat embarrassing. All *chefs de mission*, for instance, had to solve the problem of complying with the regulation prohibiting the wearing of overcoats at the funerals of deceased members of the Imperial Family, without contracting pneumonia, when death occurred in the winter months. On such an occasion most of my colleagues doubled or trebled their underwear. So did I when, hardly recovered from my customary winter asthma, I attended the funeral ceremonies in honor of a very old and entirely unknown princess on a cold March day. But how was I to obtain additional protection without violating the etiquette which made the diplomatic uniform or, in my case, evening dress obligatory? (Ribbentrop had not yet invented the gorgeous uniform which was something in between that of a Field Marshal and a paymaster of the navy.) I resorted to a desperate expedient. Instead of the low-cut black waistcoat I simply donned the leather vest which usually completed my hunting dress. It was only partly covered by the newly bestowed Grand Cordon ribbon. Bravely I withstood the dubious searching glances of the courtiers and thus saved my health.

There were two Court functions—of a uniquely Japanese character —that enjoyed great popularity among the Diplomatic Corps: duck-hunting and cormorant-fishing, neither corresponding to European ideas of sportsmanship, but invested with all the charm Japan has to offer. Duck-hunting is a euphemism for catching, with a butterfly-net, wild ducks lured by tame ducks to water-filled ditches. The keepers would then wring the ducks' necks.

Cormorant-fishing was a more complicated affair. In the heat of summer we had to travel seven hours by express train to Gifu, a town situated on the banks of a swift river. Dinner was served on boats while they were being towed upstream. The guests landed in the dark on an island from where they watched the fishing-boats lit by torches passing swiftly along with the current. At the bow of each boat there was a fisherman in charge of six or seven cormorants, which, directed by strings, were trained to catch trout. They would gorge the fish, but as their throats were narrowed by a cord their prey could be extricated again; not a very appetizing affair, although time-honored by ancient tradition. But the setting of the scene—the murmuring river, the rushing boats with the fishermen and their eager cormorants, the joyous crowds lining the banks—was unforgettable.

Though social intercourse with the Japanese was rather one-sided, those families who did entertain foreigners were extremely hospitable and anxious to make their guests as comfortable as possible. We received invitations to sumptuous dinners followed by concerts from several members of the famous Mitsui family. Baron Iwasaki, the head of the Mitsubishi, took infinite pains in showing me his collections, and after dinner a band of *shamisen* and *goto* players initiated us into the mysteries of Japanese music.

Count Mayeda, who as General in command of an army corps was killed in the war, was also fond of entertaining members of the Diplomatic Corps in his half-Japanese, half-European house, and of showing his collections of Japanese pottery and autographs and paintings by French impressionists. Professor Araki, the famous painter, invited us to his house and was kind enough to give a display of his art by painting with a few strokes of his brush a duck or a branch with a bird or a few shoots of bamboo. As is well known, Japanese and Chinese painters do not copy models. They make a most careful study of their subjects, drawing hundreds and even thousands of preliminary sketches. Then they do the actual painting from memory, integrating their impressions into a symbolic representation of the ideal behind the subject.

A peculiar charm was added to these social gatherings by the delicate beauty and high culture of the distinguished Japanese ladies dressed up in precious and colorful kimonos. At garden parties in summer, when kimonos had to be of a light blue color, the young girls, silhouetted against the dark background of firs and pine shrubs, reminded us of graceful butterflies. Nowhere is the difference between the thoroughbred and the common stock greater than in Japan. Whilst the average Japanese woman—though a faithful and efficient housewife and mother and a humble servant to a mostly arrogant husband—has a plump figure lacking feminine grace, the aristocracy produces a type of exquisite beauty, grace, and refinement.

As the Japanese were fond of visiting embassies, particularly if they had some connection or other with the respective country, we were in a position to offer hospitality to a great number of Japanese guests. There were frequent occasions for arranging a party or a concert, or, what our Japanese friends liked best, a *Bierabend*. But the beer had to be served in real *steins* and had to be accompanied by hamburgers.

Somewhat strenuous but very charming were the parties in Japanese restaurants to which we were frequently invited. The habit of kneeling and squatting forced the older generation among the Europeans to readjust their legs at intervals. The food was well suited to the taste of Europeans, at least of those who were fond of dainty dishes served in bowls of a color harmonizing with that of the food they contained. I even came to like raw fish, which, according to Japanese conviction, is a sign that the foreigner has sympathies for the country. On the whole, a European male felt a little hungry after a Japanese dinner, and the kitchen of the Embassy had to be on the alert when we returned from one. After dinner *saké* was served, the rice wine which, even if consumed in great quantities, failed to have an effect upon the European male, although a few cups sufficed to make the Japanese tipsy.

Drinking the other man's health was a performance carried out with such punctilio that even an inveterate Heidelberg *Korpsstudent* would have felt like a blundering beginner.

I had an amusing experience at one of those Japanese dinners. The *chefs de mission* had been invited to a sumptuous meal in a Japanese restaurant by Count Matsudaira, the Grand Chamberlain of the Imperial Court. My neighbor was the very charming wife of the Brazilian Ambassador. Next to her was the "ambassador" of Manchukuo, a stalwart old Chinese who could not speak a single word of any foreign language and followed faithfully the customs of his old race. When the dinner was finished he did not fail to utter that unmistakable noise by which a well-educated Chinese guest expresses his satisfaction, whereupon my charming neighbor whispered aghast, *"Mon dieu, il explode!"*

The social life of the Diplomatic Corps was to some extent comparable with that in Moscow, although the seclusion was not so strict as in the Russian capital. In Tokyo my wife and I were on very friendly terms with my colleagues, especially with the British Ambassador, Sir Robert Clive, and his wife, and with my Italian colleague Auriti, a bachelor and an ardent collector of Eastern art. The American Ambassador, Mr. Grew, knew Germany well from his appointment to Berlin and was fond of German music and Rhenish wines. I had a high opinion of his character and ability, and it was therefore disappointing to me, from a human point of view, that he did not refrain from cracking jokes about my wife and me in his book *Ten Years in Japan,* which was published during the war. Last, but not least, there were my French colleagues, Pila and Arsène-Henry, whose wife was an accomplished pianist. They were very hospitable. The Czech Minister, Havlicek, was a keen competitor of the French Embassy with regard to musical performances and hospitality.

Meetings of the *chefs de mission* were as infrequent in Tokyo as they had been in Moscow. What meetings did take place were not without a humorous touch, just as they had been in the Russian capital. While I was in Tokyo, the *chefs de mission* met only on one occasion, when the Diplomatic Corps had been startled by certain reports in a Japanese newspaper with a wide circulation disclosing the alleged love affairs of the assistant naval attaché of the French Embassy. No fewer than five Japanese ladies belonging to the Tokyo society were involved. The names and addresses of the lover and his ladies were given full publicity. This multilateral pact of love was a remarkable performance, seeing that the higher classes of the Japanese *bourgeoisie* generally kept aloof from foreigners, and that love affairs between the women of this *bourgeoisie* and Europeans were anathema (whereas their intercourse with geishas was tolerated). Little doubt was possible, therefore, that the publication of this scandal had been encouraged, if not ordered, by the Japanese authorities.

The Diplomatic Corps seethed with indignation on account of this slight inflicted on one of its members. The doyen, the chivalrous Baron de Bassompierre, the Belgian Ambassador, convoked a meeting of the *chefs de mission*. As the available rooms did not hold all the Ambassadors and Ministers, they had to work in two shifts. Among those in my shift was the Spanish Ambassador, Mendez de Vigo, who was endowed with the passionate and impetuous temperament of his race. Bassompierre gave an account of the facts with a voice trembling with emotion. When he mentioned the five love affairs of the amorous Frenchman, Mendez de Vigo, who obviously had thorough inside information, rose to correct the doyen's statement, *"Pas cinque, mais quinze!"* In view of the somewhat delicate character of the matter, the doyen was requested by his colleagues to talk things over with the *Chef de Protocole* and to avoid an official protest. He acted accordingly, and nothing was ever heard again of this love affair between West and East.

The complexity and extent of the social functions in which the German Embassy was involved may be illustrated by the fact that the number of our guests during one season amounted to 2,469, not counting those that had been invited to tea-parties. Thus, after two and a half years in

East Asia, what with the strenuous climate, my failing health, and the strain of official duties, we were looking forward to a period of well-deserved rest in Europe.

---

4. ON LEAVE IN EUROPE

Our trip home *via* Vancouver-Quebec-New York was an enjoyable recreation. We stayed for one week in New York and did not fail to notice the enormous progress which the metropolis had made since the time I visited it as a youngster some thirty years before. Crossing the Atlantic on board the comfortable North-German Lloyd liner *Europa,* we encountered a Zeppelin bound for America, and felt some justified pride in the accomplishments of a Germany that had recovered from economic plight and revolutionary unrest. On April 9 we arrived at Bremerhaven to spend six months in the old home country.

The purpose of my leave was threefold: I wanted to restore my health, to gain a general impression of conditions in Germany, and to make contact with the experts on Far Eastern politics. In my endeavor to obtain a permanent cure for my asthmatic complaint I consulted an authority in Berlin and underwent a cure at Bad Reichenhall, Upper Bavaria, a place famous for the treatment of bronchitis in "pneumatic chambers."

Between these cures and my official duties I spent weeks at Gröditz-berg, enjoying the agricultural improvements that had been brought about in the meantime. The prices for grain had been fixed at a satisfactory level and farmers knew what they would get for their crops. They were independent of the whims of grain speculators in Chicago or elsewhere, and they were no longer under pressure to sell at low prices after the harvest was over. All the farm buildings were in perfect condition by reason of a scheme which permitted arrears of taxes to be invested in repairs. By this simple device the craftsmen and artisans who had suffered most from the economic crisis had been given an incentive. I travelled up and down the country a great deal by car and by rail. We visited our relatives on the Rhine and our industrial friends at Duisburg, in the Ruhr district and at Ludwigshafen. They showed me over their plants, which had been enormously enlarged and were working at full capacity. The workers were satisfied. There was no unemployment. I was greatly impressed by some new technical processes such as the Fischer-Tropsch patent for extracting petrol from coal. At the I. G. Farben plant I was shown the laboratory where the manufacture of *Buna* (artificial rubber) was in its experimental stage. The new German process of extracting sugar from wood was also well under way.

Everywhere the roads were in perfect condition. The network of *Autobahnen* was under construction. The railway services were as efficient as ever. The people gave me the impression of being healthy, well fed, and cheerful. Compared with the miserable conditions in 1932, Germany was now a fundamentally transformed country. There was some grumbling that the party exercised a growing control of private life, and that the children were alienated from their homes by the *Hitlerjugend,* but a feeling of satisfaction prevailed on account of the general improvement in conditions. Hitler's surprise *coups* such as the restoration of German sovereignty in the Rhineland were approved by public opinion. The burden of general conscription was willingly borne. Hitler's political successes abroad filled the nation with pride. The agreement with Great Britain about the limitation of naval armaments was especially popular, because it seemed to have removed the causes of the most dangerous friction that might arise between the two countries. As for myself, I could not help being enthusiastic about the results achieved within so short a space of time.

In the Foreign Office, too, there were no signs of any radical changes. It was staffed by the same officials who had been in office before 1933, with Neurath as Minister and Bülow as Secretary of State. The thinly veiled anti-Nazi sentiments of the latter were common knowledge. When he succumbed to an attack of pneumonia shortly after my arrival, the obsequies were held with the greatest possible solemnity in the presence of the Führer. His successors, Mackensen and Dieckhoff, were also old career men. There was not a single party "bigwig" among the higher ranks of officials. Membership in the party was a minor issue. Most members of the foreign service joined the party as time went on. When I called on the chief of the *Auslands-organisation* of the National Socialist Party, Bohle, he asked me to become a member of the party, which I did. On this point it had been my line not to take the initiative but to comply with a corresponding request, as I did not wish to shirk the duty of professing my loyalty to the régime I was serving.

As to the Foreign Office, a growing menace loomed in the background: the half-sinister, half-ridiculous Ribbentrop. As his ambition had not been satisfied by the Foreign Office, he had started a competitive firm by founding the "Bureau Ribbentrop," which was housed just opposite the premises of the legitimate representation of German foreign policy—in the Wilhelmstrasse. Ribbentrop's staff was composed of characters from all walks of life, mostly young men who were more proficient by their eagerness and self-assertion than by their training and tact.

The fact, however, could not be overlooked that Ribbentrop was gaining ground. His "bureau" was an institution too much in keeping with Hitler's secret strategy of playing off one of his collaborators against the other to give Neurath a chance of putting this upstart out of action. Neurath was a gentleman, a man of character, with a political flair and the courage to stick to his guns in critical situations. But he lacked the zeal for work indispensable for a Minister of Foreign Affairs. His passion for hunting prevailed over his passion for work. This is what Bülow replied to my question when Neurath, who was absent from Berlin, was expected to come back "as soon as he has shot three roebucks."

Bülow himself was too deeply convinced that Nazism would be only a passing show, and that the bureaucracy would survive any other combination, to enter into a competitive struggle with Ribbentrop. This attitude was justified in so far as we permanent officials were lacking the most effective weapon used by Ribbentrop, namely to be Hitler's lackey, watching every one of his steps, sneaking into his presence through a half-open door to catch a glimpse of, or a word from, the Führer, and then to start on this new inspiration as if it were his own idea. Besides, there remained the fact that Ribbentrop had scored a considerable success by the conclusion of the naval agreement with Great Britain. Thus the Foreign Office found itself gradually sliding back into a state of utter insignificance, and merely dealt with the technical tasks of foreign policy.

To what extent the Foreign Office had been eliminated was brought home to me when I started my inquiries concerning the German-Japanese negotiations about a political agreement that was to become well known as the "Anti-Comintern Pact." I knew that Ribbentrop was conducting these negotiations, but I had assumed that the Foreign Office was kept informed about what was going on, in some way or other. In this assumption, I was, however, mistaken. Nobody in the Foreign Office knew anything about the matter. So I decided to walk into the lion's den and put a few questions to Ribbentrop himself, with whom I was not yet acquainted.

Evidently puzzled by my initiative, he at first showed some distrust, but eventually released some information and listened attentively to my *exposé* of the political situation in Japan. I took leave of him saying that I thought he would agree to my informing Herr von Neurath about our conversation. He said he would. The most detailed information that I received, however, came from my Japanese colleague, Count Mushakoyi, with whom I was on very friendly terms. He is one of the most intelligent, open-minded, and sympathetic Japanese I have ever met. The negotiations were proceeding smoothly and most of the clauses which were to be embodied in the treaty later on had already been agreed upon. I was definitely in favor of the basic political idea of a closer understanding with Japan.

As regards the formal aspect of the matter, I thought the reference to the activities of the Comintern, which had constantly been disowned by the Soviet Union, to be a rather clever device. It had been designed by one of Ribbentrop's collaborators, Herr von Raumer, an able and intelligent man who, therefore, soon came into conflict with his chief and left his office. I was also satisfied that the pact was not going to contain any aggressive clauses against the Soviet Union, the two parties only agreeing on consultation about their policies towards Russia and giving an undertaking that, in the case of one party being involved in a war with the Soviet Union, the other would abstain from any acts likely to assist the enemy.

When I communicated these facts to the Foreign Office, I was effusively thanked for having procured such extremely valuable information. This made me realize to what extent the Foreign Office had allowed itself to be excluded from knowledge of what was going on. It need hardly be mentioned that the Foreign Office was dead against the pact with Japan.

There was another important authority in disagreement with Hitler's pro-Japanese policy, though one might have assumed that this policy was just to its liking, the War Ministry. Whereas the Japanese Army was violently pro-German, only those officers in the German Army responded who had been instructors in Japan or who had some other affiliations with that country. The bulk of the German General Staff was developing increasingly pro-Chinese tendencies the stronger the position of the German military mission to Chiang Kai-shek became. These tendencies were backed by other partly commercial, partly military interests, which centered in the person of a German merchant and former officer, Captain Klein. He promised to secure from China considerable quantities of precious metals, such as tungsten and wolfram, required for German rearmament in exchange for the supply of weapons to the Chinese Army. Trade in war materials had always been a highly profitable, though not highly respectable, business. It was also true in this case, and Klein as well as some other German firms domiciled in East Asia did a roaring business selling arms to China.

Somehow Klein succeeded in inducing certain official persons to commit themselves to a pro-Chinese attitude. General von Seeckt, the founder of the *Reichswehr,* out of office but still full of ambition, received an invitation from Marshal Chiang Kai-shek to pay a visit to him and to inspect the new Chinese Army. Seeckt gladly accepted and spent some months in China, carefully avoiding a visit to Japan in order not to offend his host. General von Reichenau, still on regular service and one of the key men of the War Ministry, followed suit, and was also contemplating a visit to China. As I knew him personally, I tried to get into contact with him in Munich, where he was *Wehrkreisbefehlshaber,* in order to inform him that things were developing along different lines. Somehow or other we missed each other and so he started on his voyage. Once out in China, he rather limited himself to enjoying the more amenable side of life in the Far East. Nevertheless, the visits of the two well-known German generals could not fail to produce a deep effect on political circles in Eastern Asia. A few months later the War Ministry had to follow the line of the official Anti-Comintern Pact policy. The German military mission to China, however, continued to be a stumbling-block in our relations with Japan, as will be seen later on.

My next and last move on the political chessboard while I was on leave in Germany was an audience with Hitler. Shortly after my arrival in Berlin he had received me at the Chancellery of the Reich. I had been looking forward to this event with great expectation, hoping to get a chance of giving him a full account of the political situation of the Far East and receiving some flashes of his genius. After only two or three minutes he began to move uneasily in his chair, and suddenly he apologized for having to interrupt our conversation as he had some other urgent duties to perform. He hoped to see me at Berchtesgaden, he said. I left, utterly perplexed and furious. It was characteristic of the atmosphere of rumors and gossip which furtively spread in Berlin that a few days later I was asked by a friend, who was in no official position, whether I had fallen into disgrace with Hitler because my interview had lasted only a few minutes.

During my stay at Reichenhall, which is not far from Berchtesgaden, I tried again. This time Herr Meissner, the well-known chief of the *Präsidialkanzlei,* whom I had known very well since our stay at Kiev in 1918, arranged an audience for July 8. I arrived at the Berghof for the longest and most harmonious interview that I ever had with the Führer. Göring and Meissner were also present. I entered his large, beautifully furnished room, which, through enormous windows, offered a magnificent view of the Alpine scenery round the Watzmann and of the valley and plain stretching towards Salzburg. The conference lasted for more than an hour and I had ample opportunity to expound my views.

The chief problem I considered was whether the structure of the Japanese State was being undermined by the revolutionary uprisings of the army or whether Japan could be trusted as a partner to the Anti-Comintern Pact. My answer to this question was in the affirmative. Göring also spoke at some length. He shared my views. So did Hitler, without, however, starting the avalanche of his oratory. I must confess that again no word he uttered imprinted itself upon my memory and that I did not feel hypnotized or awe stricken in his presence. The conference was remarkable in so far as no offensive utterance against the Soviet Union were made.

During our discussion a thunderstorm had gathered. There were constant flashes of lightning followed by the echo of rumbling thunder. The whole view was veiled by a downpour of rain. But as in a romantic opera the thunder died down, the clouds were drawn aside as if by an invisible producer, and the sun shone again upon a rejuvenated landscape. Hitler concluded the interview by dedicating to me, on Meissner's initiative, his portrait signed and dated by himself.

My stay in Germany was rounded off by two memorable events which left a lasting mark upon my memory: the Olympic Games in Berlin and the party rally in Nuremberg. Both displays were fully reported at the time, so that I need not go into details. But I feel I must say a few words about the rally.

The masses assembled at Nuremberg were moved by the deep faith of a whole nation willing to make sacrifices for a better future, a future which was perhaps near at hand despite the deficiencies and blunders, vaguely anticipated rather than clearly experienced, of a régime that was anxious to hide its ultimate aims. When one looks back on that period which ended in disaster, bloodshed, and cruelty, this wasted enthusiasm of a great mass of honest people who were cheated by a gang of reckless revolutionaries will perhaps appear to be the most tragic thing of the German tragedy.

The performance of the "Labor Service" left the deepest impression. These 40,000 boys who solemnly recited a dialogue between a massed chorus and its leaders and then—without any loud orders, silently and with minute exactitude—did a few exercises with their spades, so that for a fraction of a second the shining blades flashed in the sunlight. It seemed to me to be the very incarnation of mass discipline.

Spectacular, too, was the night rally of certain party formations. The beams of super-searchlights converged in a huge dome several thousand feet high, whilst the boys and girls of the Hitler Youth provided a lively and invigorating scene with their songs and dances.

The most important political event on the occasion of the rally was, of course, Hitler's great speech, which was to strike the keynote for the political development of the coming year. On both occasions when I attended the Nuremberg Rally, Hitler lived up to the expectations of the outside world by giving them food for thought in the form of a ponderous slogan. In 1938 it was the cry against Czechoslovakia and in 1936 a terrific diatribe against Bolshevism. The whole make-up of the gatherings, with its standard-bearers, grandstands, and swastika decorations, had worn a little thin in the latter years of the régime. But seeing the scene for the first time, one did not fail to be impressed.

Nor could I help being fascinated by Hitler's oratorical fireworks. I felt myself much more under his spell than I did when I met him privately. As to the program which he expounded, there was nothing very startling about it, for German-Soviet relations were already bad enough, so that a further deterioration could not alter the picture materially. There was nobody who believed in the possibility of a war. To many Western politicians the prospect that National Socialist "dynamism" would be diverted towards the East was quite appealing, and some of my colleagues in Tokyo, who were anti-Bolshevik themselves, gave their hearty approval.

After the speech the German Ambassadors and Ministers present at Nuremberg gathered to express their heartfelt sympathy for their colleague in Moscow, Count Schulenburg (executed after July 20, 1944), on account of the terrible task and the unpleasantness awaiting him in the Russian capital. I was the only exception, in so far as I congratulated him that he would now no longer be bothered by requests from Berlin, that nobody would expect him to press our demands, and that he would be able, at long last, to live perfectly at his ease. And so it was. Schulenburg, a genial, easy-going *grand seigneur,* who enjoyed the esteem of the Soviet government, was able to travel extensively to all parts of European Russia, collecting icons and carpets, and to bathe in the pleasant atmosphere of German sympathy and compassion.

After Bülow's death our diplomatic service suffered another severe loss by the untimely death of our Ambassador to the Court of St. James, Herr von Hoesch, one of our ablest men. With regard to the successorship, Ribbentrop was the favorite, whereas Hassell and I were quoted with longer odds. When Ribbentrop was appointed, everybody was sure that he had attained the goal of his ambition. It was only after the Second World War that it became known that he was furious about this appointment, as he had been striving for the post of Foreign Minister and had been quite sure that he was going to replace Neurath.

I never would have predicted such a dismal failure of his London mission as it ultimately proved to be. His appointment was greeted with satisfaction in London. *The Times* published an editorial with the heading "A Welcome Visitor." After all, Ribbentrop possessed one of the most important qualities of an Ambassador, he was on close terms with the chief of State and of the executive, he was pro-English to a degree bordering on snobbery, and, at least so I thought, he was clever enough to adapt himself to the requirements of his new profession. Hitler wanted friendship with Great Britain above all. Yet, in spite of these propitious omens, Ribbentrop failed at the very beginning, when, alighting from his airplane in London, he gave an interview to the press in which he admonished Great Britain with regard to her policy towards the Soviet Union.

I was glad to return to Tokyo. I liked the Far East; I loved my independence, and I felt sure about the eventual restoration of my health. On October 9, in Genoa, we went on board the *Gneisenau,* the most comfortable North-German Lloyd liner, and thoroughly enjoyed the voyage, in the course of which we paid short visits to some of the most beautiful spots in the world: Ceylon, the Dutch East Indies, Manila. In Shanghai we spent two days in the hospitable house of our Consul-General, Herr Kriebel. A former officer who felt very strongly the humiliation of the armistice negotiations in which he had taken part at Spa, he had been one of the first to join the Nazi party. Full of enthusiasm for the new gospel, honest and straightforward, he soon fell a victim to the intrigues engineered by the clique surrounding Hitler and was eventually sidetracked to Shanghai. Later on he was appointed chief of the personnel department of the Foreign Office, but without regaining any influence on the inner party circle.

Shanghai was at the time slowly recovering from the wounds inflicted by the Japanese bombardment in 1932. The Chinese mayor, upon whom Kriebel and I called—he was of course a General like most influential men in China—showed great enthusiasm in setting forth his plans for a new civic center. We also attended the opening of a luxurious new nightclub owned and run by a German refugee. Seeing Chinese ladies dancing with questionable European types, I was once more impressed by the unhealthy atmosphere of this Far Eastern metropolis which blended the vices of Asia with those of Europe.

On November 9 we arrived at Kobe.

---

5. MY SECOND TERM IN JAPAN

On the day after our arrival in Tokyo we attended the customary chrysanthemum garden party, to which the Emperor invited the Diplomatic Corps together with the prominent Japanese. Both Imperial garden parties—the cherry-blossom and the chrysanthemum party—were charming entertainments, though one cynic remarked that there were more *cops* than chrysanthemums." As I walked up to my car to drive home, I had some difficulty in breathing, and it was evident that my asthma was returning. My efforts to get rid of it in Germany had been in vain. I hurried to Kobe to get some treatment from a renowned German physician, but some days later I was laid up with pains more tormenting than ever. During the following months I was unable to leave my rooms for weeks on end, and walking slowly in the garden was a recreation in which I could indulge only a few times. My wife nursed me with unfailing devotion, fulfilling at the same time the duties of representation. Two eminent and personally charming Japanese doctors, Professor Inada and Dr. Ikeda, did their utmost to alleviate my pain.

Thus the most important event of my Ambassadorship, the conclusion of the Anti-Comintern Pact, passed without my entering into the picture. The effect of this pact on public opinion was tremendous. There were influential political circles opposed to such an unqualified declaration in favor of totalitarianism. The "men behind the throne"—the Genro, Prince Saionji, Count Makino, the Lord Privy Seal, Count Matsudaira, the Minister of the Imperial Household—and the majority of the industrialists were all silenced. It was the militarists and nationalists who dominated the scene from now on. The broad masses felt relieved from an isolation that had been weighing heavily upon them, and they were carried away by a wave of genuine sympathy and enthusiasm for Germany. Deputations appointed by mass meetings and presents made by individual patriots kept the Embassy staff busy. From now on the political going was even smoother than it had been before. That the economic relations were thriving on a sound three-cornered basis (Germany-Japan-Manchukuo) has already been mentioned. It was an ideal time for a German Ambassador.

In July, 1937, events took a tragic turn by the outbreak of the conflict with China. Between 1932 and 1937 the characteristic feature of Japanese home and foreign policies had been an uneasy compromise. The tug-of-war between the moderate and the extremist faction had resulted, in the field of internal politics, in the gradual receding of the moderates with occasional victories such as the quelling of the revolt of February 26, 1936, and with an outward maintenance of democratic procedure. In the field of foreign affairs frantic efforts were being made by Hirota and the pro-Anglo-Saxon circles to keep up friendly contacts and to come to an arrangement with China. On the other hand, the nationalists managed to secure the Anti-Comintern Pact with Germany, to free Japan from the limitations on her naval rearmament by denouncing the respective agreements, and to push on in China by dismembering Northern China into several semi-autonomous puppet states. General indignation was aroused by the shameless corruption, dope-smuggling, and other abuses tolerated and instigated there by the Japanese wire-pullers.

The spark which touched off the explosion was the skirmish between minor Chinese and Japanese detachments at the Marco Polo Bridge near Pekin on the night of July 8, 1937. It will never be possible to determine whether this clash was engineered by the Japanese or whether it took place accidentally as the result of an atmosphere laden with electricity. I am inclined to believe that the latter was the case. Otherwise it would be inexplicable that the Japanese Army, generally adverse to taking any risks and noted for the careful preparation of its *coups,* such as the assassination of Chang Tso-lin, should so obviously have bungled this big undertaking.

Even a week after the Marco Polo Bridge incident the Japanese were in grave danger of losing vital strategic points like the airfield at Tientsin because the local Japanese garrison was entirely insufficient. On the other hand, the hope for a peaceful settlement of this seemingly local affair appeared to be too well founded to be dismissed as a mere fabrication of Japanese propaganda. From my first conversations with Hirota, whom I knew very well indeed, I personally had the impression that his belief in a peaceful solution was sincere. But responsibility for the Marco Polo Bridge incident is a minor issue. The paramount fact is that Japan must be held responsible for the outbreak of the war with China for the reason that she pursued a continuous policy of aggression.

It need not be particularly stressed that the outbreak of hostilities in China was a most undesirable event for Germany. After all, the Anti-Comintern Pact had not been concluded in order to embroil Germany in an adventure of unforeseeable consequences on the Asiatic continent. Although I am firmly convinced that this pact did not aim at a potential attack on the Soviet Union (as far as I can ascertain, the German documents published since do not prove the contrary), the effect of a certain pressure on Russia, which was certainly welcome to Hitler, was reduced to insignificance by this adventure. Besides, the general trend of our policy towards China was friendly, and our economic relations with that country were highly profitable and of great importance to Germany. Consequently, in my conversations with Hirota I expressed in no uncertain terms the hope that the "incident" (which was the euphemistic term used by the Japanese throughout the years of war) would find a peaceful settlement.

As I have already said, Hirota appeared to me to be sincerely optimistic, and for some days indeed fighting in Northern China was of no more than local importance. But soon matters got out of control, or else the military clique in Japan succeeded in turning local fighting into a full-scale war. Eventually Marshal Chiang Kai-shek's decision to open up a new theater of war in Shanghai—probably in order to attract the attention of the whole world by extending the hostilities to such a sensitive spot as the metropolis of the Far East—smothered every prospect of localizing the war.

In the course of some lengthy conversations General Ott, our Military Attaché, and I agreed that the most effective means that Germany had of mediating with a view to restoring normal conditions was to continue the activities of the German military mission to China. That these activities were not looked upon with benevolence by the General Staff in Tokyo was evident. But so far we had turned a deaf ear to relevant hints, and we felt bound to try and continue to allay Japanese concern in this respect so long as our relations with China were not seriously in jeopardy. The German military mission, led by the very able and politically clever General von Falkenhausen, enjoyed the full confidence of the Nanking Government and, above all, of the Marshal. If there was any prospect at all of mediation between the two belligerents, the mission had a chance of rendering invaluable services by exonerating the Chinese leaders from their responsibility towards their own compatriots. If the mission advocated a compromise on purely military grounds, taking into consideration the unpreparedness of the Chinese Army and the hopelessness of a continued warfare, there might be a chance of restoring peace. This trend of ideas was put forward in a long telegram to Berlin, and we thus prevented rash measures to the contrary likely to be adopted by the party extremists.

After a few months of warfare the situation seemed to be ripe for another effort at mediation. In spite of heroic resistance and huge sacrifices, Shanghai was definitely lost by the Chinese, who had also suffered defeat on the other fronts. Nanking had been captured. The Brussels Conference, which had been convoked in accordance with the Nine-Power Treaty, failed to yield any practical results. The Nanking Government was faced with the necessity of resisting the invader with no more moral assistance from the outside world. The Japanese, on the other hand, had won cheap but numerous military laurels. Now, however, they began to realize that they would yet have to make enormous sacrifices to conclude peace on their own terms. The international implications of the war in China, the foreign settlements in Shanghai and other towns, and American and British men-o'-war cruising on the Yang-tse made them feel uneasy. The sinking on the Yang-tse of the American gunboat *Panay* by Japanese planes brought them to the brink of war with the United States. There was a lull in the fighting, and both adversaries were, it seemed, considering what to do next.

This situation suggested that it might be worth while for Germany to try and act as a mediator. I obtained the approval of the Foreign Office, and our Ambassador to Nanking, Trautmann, was instructed to make a corresponding *démarche* with the Chinese Government. The Japanese Government, the *Gaimusho* as well as the General Staff, raised no objections, though they were frankly skeptical about our efforts with the Chinese. At least they agreed to avoid any action that might add fuel to the flames.

While we were waiting for a reply from the Chinese Government, week after week passed without any sign of a conciliatory spirit. The Chinese made no secret of their dilatory tactics. Whether they pursued this policy to gain time for military preparations or merely on account of internal dissensions was hard to determine. Meanwhile the Japanese had been growing more and more impatient. The General Staff became increasingly angry about the alleged active participation of the German military mission in the "shooting war." They asserted—and this was later on confirmed—that members of the mission were engaged in directing the fighting activities of Chinese divisions in sections of the trenches round Shanghai. One of them, General Streccius, even went so far as to take one of the Chinese war lords in Shantung severely to task for his slackness in fulfilling his duties toward the Marshal.

The war profiteers also saw their chance. Several German firms in Shanghai and Herr Klein, of Berlin, who has already been mentioned, were busy dispatching to Hong Kong freighters laden to full capacity with war material. Small wonder then that the Japanese officers harbored feelings of bitterness about the activities of their Anti-Comintern partner, and that they nicknamed the hostilities "the German war."

Early in January, 1938, one month after starting our mediatory effort, we at last got word from Trautmann that the Chinese reply would be available within a few days. I begged Hirota to come and see me in my bedroom, as I was laid up again with severe asthma. I had a long conversation with him, urging him to have patience and wait yet a little longer. But it was evident that he would not be able to keep back his wild men very much longer. Once again we had to wait many days. A Cabinet meeting was called for January 13 or 14. Soon we were to know what had been the subject of deliberations. I received word that the Japanese Government had decided to consider mediation as having failed and to cancel all restrictions on warfare. By a tragic irony of fate, a reply from the Chinese Government, which had been submitted to Ambassador Trautmann, was being decoded at the Chancellery of our Embassy at the very time that the Japanese message was delivered. But it turned out that Chiang Kai-shek's reply would not have brought matters any further. It boiled down to nothing more than a polite acknowledgment of the receipt of our proposal for mediation. At best it could be taken as an expression of his not entirely unqualified readiness for further talks. For righteous indignation against the aggressor, over-valuation of Chinese strength, inner political expediency, or whatever reason, the Nationalist Government had not deemed it feasible to enter into formal negotiations and found it a better policy to continue the fighting.

While my political mission to Tokyo ended with a failure—though an honorable failure—I was able to score a success in the cultural field. In my capacity as President of the German Society for East Asiatic Art, my conversations with Professor Kümmel, Director-General of the Berlin museums, with a world-wide reputation as an expert on Japanese art, as well as with Professor Reidemeister, had encouraged me to realize a long-cherished plan, namely to organize an exhibition of really first-class Japanese art in Berlin. I was fully aware of the almost insurmountable difficulties of such a venture.

The Japanese, with their blend of pride, shyness, and sensitiveness, were always suspicious that their art would not be sufficiently appreciated abroad. Many years back they had had some discouraging experiences in this respect either in London or in America. For them to send their art treasures abroad is more than a mere act of cultural propaganda; it is a sign of sincere friendship inspired by the confidence that the others will really understand the things that are so dear and near to their hearts. These sentimental considerations are coupled with technical difficulties: in addition to the normal dangers of transport, the delicate paintings and other objects of art are liable to suffer from the influences of the climate. There were also certain political considerations to be taken into account. Years before, an invitation by Great Britain to organize a similar show in London had been declined, and now the Japanese were afraid that the British might be offended.

Slowly but gradually I became familiar with all these difficulties which were set off against the personal likes and dislikes—pro-German or pro-Anglo-Saxon sympathies—of the officials and owners concerned. It took me almost a year to overcome all obstacles, overt and secret. Had it not been for the fact that I was sailing before the wind of the Anti-Comintern Pact, and that there was a feeling of genuine friendship for Germany and of deep respect for her achievements in the field of East Asiatic culture and philosophy, I should never have succeeded. Besides, I had a powerful ally in the person of Professor Kümmel, whom I had invited to Tokyo. As he knew everything and everybody connected with Japanese art, nobody could resist his efforts to persuade collectors to part for some time with their treasures. Thus when I left Tokyo I had the gratification of having brought at least this undertaking to a satisfactory conclusion. But, as will be seen later, even in this case there was a fly in the ointment.

Meanwhile my departure from Japan could no longer be postponed. I had been advised by the doctors to avoid another asthma winter in Japan, and accordingly I asked the Foreign Office to relieve me of my post on account of failing health. A passage had been booked for me on the *Gneisenau* for September. When the "China incident" occurred, I had felt it my duty to stay on. My asthmatic trouble had always set in punctually about mid-October, all precautions and counter-measures having proved futile. So I had no alternative but to give up my post, and I decided to leave Japan on Sunday, February 6, on board the well-known liner *Empress of Canada.*

The sympathy shown to me by Japanese people from all walks of life when they got to know about my ailment was really moving. Dozens of more or less helpful medicines and suggestions reached me from well-meaning people all over the country: from farmers' wives, artisans, retired officials. Several weeks before, a Japanese officer, without a formal introduction, knocked at my door. He was a military doctor who had been dispatched by the General Staff. They wanted to make sure that the German Ambassador, whom they respected, received decent treatment at the hands of the "incompetent" civilians. Prince Kanin, Prince and Princess Chichibu, and many other notable people invited us, asking me to fix the date at my own discretion. I could not accept any of these invitations, nor could I pay my respects to the Emperor or make farewell visits to my colleagues. It was for my wife to perform all the social functions and to do all the packing. I just managed to go to a tea-party to which the Counsellor of the Embassy and Frau Noebel had invited all the German and Japanese members of the staff. On that occasion I received the somewhat vague information that the press had published a report from Berlin announcing that, together with two of my colleagues, Herr von Hassell, Ambassador to Rome, and Herr von Papen, Minister (with the title of Ambassador) to Vienna, I had been put on the retired list. Attempts were made to console me by adding that the report seemed untrustworthy. I did not pay any great attention to it.

On the morning of my departure I received a personal telegram in secret code signed by Herr von Neurath saying that the news of my retirement was erroneous and unfounded. I was somewhat bewildered, failing to see how it could possibly happen that such controlled news as changes in diplomatic posts were subject to error. I had no time to ponder over this matter, as the car was waiting to take my wife and myself to Yokohama, where I went on board the *Empress of Canada*. I immediately retired to my cabin, accompanied by my inseparable little Japanese doctor, while it was left to my wife and to the Embassy staff to look after the numerous Japanese and German visitors who wanted to say good-bye to us in spite of the fact that it was a Sunday.

Gradually, as we proceeded along the Chinese coast, it came home to me that I had been somehow involved in the February crisis in Berlin. In the first days of February, Hitler and his party lieutenants had started their *coup* against the generals. The Commander-in-Chief of the army, Colonel-General von Fritsch, one of the ablest officers, and a man of undisputed integrity, had been dismissed from his post on a charge of homosexuality —an infamous lie cooked up by Himmler and the S.S. Together with him, a considerable number of commanders who were distrusted by Hitler had been relieved of their posts.

At the same time a reshuffle of the Cabinet had taken place, Neurath and Schacht being made to resign. Ribbentrop was appointed Minister of Foreign Affairs, thus reaching the goal of his ambition. Evidently in order to round off the picture, several Ambassadors were affected by the purge. Hassell because he was due to be recalled in compliance with Mussolini's request; Papen because his post was to be cancelled in any case; and myself.

Probably because some bright party youngsters had heard that I was quitting my post in Tokyo and thought it was nicer to have three Ambassadors on the purge list than only two. After my return to Berlin I tried by all available channels to find out what exactly had happened, but nobody was able to tell me anything. But what I had heard on my voyage sufficed to rouse my deep indignation. At every port which our boat touched I had to stand the indiscreet questions of journalists who wanted to know whether I had fallen into disgrace with Hitler. Thus the depressing feeling of having left behind an unfinished task on account of my ill health was strengthened by the embitterment of having been slighted.

---

6. BACK TO EUROPE

It was almost an irony of fate that my asthma disappeared and my health was almost completely restored as soon as the coast of Japan receded in the mist of a grey winter day. Even in Kobe I was able to greet the numerous visitors—the German community headed by Consul-General Wagner, Japanese officials, and the professors of Kyoto University—who had come to take leave of me, bring along valuable presents. Only forty-eight hours later I drove through Shanghai, inspecting the ravages of war. Blocks and blocks of houses had been smashed up by air raids and artillery bombardment; 140,000 soldiers—40,000 Japanese and 100,000 Chinese—and uncounted civilians were buried under the ruins—an appropriate prologue to what was in store for Europe. The fashionable European quarters were comparatively undamaged.

On the river the majority of the Chinese barges and junks were flying German, many also British, colors—an astonishing sight which could only be explained by the fact that after the conquest of the city by the Japanese, the Chinese colors had to disappear. And now it was the speculation of the astute Chinese that the German colors would secure for them the best protection against their new rulers. Probably they were eventually disappointed, as it was obvious even then that the Japanese were discouraging Chinese trade with foreign nations, including those allied with Japan. German merchants bitterly complained that permission to visit their godowns (storehouses) was being withheld, and that valuable goods were rotting there. This time again I was glad to leave Shanghai. The hectic, luxurious life of the European quarter was going on unaffected by the ravages of war. Against the background of the material damage and the

Dr. von Dirksen visiting Divisional Commander Prince Higashi
Kuni in Nagoya

loss of life sustained by the city only a few months before, it appeared to be even more ghost-like and unreal than it had ever been.

While Shanghai was going down, Hong Kong had advanced to the position of the metropolis of the Far East. There was a roaring trade in war materials and goods of every kind. The smuggling of arms sought the most adventurous ways, 10,000-ton freighters being used along with junks and sampans. Undismayed by the vicissitudes of war, the imperturbable Chinese traders had found ways and means to keep up a lively business across the fronts. Politicians and speculators from all over the world had gathered in Hong Kong, wealthy Chinese people had fled thither and were leading a sumptuous life; representatives of the Chinese Ministries had their offices there. Patrolling the straits with torpedo-boats and small craft, the Japanese were making frantic efforts to suppress the smuggling of arms, while the explosions of the bombs dropped by them on the neighboring Kowloon area were to be heard. Alongside our boat there moved a German freighter with a cargo of war material for the Nationalist Army. At a luncheon in the German Consulate-General I met again the famous American journalist Carl von Wiegand, Frau von Falkenhausen, the General's wife, and several of our Consuls stationed in Southern China. The war was spreading well to the south, and a Japanese landing on the rich and strategically important island of Hainan was imminent. The Japanese had baffled the world lately by a number of brilliant amphibious operations on the Chinese front.

In Manila we left the *Empress of Canada* for a three weeks' holiday at Baguio. It had been prescribed by my doctors and it was entirely justified, as I was still rather weak. From Hong Kong to Manila I had been laid up with 'flu and a high temperature. Thus I still felt rather miserable when we were welcomed by official representatives in Manila: the Chief-of-Staff of the American Army, the A.D.C.'s of the High Commissioner and of President Quezon, the Japanese Consul, and, of course, the German Consul and Frau Sakowsky came on board the boat. This friendliness was due to the courtesy of the American Ambassador in Tokyo, Mr. Grew. Throughout our stay in the Philippines the authorities proved to be most kind and helpful. President Quezon even put a motor car at my disposal.

It was not due only to this courteous reception that I came to develop a definite predilection for this earthly paradise. Manila blended the charms of a tropical city with those of a thriving and elegant modern metropolis. We enjoyed the amenities of the Manila Hotel—one of the most efficiently managed hotels I have known—the polo club, the modern *avenidas* as well as the narrow old Spanish streets. In the clear cool air of Baguio, which is the Simla of India or Karuizawa of Japan, I recovered from my illness. I spent an interesting day as the guest of Mr. Weinzheimer, inspecting his sugar plantation. President Quezon invited us to a luncheon; he impressed me as a strong and sympathetic personality who had friendly feelings for Germany.

What appealed most to me and aroused my admiration were the spirit and the results of the American colonizing effort during the last forty years. Especially on the 200-mile drive from Baguio to Manila I had ample opportunity of observing the high standard of living, the clean villages with their neat houses, and the agricultural prosperity. Sign-posts bearing such inscriptions as "Drinking water ahead" or "Long-distance telephone calls" testified to the circumspection of the administration. I also learned that the scourges of these tropical islands, yellow fever and malaria, had been entirely eliminated by the sanitary measures of the Government. Now Congress in Washington had passed a bill granting the Philippines independence. But I kept wondering whether this statesmanlike act would not entail grave consequences for these islands. No longer benefiting by a customs union with the U.S., the Philippines would have to sell their products on the world market on a free-competition basis. I was doubtful whether they would be able to do so in the face of the higher production costs caused by their standard of living, which was higher than that of their backward competitors. So the Philippines might one day be facing the cruel alternative of lowering production costs and forgo the blessings of their higher standard of living or of keeping it up and suffering a deterioration of their general economic situation.

When the North-German Lloyd liner *Gneisenau* arrived in Manila, I went on board with the feeling of having regained my health. There a telegram from personnel department of the Foreign Office was handed to me, asking me whether I felt strong enough to be appointed to another post after my return home.

I was rather dumbfounded by this offer. Even before I had received the news of my retirement, which was subsequently denied, I had not expected to get another appointment and I had been looking forward to returning to Gröditzberg after an absence of more than four years. The false alarm about my dismissal had confirmed my view in spite of Neurath's denial. The prospect of getting a new post was rather tempting, inasmuch as it was a very effective refutation of the slight that had been inflicted upon me. As the news of my dismissal had been broadcast all over the world, whereas the denial had been addressed to none but myself, I felt that my honor had been violated, and I was anxious to see it restored. That it was perhaps more honorable not to serve the Nazi Government at all was a point that did not strike me at the time. The Hitler régime had reached the climax of its successes and things seemed to be on the way to a normal state. I was unaware of what was going on behind the scene. Even the

Anschluss had not yet been perpetrated. I felt that my health was good enough to enable me to take another post. So I wired back to the Foreign Office that I was willing and physically fit to accept another post provided the climate was favorable.

Now came the most idyllic part of our voyage. From Singapore to Suez we crossed the Indian Ocean: twelve days of wonderful weather, no oppressive heat, perfect leisure. Our calls at Medan (Sumatra), from where we made an excursion to the mountain resort of Bragasti, and at Colombo were pleasant breaks in the alluring monotony of the sea voyage. Another, less agreeable, interruption of our leisure was created by the broadcast news of the *Anschluss*, which we received in mid-ocean. Although the fact as such appeared to us to be only the realization of a justified demand denied to Germany for the last twenty years, we could not help feeling uneasy on account of the methods employed. Why the immediate military occupation of Austria? Why the absolute integration of the country in the Reich? That the reaction of the outside world was strong and unfavorable was a fact that did not astonish me at all when I remembered the countermoves that were made in 1931 when the democratic Governments of Germany and Austria tried to establish a customs union.

At Suez we left our boat for a fortnight's stay in Egypt. We spent unforgettable days at Cairo, Assuan, and Luxor. Having heard and read a great deal about the land of the Pharaohs, and having seen the most important and beautiful places all over the world, I did not expect any sensational things. But I was overwhelmed by the impressions which every day, every hour, had in store: the delicacy of the colors; the grandiose majesty of the monuments built of stone or carved in rock; the refined perfection of the objects of art found in Tutankhamen's tomb; the elegance and genius of the archaic frescoes in the tombs of Luxor and Assuan; and the magnificence of Egyptian art in general.

I was, however, struck by the incredible backwardness of the country. Certainly I had not expected to find motors, tractors, electric light everywhere. But the fact that the population lived and worked like their ancestors of Biblical times, that vast crops of grain were cut with the sickle, that threshing was done by men and oxen trampling on the ears of corn, that the chaff was sifted from the wheat by throwing it in the air with shovels— that all this was done in a country that had been in close contact with Europe for a long time, and been under British administration for the last fifty years, was certainly a revelation to me. I was now inclined to believe everything I was told about the illiteracy of the *fellaheen* and about the epidemics which demanded such a heavy toll. A striking contrast to these miserable conditions was provided by the great technical achievements, the irrigation and cotton-growing schemes, although the exclusive cultivation of cotton had proved more profitable to the foreign investors than to the natives, who thus became dependent on imports from abroad.

At Luxor I had a telephone call from Cairo. A member of our Legation staff informed me that according to a message from the Foreign Office the new post to which I had been assigned was that of Ambassador to the Court of St. James. So the veil was lifted at last! In my mind the joy of having been entrusted with a great and important task prevailed over the doubts as to whether I was going to stand the wet and foggy climate of England. Ribbentrop, as Minister of Foreign Affairs, would be a hard nut to crack—of this I was sure. But just as a poacher, when appointed to the post of gamekeeper, will become a respectable member of the hierarchy, so Ribbentrop, I thought, having reached the goal of his ambition, might also become amenable to reason and good counsel. Moreover, the competition between the *Auswärtiges Amt* and the "Büro Ribbentrop" was now bound to be discontinued, for, as I put it, nobody can, after all, intrigue against himself. That Ribbentrop was to perform even this miracle came home to me only much later.

Concerning the task awaiting me in London, I felt quite confident. I knew for certain that one of Hitler's really deep convictions was his belief in a friendship between Germany and Britain. I also knew that Ribbentrop was nothing but the Dictator's messenger boy, and that even if he had a grudge against the British (his Nazi salute to the King had been given broad publicity even in the Far East), he would not dare to show it. Anglo-German relations had in my opinion reached quite a hopeful stage: the stumbling-block of naval competition had been removed when the Chamberlain Cabinet took office. A number of anti-German politicians left the scene; Lord Halifax, the Foreign Secretary, was a man who had established personal contact with Hitler by his visit to Berlin in November, 1937. So I expected that by a cautious handling of the political problems and personalities the harm caused by Ribbentrop's clumsiness and arrogance might be undone to a certain extent and some further progress might be made. That I was out of touch with British affairs owing to a twenty years' career in the Eastern political field was undoubtedly a handicap, although not an insurmountable obstacle.

As regards my personal feelings, I was Western-minded and especially Anglo-Saxon-minded, despite my Eastern antecedents. That the efforts of Mr. Joseph Chamberlain to bring about an alliance between Britain, Germany, and Japan at the turn of the century had failed was, in my opinion, an irretrievable loss. Had he been successful, the disaster of the First World War might have been averted. There was, perhaps, some hope of following in the footsteps of the great British statesman. It would perhaps even be possible to win over Japan to an Anglo-German scheme of co-operation.

While in Tokyo I had persistently urged Hirota to adopt a moderate attitude towards the Anglo-Saxon powers. That he had not only taken this
advice to heart, but divulged it to the Anglo-Saxon representatives in
Japan, was evident when my British colleague in Tokyo, Sir Robert Craigie
(who had succeeded Sir Robert Clive), asked me whether it was true that
I had been counselling restraint and moderation on the part of the Japanese Government towards Great Britain. Thus I was inclined to be optimistic regarding my new task.

As I was requested to accelerate my return to Berlin, I had to cut
short the pleasant days in Egypt. After a short stop at Cairo for the purpose
of making the necessary preparations and calling at our Legation, we proceeded to Alexandria. There we took the Italian boat to Brindisi. When I
was about to leave my hotel for the quay of embarkation, I was called back
to answer a telephone call from Cairo. The Legation informed me that my
appointment to London had been broadcast on the previous evening. It
was April 2, my birthday. At the end of two restful days on board we
arrived at Brindisi, where my sister awaited us. We spent the night at Bari.
A good performance of *Madame Butterfly* at the provincial opera house
conveyed to us the last greetings of the Far East. A few days spent with my
sister and brother-in-law at the Villa Bonaparte reconciled me to the fact
that I was now back in Europe. Then we hurried to Berlin, where we arrived on April 12, 1938.

V

Ambassador in London

1938–1939

With the assumption of power by the National Socialists a new and more hopeful chapter seemed to have been introduced into the tragic history of Anglo-German relations. Just as Hitler's *Mein Kampf* displayed, in respect to his policy toward France and the Soviet Union, views calculated to cause forebodings of disaster, so his wish for friendly relations with England was clearly consistent with his convictions.

And the more it became apparent in subsequent years that the program set out in his book was not the irresponsible tirade of a youthful hothead, but a plan pursued with relentless tenacity, the more the conclusion was justified that he would adhere just as unswervingly to his cherished ideal of friendship with England.

Nevertheless, even the first period of mutual relations extending to the Austrian annexation did not indicate a successful attempt at a *rapprochement*. It rather indicated discord, with one bright exception: the naval agreement.

Undoubtedly this unsatisfactory development was largely caused by the wholly misdirected choice of men whom Hitler entrusted with the execution of his plans. Rosenberg's appearance in 1933 in London developed into a tragi-comic episode, whilst Ribbentrop's activities as Ambassador caused lasting and severe damage. The real reason for the failure of these efforts at mutual understanding lies deeper and is based on Hitler's tactics and on Great Britain's political position in the world.

Hitler's tactics in these years can be described as an endeavor to keep conversations with Great Britain alive, while exploring her intentions, partly by reproaches and partly by far-reaching proposals, and then to evade clear answers whenever concrete proposals were made to him. The British Government, on the other hand, was influenced by the strength of her alliances with other powers.

As these alliances were subject to variations, Mr. Baldwin's Cabinet lacked firmness and consistency towards Hitler. The policy of Downing Street was rendered difficult by the French Foreign Minister Barthou, whose lodestar was the integral maintenance of the constellation created at Versailles. Hitler would have been a bad tactician if he had not aimed his shafts at the weakest spot in his adversary's armor, namely the question of disarmament. Here Germany had a clearly justifiable claim. Again and again the various Cabinets of the Weimar period were denied equality in disarmament, although a joint declaration of the Western Powers and Germany in December, 1932, had recognized this equality in theory.

On the contrary, it was the British Government, represented by the Foreign Secretary, Sir John Simon, which at the Disarmament Conference in October, 1933, submitted the proposal that equality should be granted to Germany only after a first stage of four years. Hitler had only waited for such a catchword to retire from the Disarmament Conference and the League of Nations. During the ensuing period the activity of the British Cabinet exhausted itself in toning down hostile advances by France on the disarmament question, or acting as mediator.

No decision was reached concerning the comprehensive German memorandum of 1933, with its proposal to establish a short-term army of 300,000 men restricted to the use of defensive weapons. The breaking off of disarmament discussions through the positive Barthou note of April, 1934, was equally unavoidable.

And furthermore, in 1936 the Baldwin Cabinet made the serious tactical blunder of irritating Hitler's Government with a sarcastic questionnaire which remained unanswered and which did not achieve either of its two aims, which were either to take Hitler at his word (if he was carrying out propaganda), with far-reaching proposals for disarmament, or to expose Hitler's ill will to the world. Still less was the alternative course pursued, namely to arrest with all energy Germany's secret rearmament and thus jeopardize Hitler's prestige. By mixing pin-pricks and feebleness nothing else was attained than to drive Hitler to greater exasperation and to increase his contempt for his opponents.

The attitude on the part of Britain towards German rearmament was not calculated to make an impression on Hitler. By means of a White Paper laid before Parliament on March 1, 1935, the British Government made known its conclusions about rearmament. The German Government's military preparations, which infringed the Treaty of Versailles, and the threats to peace by the National-Socialist régime, served the purpose of this publication. By itself this proof of resolution would have made an impression on Hitler if it had not been accompanied by procedure of a different order.

When the French Government, on March 6, introduced the two years' military service again and thus gave the Government of the Reich occasion to announce the introduction of conscription, the British Government, it is true, was the first of the Western Powers to protest. But it could not even make up its mind to call off the prospective visit to Berlin of Sir John Simon and Mr. Eden. It even asked if the planned visit should take place. The inconsistency of this attitude was strengthened by the fact that during these days the Western Powers had settled the date of the conference at Stresa which was to demonstrate to the German Dictator the close co-operation of the European defensive front, which included the Italian Dictator.

Hitler drew his conclusions from this defensive attitude, which was based more on words than on deeds, and so triumphed when the talks with Simon and Eden had given him contact with the other side. And the purely political events of the year 1935, so far as they affected Anglo-German relations, cannot be brought under one denominator.

In the previous year the British Cabinet had let itself become entangled by its French ally in a political maneuver, which had to be felt as a threat not only by Hitler's Government but by the entire German public. This was Barthou's plan of an Eastern pact, which subjected Germany's Eastern flank to pressure of a united alliance with French guarantee and including the Soviet Union. Besides, the Eastern pact bolted the door against revision of the Eastern frontiers and knocked the bottom out of the Locarno Treaty. Not only did the British Government agree with this plan, it also had it submitted with a recommendation, to the German Foreign Office through the Ambassador.

The speech made in the same year by Mr. Baldwin in the House of Commons, stating that Britain's frontier was on the Rhine, was hardly calculated to convince the German public that Great Britain was showing any understanding of the German demands. Therefore, when the conference of Stresa in 1935 united the Western Powers for a defensive front against breaches of international treaties, Hitler interpreted the participation of Great Britain as bondage to the aggressive policy of France. The agreement soon proved itself a hollow demonstration when Mussolini, one of the co-signatories, attacked Abyssinia. It was, in any case, shown to be unworkable by the failure of sanctions.

The publication of the Anglo-German Naval Treaty made shortly after, in June, 1935, had a still more disuniting effect. By the British proposals made during the Berlin talks this agreement granted Hitler the required rearmament at sea up to a limit of 35 per cent of British naval strength—after this demand had been decidedly rejected on the first day of the conference.

Politically speaking, this agreement, which seemed to have eradicated the main cause of Anglo-German rivalry at sea, was shown to be impracticable. In the confusion of disjointed political clauses inserted before and after, it brought to the British only a transient brightening of the political horizon. It seriously offended her French allies and made Downing Street an easy prey to the German mediator, Ribbentrop.

The dispatch of Ribbentrop to the Court of St. James must be assessed as an important and positive manifestation in the Anglo-German relations of those years, however much the good intentions of this prodigy from Hitler's own school were reduced to absurdity within one year. Without doubt, by sending one of his trusted men, Hitler intended to realize his wish of friendship with the island kingdom. The complete reticence which was imposed upon the German press during the royal crisis in 1936, whilst the American newspapers exploited the situation to the full, must have been welcomed by the British public, so deeply shaken by these events. But in the important matters no progress was made when, after the retirement of Prime Minister Baldwin, who was more concerned with domestic and Empire policy, the direction of foreign policy was placed in the hands of Neville Chamberlain.

It is the fate of the statesman whose aims have been shattered to be condemned to silence and to endure the criticism of world opinion, which retrospectively and mercilessly assumes the right to break the rod on a man who has had the courage of initiative, particularly if his initiative proves to be unsuccessful and barren. However understandable such judgment may be, Chamberlain's contemporaries should surely now recognize that he was an international figure of outstanding stature and of clear and courageous aims. Even if not adept in the immediate technique of foreign affairs, he had, in the training which England automatically extends to her public men and politicians, enough opportunity to give proof of his statesmanlike qualities. During a long and honorable career he rendered signal services to his country and the Empire, especially in the important Ottawa Tariff and Trade Agreement.

Also in regard to the most important question for British foreign policy, the attitude towards the newly risen authoritarian States, he was guided by rigid, honest ideas. He started with the belief that people would turn to him and achieve a *modus vivendi*. Thus he committed an error, which is not rendered less grave by the fact that later on it was committed by Roosevelt towards the Soviet Union.

This being his conviction, he took the necessary steps towards its fulfillment. He replaced those who stood aloof from his views by men of his choice. Anthony Eden and Lord Cranbourne resigned from the Foreign Office. Lord (then Sir Robert) Vansittart, whose political opinions were too unequivocal, was excluded from the executive and restricted to the position of diplomatic adviser. The direction of the Foreign Office was undertaken by Lord Halifax. As next adviser, the new Prime Minister chose Sir Horace Wilson. Sir Nevile Henderson was appointed Ambassador in Berlin. Even before these changes, Chamberlain sought contact with Hitler. This was brought about by Lord Halifax, then Lord President of the Council, at a hunting party in Berlin in November, 1937. But the incompatibility of the two men proved an insurmountable barrier, apart from the fact, made known by the Hossbach Protocol, that Hitler had during these very days laid down his aggressive plans for the ensuing year.

The careful and tentative explanation of his mission through Halifax, who declared himself only authorized to investigate the German point of view and to bring about a basis for negotiations, had already irritated Hitler, accustomed as he was to terse and immediate resolutions. Hitler took no notice of Halifax's acknowledgment of Germany's merit as a bulwark against Bolshevism. He overwhelmed the English statesman with lengthy expostulations about the ruinous consequences of Versailles, thoroughly rubbed in the omissions relating to armaments, and then turned to the Colonial question, which he described as the only outstanding difference between Germany and Britain. He even evaded Halifax's proposal that the discussions should be continued by indicating that the worn-out road of diplomacy should be taken. To the suggestion, made by Halifax, that the *status quo* was no irrevocable dogma for Britain and that the Colonial question could be discussed, he made no response. On the other hand he allowed Austria and Spain to become threatening clouds on the international horizon.

Chamberlain did not fail to follow up the Colonial question propounded by his adversary. In a written inquiry, handed over by Henderson in the autumn of 1937, he developed ideas which some months later found a tangible result. Hitler having left this inquiry unanswered, Henderson took it up with the Foreign Minister Neurath in January, 1938. Acting on instructions, Neurath answered evasively. Thenceforth the British Government resolved on official proceedings. Chamberlain instructed Ambassador Henderson to call on Hitler personally and hand him a memorandum which should be subject to thorough political discussions.

The interview took place on March 3, 1938. Henderson pointed out that neither the French nor any other powers had been informed of the substance of the discussion. He explained the purpose of the British *démarche,* that it was not a question of bargaining but an attempt to establish a genuine and cordial friendship towards Germany, beginning with an improvement in the general atmosphere and aiming at the creation of a new spirit of friendly understanding. The British Government proposed means whereby confidence in respect to the Austrian and Czechoslovakian questions could be established.

Suggestions for discussions with regard to the limitation of armaments on the basis of the latest German proposals were touched on. The main emphasis was laid on the Colonial question. The British proposal visualized a new system of Colonial administration. A region approximately corresponding to the Congo Basin should be administered by the participating powers, according to certain common principles, even if each individual power should be responsible for its own region.

The allotment of its own Colonial territory was provided for. Would the German Government participate in the new Colonial régime? To that was added the ominous question, which Henderson had to ask Hitler: What contribution would Germany be prepared to make towards the general tranquillity and security of Europe? That no such contribution could be considered by Hitler, who was on the eve of his invasion of Austria, need hardly be mentioned. He once more replied, if one can trust the German minutes, that he would not be deterred by third-rate powers in Central Europe. If Britain were to oppose a just and reasonable solution in the Austrian question, then war might result. Apart from this, Hitler evaded a clear attitude to the British proposals, adding a tirade against the international *Hetzpresse* (as he called the violent anti-German press) and the complaint that he had been ill repaid for his friendship to England. The Colonial question was not ready for a solution. One would have to wait patiently for another ten years. Besides, Germany was interested only in the return of her own colonies. But owing to the importance of the question, he would give a written answer. If Hitler had not already trampled on the delicate plant of reconciliation by his brusqueness, it would have withered at the icy blow of the invasion of Austria.

The British Government had, in fact, shown far-sighted comprehension of the German people's wish for harmonious relations. It had broken away from the French policy of unconditional opposition. The British Government was not opposed to harmony by mutual consent. A French inquiry as to a new joint advance was answered by Halifax in the negative. Great Britain would undertake no steps which could be interpreted by Schuschnigg as an incitement to resistance. Hitler had succeeded in eliminating this extremely conciliatory attitude by the brutality of his methods. He turned acquiescence in the annexation of Austria to a storm of resentment on the part of British public opinion. If the discussions at Berchtesgaden with Schuschnigg had already set world opinion thinking, the compulsory retirement of the Austrian Chancellor and the occupation did the rest. Aversion against the transformation of the balance of power in favor of Germany showed itself. At the same time English society, above all, mourned the disappearance of a fairyland which was now subjected to the unsympathetic Nazi administration. And to rub more salt into the wound, Ribbentrop's farewell visit to Chamberlain synchronized with the invasion of Austria. The newly appointed German Foreign Minister had not been informed by his chief and therefore replied in the negative to the Prime Minister's question as to Hitler's plan of occupation.

The hopeful picture which I had made, when I returned to Berlin, of the chance of positive achievement in London had been substantially dimmed by the events of the previous few weeks. Only the publication of documents in recent years have shed light on Hitler's aggressive plans. But the talks that I had with him were destined to pour more water into the wine even of my limited optimism.

---

2. THE FIRST PERIOD IN LONDON, SUMMER, 1938

In spite of a two years' absence from Germany I had to compress my stay in Berlin into barely three weeks, in order to step as quickly as possible into my post in London, vacant since February, so I had only time for official visits and for a rapid study of the questions which would be awaiting me in London. Ribbentrop handed over my credentials as Ambassador in London and explained that he had proposed me to the Führer for this task for two reasons: on account of my loyalty and because of my reports from Tokyo. He was pleased with these and he was convinced of my loyalty when I had told him, after our talk in 1936, that I would give a report of its substance to Foreign Minister von Neurath. That Ribbentrop had thought it worth while to mention these obvious facts throws a significant light on his character.

The further talks with the Foreign Minister on the tasks awaiting me in London gave me few clues. He talked in generalizations; that we should have to foster friendly relations with England and convince her that our claims were justified. Unfortunately Great Britain had shown little understanding of these claims. In spite of a certain ill will towards the British, the substance of his talk was moderate in tone. Above all he avoided expressing bitterness at the failure of his London mission. In what measure these subjective considerations swayed him and how consistently he agitated against Great Britain I first realized by my experiences and observations in the following year. When I grew completely aware of his attitude, and when, at the same time, I realized that in all these discussions he carefully avoided giving expression to this hostility, I drew the obvious conclusion that he looked upon me as a screen to conceal his true attitude and intentions towards the British Government. I hoped that co-operation with him would be possible. He had, after all, achieved his purpose to be Minister of Foreign Affairs. As dutiful servant of his master he would have to steer Hitler's course, a course in principle friendly to England.

My talk with the Führer gave me food for thought. When I reported to him in the presence of Ribbentrop he received me with the words, "You are taking over a difficult task," and he criticized bitterly the attitude of the British Government and its lack of understanding of Germany's just claims. With rising anger he dwelt on the Colonial offer which Henderson had submitted. It was unacceptable to him. Besides, some of the territory in Africa stretched into Italian territory: he could not place an ally at a disadvantage. When I asked what answer he intended to send to London, he replied that he had not made up his mind.

The conversation turned to the Far East. I explained to Hitler that the continued activities of our military mission in China were seriously harming our relations with Japan. I informed him of the attempts made by General Ott and myself to harmonize the work of the German officers in China with our friendship with Japan. The tension was increasing substantially. Hitler ordered Ribbentrop to have the mission recalled. This instruction was carried out by the Foreign Minister on the same day by means of a rude and tactless telegram.

Although I made a note that Hitler's displeasure towards Great Britain might give way to a better mood, the answer that Ribbentrop gave me a few days later in reply to my question about the Colonial offer showed the same negative attitude: the Führer had made up his mind not to reply at all. Thus this proposal was laid in its grave, and in London I was never spoken to on the matter. In view of the great political risk of this offer, which if rejected would only have increased the vulnerability of the Government had the terms been published, official circles in England were chiefly interested in letting the grass grow over this wretched offer. In the following year, before the gates were closed, it was renewed on a larger frame.

My visit to the leading men in Berlin produced no important incidents, although they helped me to become used to the Berlin atmosphere and to pick up broken threads. The deepest impression was left on me by General Beck, Chief of the General Staff. His quiet dignity and well-balanced judgment reminded me of Moltke, to whom he bore a marked resemblance. Goebbels, in whose anteroom I had to wait for half an hour until a well-known film actress appeared from his study, promised me every conceivable help in "my enormously important task." Göring had no time to receive me. Having tried until 1938 to establish personal contact with the heads of the party, I now desisted, as the value of these talks was not great enough to warrant the waste of so much time.

One of my first visits I paid to my opposite number, the British Ambassador, Sir Nevile Henderson. From the very beginning we liked each other, probably because we both had to bear heavy responsibility and were approaching our task with equal good will. We gave advice to each other, as to which men to turn to in our respective countries. I recommended Göring, Weiszäcker, and the Generals to him. After a colorless farewell visit to Ribbentrop, I began my journey to London accompanied by my wife. On May 2 I arrived in the English capital. A few days after my arrival I was received at Buckingham Palace, together with two other heads of the mission. My official duties would begin at last.

My initial visits were made to the Foreign Minister, Lord Halifax, the Permanent Under-Secretary, and Sir Alexander Cadogan, whom I had known since we crossed the Pacific Ocean together when he left his post in Nanking and I was travelling to Germany on leave from Tokyo. His parliamentary colleague Mr. R. A. Butler was responsible for representing British foreign policy in the Commons. With Lord Vansittart, whom Chamberlain had removed from active politics but who had formerly been one of the most decisive men in the Foreign Office, I never came into official contact, except for one introductory visit. The most important personality for the daily work was the head of the Central European section of the Foreign Office, Sir William Strang. I was able to resume the personal relations with him which we had formed during a three-years' joint stay in Moscow, where he was attached to the British Embassy. My main discussion at my introductory visit I naturally had with Lord Halifax. I first had to tender Ribbentrop's thanks for the information which the British Foreign Minister had conveyed to him through the German Chargé d'Affaires, Counsellor of the Embassy Theo Kordt, about the Anglo-French discussions at the end of April. The main part of our conversation was devoted to the Sudeten question. Although there was no actual cause for an open crisis, the danger signal appeared very clearly through the growing differences between the Sudeten Germans and the Government in Prague. Lord Halifax expressed his willingness to help to bring about a peaceful solution of this problem. Even if he recognized the special interest of Germany in the destiny of the kindred and neighboring Germans, he nevertheless hoped that British willingness to play a mediating part would not be rejected on Germany's part because the subject in question was one which did not concern Great Britain. I replied that much would depend on the manner in which mediation was offered. On the one hand

Hitler might be inclined to be offended at any intervention; on the other it was quite possible that he might welcome valuable co-operation. As to the problem itself, it would depend on the Sudeten Germans receiving full equality with the Czechs. Possibly this could be achieved by granting autonomy in the frame of the Czechoslovakian State. From this conversation I gathered that Lord Halifax wished to bring about a general settlement between Germany and Great Britain.

The Sudeten question soon stepped out of the Council Chambers into the dazzling searchlight of an acute and dangerous conflict. The crisis indubitably originated in Prague. Having received reports of alleged threatening German troop movements in the direction of the Czechoslovakian border, the Czech General Staff, without communicating with their French allies, ordered the mobilization of several army groups. The international press was overwhelmed with reports of coming attacks on Czechoslovakia. Great excitement reigned in European capitals. London, too, was shaken by a crisis fever. One head of a mission after another appeared in Downing Street for discussions and questions.

The German Embassy was completely surprised by this panic. I had neither clues of aggressive intentions on the part of Germany nor news of a threatening situation on the frontier. A telephonic inquiry to Herr Weiszäcker gave the answer that in Berlin the same surprise was felt at this world-wide excitement. This time we really seemed to have a good conscience when Lord Halifax asked me to see him on Sunday afternoon. I was able to give him my reassuring impressions from Berlin. I asked the Foreign Minister to exercise strong pressure in Prague, so that normal relations could be re-established as quickly as possible. The chief danger lay in unexpected incidents. Halifax replied that he had already done everything possible. Then he told me of a personal letter to Ribbentrop in which he advised calm and moderation. Two days later the conversation was continued, and the attitude of the press on both sides and the influence that could be brought to bear on it was discussed.

As soon as the Czech alarmist news had been proved unfounded by the military attachés sent to the frontier, the situation became less tense, in spite of the fact that the shooting of two Sudeten German motorcyclists, owing to an alleged failure to observe a halt signal, might easily have led to a dangerous flare-up. The week-end crisis, as it was called after the day of its outbeak, faded away as quickly as it had arisen. The extent of the excitement in which the European Cabinets were involved can be proved by the fact that in the British official documents the telegrams between the Foreign Office and its foreign representatives fill 180 pages. But for Hitler the week-end crisis, with its subsequent reassurance, had by no means ended. For him it had only just begun. It was perhaps not so much the thought that he had grown suspect as the triumphal cry of a section of the world's press, which boasted that the energetic bearing of the Czechs had forced him to withdraw. Once more he had received the cue to convert his secret intentions into action. He did not hesitate. On May 28 he called his confidential men in the party and the State to a secret discussion in the *Reichskanzlei* and informed them of his resolution to crush Czechoslovakia that very year.

During the succeeding months the British Government busied itself seriously with the Sudeten-German and Czech problems. It never tired in urging the irresolute Cabinet in Prague to conclude a rapid and generous agreement with the Sudeten Germans. It urged moderation and reciprocity upon the latter and, at the same time, tried to pacify Berlin. In the business sphere of the Embassy, after an exhaustive talk with Lord Halifax, on June 8, when I had discussed it comprehensively, this question remained in the background for a time. As a decisive factor in Anglo-German relations, however, great importance was attached to it. Together with the *Anschluss,* the generally aggressive tone of the Nazi press and Nazi potentates, as well as the fear of a surprise *coup* by Hitler, the threat to Czechoslovakia provided the essential reason for the change in British mentality in favor of quicker rearmament. Whereas dictators can complete rearmament in secret whilst keeping the press at a normal temperature, democratically governed countries have to convince their public that new sacrifices for the defense of their land must be made. This conviction can only be reached by Parliament, press, and public, if they become aware of definite threats by an adversary. Such threats were felt to be implicit in Hitler's policy, even if he at the time still refrained from other open attacks and although his plans were hidden from the world. By bringing this question into the daylight, and through the press campaign on both sides, the "man in the street" was overcome by an excitement that bordered on panic. Domestic servants refused to take jobs in houses on the South Coast because they were afraid of German bombs. The Counsellor of the Embassy, who wished to rent a house, had three agreements ready for signature withdrawn by the lessor because, owing to the coming war with Germany, an agreement with a member of the German Embassy would be useless. Everywhere one heard the complaint that a house in London was hardly salable—this, too, from fear of German bombs. The voice of the people gave vent to strong pressure on the Government in respect to stronger rearmament in the air and more efficient anti-aircraft protection. The responsible Ministers, Lord Winterton and Lord Swinton, had to yield to these voices. Thus England became conscious of the fact that she was no longer an island. The same consciousness robbed the naval treaty of its real and intended value.

This feeling affected the attitude of the Government. The Home Office terminated the Anglo-German passport agreement. That the alleged technical reasons for this were not authoritative was proved when, on the German side, these objections were considered. Nevertheless, the termination was not revoked. It became clear that the Home Office could refuse the entry of visitors and undesirable travellers and that anyone conspicuous as a National Socialist would be regarded as undesirable.

On the other hand the question arising out of the *Anschluss* was dealt with in a more positive way. The discussions about the Austrian debts, which Germany had taken over, produced a somewhat violent exchange of opinion during which the English side threatened to retain sums alleged to be owing *in contra* account. The introduction of compulsory clearings would have meant a trade war. At length discussions about Austrian debts and economic questions in general on a broad basis were agreed upon. Held in London, they ended in agreement on July 1. These agreements not only exercised a favorable influence in the City and on economic relations, but they also created a more favorable atmosphere in foreign policy.

Another highly explosive question which brought the world to the verge of war in 1937, the Spanish Civil War, had in the meantime lost its inflamatory effect. The powers had at that time agreed upon a "Non-Intervention Committee," which sat in London. To it had been delegated the task of finding the means of localizing the civil war in Spain, so that the powers should not be drawn into a world war. This body had held numerous sessions under the chairmanship of Lord Portsmouth and the able management of the Secretary-General, Hemming, and had amassed a mountain of resolutions and memoranda. Thus a complicated and involved machinery had developed which, on account of the slowness and transitoriness of its proceedings and the lack of unity among the principal participants, reminds one vividly of the League of Nations. Only gradually did I realize that this complication and slowness served to cool the heat of the passion which reigned behind the red and white front in Spain. The bureaucratic machine was to act as a brake until a decision had been reached on the battlefield. As this decision was approaching in the summer of 1938, the deliberations of the committee slowed down imperceptibly towards a complete stop. During the concluding sessions I had to appear as representative of Germany, and I had to give explanations and make proposals where coherence was entirely lacking. To get well into these questions would have been a hopeless undertaking. I simply had not the time for that. But the able experts at the Embassy, Herr Brückmayr (he was executed after July 20) and Herr Schlitter, succeeded in steering me through all the deliberations of the committee.

The most important political event of the summer was the attempt at an understanding initiated on the German side. It showed glaringly the methods of Hitler's diplomacy: the many sidetrackings, the circumvention of pertinent situations, the insincerity, as well as complete incapacity to appreciate the mentality of the opposite side. In the middle of July the personal adjutant of the Führer, Captain Wiedemann, called on me and introduced himself as the bearer of a secret, highly important, political mission. With Hitler's full knowledge and by order of Göring, and ignoring Ribbentrop, he was to sound the British Government as to whether the visit of a highly placed personage, i.e. Göring, for the purpose of a frank talk on the possibilities of an Anglo-German understanding would be acceptable. Wiedemann, a straight-forward, intelligent soldier but no politician, had known Hitler in the First World War. As regimental adjutant he was, for two years, the superior of the corporal and orderly, whose courage he had valued without having perceived any unusual gifts in him. Having achieved power, Hitler appointed his former superior to the position of personal adjutant. The idea of this London mission seemed to spring from two sources: on the one hand Göring's urge for recognition and his wish for the maintenance of peace through an understanding with Great Britain, and on the other the initiative of a skillful woman. This woman, Princess Hohenlohe, a Hungarian by birth, divorced from her husband and living in London for years, had succeeded, by reason of her friendship with Wiedemann, in obtaining access to Göring and even to Hitler. The latter had received her for a discussion lasting several hours, a distinction which, as is well known, he denied to the official representatives of the Reich abroad. But as the Princess was a clever woman working for peace, her influence on the Führer was to be welcomed. Guided by her, Wiedemann stepped on to the smooth London parquet floor. As his task was clearly similar to my own endeavors and as he informed me loyally about everything worth knowing, I did my utmost to help.

Lord Halifax received Wiedemann for a detailed discussion on July 18 in his private house in the presence of the Permanent Under-Secretary, Cadogan. Wiedemann honestly let them have an insight into the intrigues of the party hierarchy. Hitler, he said, had agreed to the London journey; Göring had emphatically fostered it; Ribbentrop, whose position had been weakened, knew nothing about it, and would only be told about it if it were unavoidable. Hitler, he said, felt admiration and friendship for England, but he considered himself rebuffed and misunderstood; he was disappointed that Halifax, on the occasion of his Berlin visit, had not brought any clearly outlined proposals. He had made a great sacrifice over the naval treaty, without its having been appreciated. And finally he was exasperated that England should have given credence to alleged German troop movements. As the best means of furthering the intense wish for the establishment of more friendly relations, the visit of an authoritative German personage, i.e. Göring, was suggested. This plan was welcomed by Halifax, but with the proviso that a favorable opportunity should be chosen for such a visit. As long as the tension which had arisen through the situation in Czechoslovakia oppressed the world, the visit would be inopportune.

Captain Wiedemann emphatically contradicted the rumor that warmongers in Germany wanted to solve the conflict by violent means, a proof of how secretly Hitler had kept his closest entourage in the dark. Wiedemann's character being what it was, it can be reckoned as out of the question that he gave such assurances without conviction. The talk closed with a discussion about the possibility of solving the question of the Sudeten Germans, and with the agreement that the British participants should be informed of further German decisions either through me or Henderson or Wiedemann himself. A more precise demarcation of the question to be put into the program did not take place.

When Wiedemann took leave of me, he asked me not to mention his visit to the Foreign Minister. Upon my objection that I could not withhold such important occurrences from my superior in the Ministry, he expressed his willingness to bring Ribbentrop into the picture. He kept his word, with the expected result. The distrustful Ribbentrop, who, nervous about keeping his position, never forgot that he had been passed over, dismissed the member of his special mission whom he could get at, namely Wiedemann.

After a few months Wiedemann was taken into the foreign service and sent as Consul-General to San Francisco. When America entered the war, Wiedemann went to Tientsin. As long as he was in Europe, I kept in contact with him. During the talks I found him very depressed by the growing tension and the prospects of war. Apart from his genuine and honest wish for peace, he regarded an aggressive war by Germany as a crime, because of her unpreparedness. He held that the available number of her serviceable aircraft and guns, down to the supply of uniforms, was so incredibly low that she would not have the least chance of winning. His remarks strengthened my hopes that it could not be Hitler's intention to force a war upon the world, and with regard to coming developments I found consolation in the proverb, "Time gained, everything gained." Above all, I reasoned that England's rearmament would be complete and that this preparedness would deter Hitler from any possible plans of aggression.

About the time of Wiedemann's visit, Forster, the *Gauleiter* of Danzig, who was known to enjoy the closest confidence of Hitler, called on me. As interpreter and companion he was served by the Director-General of the

Danzig wharf, the clever and skillful Professor Nöe, whom I had known well in my Danzig days. Forster and his wife made a freer and more unbiased and less pompous impression than I was accustomed to from party bigwigs. But in Danzig, through his self-glorification and dictatorial manner, not only had he attracted the dislike of the populace, but he had also incurred the bitter enmity of a considerable section of the party. He pretended that the journey to London was a pure holiday trip, without giving me any clue as to the task which Hitler had undoubtedly imposed upon him.

As I took him to be on a mission, I tried to win him over to my point of view. As the *leitmotif* of my statements I hammered the fact into him that the British Government had, it was true, sympathy for Germany's justified claims, and much desired a lasting agreement, but that it would in no way agree to a German attack on small States or to a breach of the peace. Violence would be met by a declaration of war. Such a determined point of view was approved of by a vast majority of the British public. I stressed that it was altogether erroneous to reckon on England's supposed degeneration or war-weariness, although influential circles in Germany appeared to hold this opinion.

These declarations made some impression on Forster, the more so as they were proved to him by his British hosts. Although I had not discussed Forster's visit with the Foreign Office, leading circles became aware of the importance of the man as being one of Hitler's closest intimates. Above all, the tours organized for him were intended to show him Britain's might. He was given the opportunity of seeing a squadron of the British fleet. He was received at a meeting by Sir Alexander Cadogan, during which he put, in careless jovial style, such questions as: What interest did Britain have in Czechoslovakia? And were Cadogan a German, what would he think of the current political questions? In general, the Under-Secretary of State had a favorable impression of the intelligence and frankness of his visitor, as can be seen from the minutes published in the meantime. On his final visit Forster told me that the display of power and the resolution of England, of which he had been witness during his visit, had made a deep impression upon him. He felt sure that Germany would be forced to come to an arrangement with England and should not indulge in wishful thinking of a feeble Empire. He promised to report in this sense to the Führer. A few weeks later I received a letter from him, with a complete withdrawal of the ideas which he had formed in London. He wrote that he had had a long conversation with the Führer, during which Hitler had convinced him that his views of the might and resolution of Great Britain were erroneous. He had come to the conclusion that the Führer was right. That was a humble *Pater Peccavi* and a classical example of the almost mystic influence which Hitler exercised over his followers. To them he was infallible, and to contradict him a deadly sin.

A third visitor from the highest party circles did not appear in the Embassy. He was Konrad Henlein, the newly elected leader of the Sudeten Germans. As a Czech subject he eschewed the German Embassy, but I was informed about his conversations with his fellow countryman, Prince Hohenlohe (not a relative of the Princess mentioned earlier). Henlein had long conversations with Lord (then Sir Robert) Vansittart, Churchill, and Sir Archibald Sinclair. As may be seen from notes made by them, they were favorably impressed by Henlein's attitude and moderation. He considered a Sudeten-German autonomy within the Czech Union as still possible. He pressed for prompt action, as this would be the last opportunity for this, the mildest form of solving the problem. The next solution would be *Anschluss*, and the third, war. He affirmed on his word of honor that he never received commands or instructions from Berlin. He also acted on the advice of his English counterpart and called upon the Czechoslovak Ambassador, Jan Masaryk. Later on Masaryk declared to Churchill that he considered Henlein's autonomy proposal as practicable. But despite the unceasing pressure of the Foreign Office, the Czech Government could not make up its mind to grant a prompt and liberal autonomy, although such a solution would still have satisfied the Sudeten Germans.

During these initial months I gradually became acquainted with Great Britain's leading statesmen. During a banquet in celebration of the King's birthday, to which the Prime Minister had invited the Cabinet, the heads of missions, and the most prominent Admirals and Generals, Chamberlain addressed me and invited me to take a seat with him on the only sofa there was. We had a half-hour's discussion on Anglo-German relations and international affairs. Although this conversation produced no special results, the upright, straightforward, and statesmanlike manner of the Prime Minister made just as deep an impression on me as his understanding of Germany. On the other hand it seemed doubtful to me whether his somewhat old-fashioned strait-laced manner would be up to the twists of modern diplomatic methods, as applied at present by totalitarian countries. During social events and week-end visits I further made the acquaintance of Lord Runciman, Lord Templewood (then Sir Samuel Hoare), Lord Simon, Mr. Duff Cooper, and the Prime Minister's closest adviser, Sir Horace Wilson.

After an evening party, to which I had been invited, I had quite a long conversation with Churchill. He emphasized that he was no anti-German, as he was said to be. He had felt very happy in South Germany, where he had studied the campaigns of his ancestor Marlborough. He esteemed the valor of the German soldier very highly. "It cost the Allies five lives to extinguish three German ones": these were his actual words. It had also impressed him that after Germany's defeat so many officers had entered volunteer corps to fight against Bolshevism.

In numerous conversations with leading members of the Commons and publicists who visited me in the Embassy or whom I met in clubs, I had an opportunity for detailed discussions on Anglo-German relations and for a study of Great Britain's domestic political developments. After living abroad for nearly ten years, where foreigners lived more or less in seclusion and language difficulties raised additional barriers, I most thoroughly enjoyed the free intercourse with all important political circles.

I summarized the impressions thus gained in a report of July 10. I put forward the view that probably never before had discussions on Anglo-German relations been ventilated so thoroughly and in so short a time as in the past three months. British public opinion was resolved to oppose further efforts for an increase of power on the Continent without a previous understanding with England, even if it meant war. Anglo-German relations drifted ever more into the sphere of British domestic politics. Agreement with the authoritarian States outside the League of Nations was a possibility.

For the Labor party and the Liberals, Germany, with its authoritarian government, was, for obvious political reasons, an object of attack. The opposition to Chamberlain within his own party—the Churchill and the Eden group—saw the best possibility of bringing about Chamberlain's fall and of getting into the saddle themselves by accusing the Cabinet of negligence in the creation of a comprehensive defense against possible attack— by Germany, of course. A general clarification of Anglo-German relations should be attempted, if the risk of a dangerous and vast war was to be avoided. In continuation of these remarks I put the question: Had the development of the last three months reduced, or eliminated, the readiness of Chamberlain's Cabinet to come to terms with Germany? Also there was the question whether the Chamberlain Cabinet was strong enough to come to a settlement with Germany.

I replied in the affirmative to the question whether the Cabinet was willing to make further attempts to reach a settlement. For the time being such readiness was connected with a real clarification of the Czech question. Furthermore, there seemed to be a tendency to put the onus for a resumption of such conversations on Germany. I also considered the domestic position of the Cabinet as strong enough to approach, in a few months' time, the most important task of British policy, viz., agreement with Germany. Recapitulating, I endorsed the fact that Anglo-German relations were in suspense, were laden with tension, and needed agreement. Without agreement, the safety of the British Empire would require a world-wide coalition for the defeat of Germany, and any British Government—present or future—would make a decision as it had done in 1914.

The present Cabinet, I concluded, had made an understanding with Germany one of the most important items in its program. It was the first post-war Cabinet with such plans, and thus showed towards Germany the greatest understanding that any Cabinet could show. It showed growing comprehension in the Sudeten question and would be prepared to make great sacrifices to satisfy Germany's justified claims, but only under *one* condition: that such claims were realized by peaceful means. Should Germany, to gain her objectives, have resource to military means, Britain would, without a doubt, declare war along with France. The military preparations were now advanced far enough. So were the economic preparations. The moral preparedness of the British public was complete. This had been proved during the past months. Internationally, there had been a political mobilization equal in strength to the world coalition of 1914.

This serious warning concluded the first period of my London activities. At the end of July political and social life vanished from the British capital. Before beginning my leave, I said good-bye to Sir Horace Wilson. He asked me whether I would like to see the Prime Minister, and shortly afterwards took me into Chamberlain's study. He discussed the Sudeten crisis and gave warning against violent solutions. Should the Czech Sudeten negotiations fail, he reaffirmed what Wiedemann had declared in his conference with Lord Halifax to be Hitler's view, viz., a resumption of negotiations in some way or other. The British Government, he hinted, was considering a further proposal for expediting the discussions. He welcomed the visit of an important German personality, provided the success of the visit could be reasonably assured and that a favorable moment were chosen. I emphasized, in my reply, the urgency of a solution of the Sudeten question, especially as the proposals of the Czech Government had hitherto been entirely inadequate.

The visit had an aftermath, for there was a press "leakage." The initiative was attributed to me, and it was surmised that I had undertaken a *démarche* in connection with Wiedemann's visit. Such surmises were certain to arouse Ribbentrop's distrust. I begged Sir Horace Wilson to have a retraction published by the press, but this appeared only in a desultory fashion. The constant indiscretions of the English press made my work increasingly difficult, and helped nobody. They had already put the Wiedemann visit into the limelight and were also subsequently to prevent any efforts at an agreement. When on leave I was informed by a letter from Chamberlain about the intentions of the Cabinet. He wrote that the Cabinet had entrusted Lord Runciman with the mission of travelling to Prague and investigating the possibilities of a solution in the Czech Sudeten question. Chamberlain asked me to inform Hitler of this. This request was the more agreeable as it seemed to assure me of a prompt interview with Hitler. In this, as in many other matters, I was to be bitterly disappointed.

---

3. THE CZECHOSLOVAKIAN CRISIS

After my arrival in Germany at the beginning of August I made it my principal object to be received by Hitler, so as to execute Chamberlain's commission and report on the state of Anglo-German relations. From a conversation with Ribbentrop I had already gathered that Germany's reserve with regard to the Runciman mission would preponderate. The Minister for Foreign Affairs had been vague and uncertain, and although he refrained from any violent language against Great Britain and Czechoslovakia, he never gave the slightest inkling of the attack which had been resolved upon in May. He agreed to arrange a meeting with Hitler, although he did not seem inclined to hasten it. Meantime I paid my customary visits in Berlin. When calling upon Bohle, chief of the overseas organization of the National-Socialist party, Hess, his deputy and brother of the Führer's deputy, took part in the interview. I gave them my views on the policy of the British Cabinet as I had given them to Forster and in my report of July 10.

That afternoon Hess rang me up, saying that my political review of the situation had greatly interested him, that he had spoken about it to his brother, who wished me to pay him a visit in Munich. I said I was ready to leave that same evening. In Munich I was met by Hess's adjutant, who told me with obvious satisfaction that his chief had succeeded in arranging an interview with the Führer for General Sir Ian Hamilton. I then had a long conversation with Hess in his fine and elegant country seat at Hellabrun, near Munich. Hess, a reserved man and a good listener, gave me every opportunity for a detailed and frank account of the political situation in Great Britain, of the conciliatory, if firm, attitude of the British Cabinet towards Germany, and of the rearmament now in progress. With the greatest vigor I pointed out the danger of a war in case of any aggressive action on Germany's part. Hess listened attentively and seemed to be in agreement with me. He, too, mentioned with some pride General Hamilton's visit to Obersalzburg. He put a few questions without committing himself in any way. I had not the slightest doubt that he would give a faithful report of our conversation to Hitler.

After my arrival in Reichenhall, where I intended to take the cure for the remnant of my asthma, I renewed my efforts to be received by Hitler at Obersalzburg, efforts similar to those I had made two years previously when I was on leave in Germany from Tokyo. One evening when I had been invited by Herr and Frau Meissner to their small Bavarian house in Berchtesgaden I asked Meissner whether he could not arrange a visit to the Führer. He was perfectly ready to do so and added that this should be possible without much difficulty, as the Führer was staying in Obersalzburg and had nothing very important on for the next few days. Meissner called up the Chancellery and was told that the official in charge was absent. He repeated the call about an hour later, and returned to the drawing-room somewhat disconcerted. In response to his request he had been told that Hitler was not receiving during the next few days, and could not fix a later date. It was obvious that Hitler did not want to see me, although he knew that I was the bearer of a personal message from Chamberlain. The reasons for his refusal were just as evident: he knew what I would have to tell him and did not want to hear it. I have never been able to find out the real reason for the break in our relations, which later on it proved to be; perhaps it was Hess's report on the interview with me, or my own report of July 10, or all my reports. At that time I resolved not to jump to conclusions. There might also have been some mistake, seeing the notoriously confused management in Hitler's Chancellery. I simply had to make a fresh effort.

The next opportunity presented itself on the Party-Day in Nuremberg. Again I pressed Ribbentrop for an interview. At last Dieckhoff, Ambassador in Washington, and myself were told to be present in his hotel at a tea-party which he was giving to the foreign guests. There was an endless coming and going in the corridor leading to his room. Ley succeeded in forcing his way into the Führer's room, where he had to salute the uniformed workmen, the so-called "Workers' Troops," who marched past through the streets in pouring rain. Meantime Ribbentrop had expressed the opinion that he would not permit me or Count Welczeck, our Ambassador in Paris, to return to our posts, in view of the critical state of affairs. I replied that in such critical times the presence of Ambassadors at their posts was exceedingly important and necessary.

Dieckhoff and I had hardly a quarter of an hour's time before the tea-party began. I was conducted into Hitler's room, and did not even sit down for our short conversation. I gave him Chamberlain's message and mentioned briefly the reasons for Runciman's mission. "This Runciman is said to be a rabid Democrat—at least that is what General Hamilton told me," said Hitler. I answered that Runciman was not known for his radicalism. "Perhaps he has changed his views, and it is high time that he did."

Thus my interview came to an end, having lasted hardly seven minutes. It was the last I had with Hitler. An excited and hectic mood prevailed during the Party-Day. The conviction grew from day to day that some kind of blow had been planned, if only from the fact that reports of terrorism in the Sudetenland increased. Ribbentrop called the Ambassadors and Ministers to a meeting, explained the political position in his amateurish way, and emphasized its seriousness without a hint of the coming war. We all dined together. I sat on Ribbentrop's left. He complained of the unyielding attitude of the British Cabinet during the past few years, despite the liberal offers made by the Führer. I asked him to which offers he was referring. He gave no clear reply. I further inquired why such offers had not been published, so that the responsibility for failure to reach agreement could be definitely established. Again he replied evasively. I have never been able to have a continuous, sensible conversation with Ribbentrop.

The bomb burst during the height of the Party-Day, which culminated in Hitler's speech in the big hall. It was a masterpiece of demagogy. Working himself up into a passion, after gaining control over his listeners, he insulted Benes and Czechoslovakia in the grossest manner. His speech was equivalent to a declaration of war. On my way home I agreed with my friend Moltke that at least the irrevocable word "war" had not yet been spoken, so that the door to peace had not been closed altogether. But as Hitler disregarded the solemn warning given by the British Cabinet in those days, as well as the readiness of France, for a few Czechoslovak territorial adjustments, provided that they were carried through in a peaceful manner, it seemed unlikely that he would be afraid of a war.

When a few days later I visited the Secretary of State, Weizsäcker, he said that I had come at the right moment, as Chamberlain wished to visit Hitler on the following day at Berchtesgaden and that I was to go to Munich that evening as a member of the delegation. Having arrived there, we drove to the aerodrome to welcome the Prime Minister and Sir Horace Wilson. The German delegates were put up in one of the hotels and remained there until the following morning. Not one of us was consulted —I recollect the presence of Weizsäcker and Gaus—and we also heard but little of what was taking place. Then it filtered through: that, contrary to all expectations, the conference had run more smoothly than could have been anticipated. Next morning the German and British delegates started on their return journey to Munich. I travelled with Sir Horace Wilson. He told me that Chamberlain had recognized the self-determination of the Sudeten Germans. A second conference had been fixed. It was to be held within a week at Godesberg. So hope sprang up once more, despite the disloyal action of Hitler and Ribbentrop, who, contrary to what had been agreed upon, issued instructions to withhold the minutes of the conference from the British (the minutes having been drawn up by interpreter Schmidt, the sole witness present).

A few days later the same Foreign Office officials assembled once more in Berlin for the journey to Godesberg. Whilst the meeting in Berchtesgaden had been small and intimate, the Godesberg Conference resembled Locarno, or similar meetings of world-wide importance. A large German staff filled the modest Hotel Dreesen, which in ordinary times was a meeting-place for tourists who wished to drink Rhine wine on the terrace of the hotel, with a view of the majestic river. Now newspapermen from all parts of the globe congregated, whilst all approaches to the hotel were closely guarded. Party officials turned up to bathe in the sun of highest favors.

Soon after our arrival we drove to the Cologne aerodrome. Here, too, preparations had been made. A guard of honor—S.S. men, of course—had been marched up. When the Prime Minister with Sir Horace Wilson and Sir William Strang descended from the plane he saluted the guard of honor, and then we drove to the beautifully situated Petersberg Hotel, lying on the far bank of the Rhine, opposite to Godesberg. Again I sat in the same car as Sir Horace Wilson. He told me that Chamberlain had done his utmost in London to bring about a compromise. Now he was in a position to make proposals to Hitler which would surely satisfy him. But one should not hurry the Prime Minister, but give him time to bring the entire business to a successful conclusion.

These favorable reports filled me with joy, and I hastened to pass them on to Ribbentrop, whom I met at the midday meal on the terrace of the Hotel Dreesen. I took it that he, too, would rejoice at the forthcoming satisfactory solution. But when he heard Sir Horace's advice not to press Chamberlain unduly, he put on his iron face, banged the table with his fist, and called out, "Three days." These two words left a deep and lasting impression on me and completely changed my ideas about Hitler and Ribbentrop. The hopes which had filled me on taking up my post in London that something useful and lasting might result through an improvement in Anglo-German relations had indeed been shattered during recent weeks. When Hitler declined to receive me and the Minister for Foreign Affairs had expressed the view of not permitting the Ambassadors to return to their posts in times of crisis, it became fairly clear to me what these two men had in mind with regard to responsible officials assigned to responsible posts. They distrusted them, and as the Ambassadors worked in favor of peace, this distrust could only mean that Berlin headquarters was not in favor of peace.

These vague suspicions were now confirmed by Ribbentrop's words. It was quite obvious to me that he was not at all interested in obtaining autonomy for the Sudeten Germans by peaceful means, or he would have rejoiced at the coming triumph. It surely was immaterial whether this object was attained in two, three, or five weeks. His vexation and the intention of humiliating the Englishmen through a short-timed ultimatum, and so preventing any compromise, clearly proved that for him it was not a matter of achieving a political result, but of humiliating the opponent and possibly of precipitating war. From that time onwards I abandoned hopes of converting Ribbentrop to a sensible policy, and determined to make myself independent, and to work against him as best I could. My hopes that Hitler desired not war, but perhaps an honorable understanding with Great Britain, had been severely shaken.

When the conference opened, it was nearly wrecked by Hitler, who declined Chamberlain's offers, although they fulfilled almost all his demands, so the British statesman took refuge in written communications by addressing a letter to the German side. Although Chamberlain adopted this method to determine definitely in writing the responsibility for a rupture, he nevertheless offered Hitler and Ribbentrop the desired opportunity of a tactical delay, which proved itself a dangerous weapon in view of the world's feverish tension.

In any case the two locked themselves in their rooms for the greater part of the day in order to hatch a reply, without consulting one of their advisers, not even Gaus. After two exchanges of letters the fateful conference began, late in the evening. The Germans present were Hitler, Ribbentrop, and the interpreter Schmidt; the British were Chamberlain, Sir Horace Wilson, and an interpreter. We were tormented mainly lest an agreement might be prevented by differences of opinion on the delineation of boundaries, in so far as Germany might claim too extensive Czech territories as belonging to the Sudetenland and the British might draw the boundaries too narrow. Thus the conference might have broken up, even though an agreement might have been reached on principle. The hours seemed to drag out endlessly.

At eleven o'clock came the disastrous news that the Czechs had mobilized. A rupture seemed unavoidable. I was talking with Sir William Strang. At last the doors of the conference room opened. A rupture had been avoided; this, at least, was the confident interpretation ascribed to the result of the conference. Hitler had almost wrecked it with his short-term ultimatum, within which the evacuation was to be carried out. As Hitler had attained his political aims—the freedom of the Sudeten Germans—and as any serious reasons for the short-term ultimatum no longer existed, his further intentions were suspect. A catastrophe had only been avoided because Chamberlain declared himself willing to submit Hitler's demands to the Governments of the Western Powers, but without recommending their acceptance. How irresponsible Hitler's resolve had been to let the conference fail only because of the minor question of a time limit was proved by the fact that complete unity of the Sudeten territory had been agreed upon by both delegations. This problem, which might indeed have become a dangerous obstacle, offered no difficulties.

But Hitler by no means gave up his resolve to bring about a war. Mortified and disappointed by the peaceful sentiments of the people of Berlin, sentiments which he tested by the march of an armored division right through the city, he accepted Mussolini's mediation and signed the Munich Agreement. My rôle as spectator did not extend to this last act, for after the Godesberg Conference I returned to Gröditzberg, there to await further instructions. Thus I was able to observe the deep anxieties, akin almost to despair, in Silesia and especially in Breslau, when during the last days of September war seemed inevitable.

The signature of the Anglo-German protocol proposed by Chamberlain filled me with delight. But a few days later, when I arrived in Berlin, it was whispered in the Foreign Office that the signing of the protocol meant no change of policy.

4. SECOND PERIOD IN LONDON, OCTOBER, 1938–MARCH, 1939

After the danger of war had once again been averted through the Munich Agreement, I pressed for my return to London. But Ribbentrop only gave his consent after repeated requests. I said good-bye to the Secretary of State, seeing that the Minister for Foreign Affairs gave me no opportunity for an interview. In London I found that opinion was by no means unanimous. The great majority of the people regarded the past critical weeks and the dramatic Munich solution like a heavy thunderstorm, clarifying and purifying the atmosphere. But a counter-current made itself felt amongst the general public: a feeling of shame and degradation in having been compelled, under pressure, to a solution which meant desertion of a small ally.

Government circles were pushed to and fro by diverse tendencies and currents. It is true that for the Prime Minister, the Anglo-German Agreement, the signature of which he had extorted from Hitler in Munich, was fundamental to relations with Germany. It had enabled him to give his journey a positive and constructive appearance. The honest joy of Chamberlain, on his arrival at the aerodrome, when, returning from Munich, he uttered the famous words "Peace in our time" and showed the people the document, was perhaps unintentional. But in effect it proved to have been a skillful tactical move. It certainly helped him against the first assaults of his critics. But the pressure became ever more severe. It forced him to take the wind out of the sails of the Opposition as far as possible. The accusation of being an "appeaser" kept increasing in vehemence, strengthened by the indignation of America over Munich. Duff Cooper, as a protest against Chamberlain's submissive policy, resigned from his ministerial post, and that powerful orator Churchill condemned it root and branch. The lack of military preparation in Great Britain demanded immediate and thorough measures of rearmament, which went hand in hand with a press campaign to stir up public opinion. The Prime Minister took these circumstances into account in his declaration in the Commons on October 3 that Britain had resolved upon rearmament so as not to stand defenseless should a new crisis arise. Thus the Munich Agreement changed from a sacrifice, made for the sake of peace, into a skillfully calculated means of gaining time for full military preparedness. Hitler immediately used these currents to voice his displeasure at the compromise forced upon him in Munich and to depreciate the Anglo-German protocol which was so distasteful to him. In a speech at Saarbrücken on October 9 he emptied a bowl of scorn over the British attitude, which he compared to that of a governess. He complained about the hostility of British opinion towards the agreement, which had only just been concluded, and attacked the Eden–Duff Cooper–Churchill opposition in the severest manner. With that all hope of a fresh Anglo-German *détente* was killed in the eyes of the general public.

Nevertheless, leading British Cabinet Ministers were loath to let the links with Germany break during these weeks. In various speeches Chamberlain, Lord Simon, and Lord Templewood, amongst others, directly or indirectly requested Germany to produce a program of her wishes for negotiations; colonies, raw materials, disarmament, and limitation of spheres of interest were mentioned. In a long interview during a week-end visit Sir Samuel Hoare approached me with these ideas. I had to temporize until a clarification on a broad basis could be achieved. Clarification then came in a terrifying shape, in the persecution of the Jews, which Goebbels set in motion on November 10, after the murder, by a young Jew, of the Secretary to the Paris Embassy, von Rath. The infamies committed on that day, the burning of synagogues, looting, and ill treatment, set free such a wave of hatred and indignation throughout Europe that all discussions came to an end. The brutality of Goebbels was the more incomprehensible as just in those very weeks the first step had been taken for an organized and humane international solution of the Jewish question. As the negotiations during the next few weeks showed, the plan was based on the following idea: that the emigration of the Jews should be organized so as to take place gradually, into countries to be declared suitable by an International Commission. The transfer of funds conceded to the Jews was to be combined with an annual export of 3 per cent, plus a 3 per cent sinking fund, and so discharged.

The conversations ran their course, thanks to the initiative of President Roosevelt, who had sent two plenipotentiaries to Europe in order to study the Jewish question. They were Mr. Rublee, later on Chairman of the so-called Evian Committee, and Mr. Pell. Göring, with the Ministers for Agriculture, Finance, and Home Affairs, made special efforts to promote the start of negotiations with the American representatives and to further the elaboration of practical plans. The establishments of contacts were set up *via* the German Embassy in London. In a report I had declared myself most emphatically in favor of active furtherance of these efforts, as by our co-operation we would serve not only our own interests, but set in motion favorable feelings abroad.

After the first contact had been made with Rublee and Pell, through the Austrian Chancellor of the Exchequer, Fischböck, and the well-known German press representative, Abshagen, these contacts gradually grew into a discussion of Rublee with Göring and Dr. Schacht, the President of the *Reichsbank,* who had worked out the financial side of the plan. Schacht also carried on negotiations in London, with Mr. Rublee and leading British economists, such as the Financial Adviser to the British Government, Sir Frederick Leith-Ross, and Lord Winterton. American and British capital had been induced successfully to take an interest in the financial side, and Herr Wohlthat, who then carried on the negotiations by order of Göring, was invited to London. Here he established contact with British high finance until these hopeful expectations were brought to naught by the war.

Schacht's three-day visit to London in December, 1938, had still further far-reaching effects, although it was only a matter of a private visit to his friend Mr. Montagu Norman, Governor of the Bank of England. How highly Norman esteemed his guest could be seen from the remark made to me on the occasion of a visit to the Embassy—"Schacht ought really to become a British subject." In his discussions with the President of the Board of Trade, Stanley, Sir Frederick Leith-Ross and other important City financiers, Schacht met the greatest readiness on the part of those attending the discussion for commercial negotiations on the broadest basis with Germany. Increased exchange of goods between the two countries, exchange equalization, and other subjects were broached as suitable for negotiations. Stanley had even hinted at his readiness to visit Berlin to take part in the discussions. My conversations with Schacht on the complexity of this question brought an idea into my mind, which I had already cherished during the last few weeks, and which I tried to promote. It was an improvement in Anglo-German relations on an economic basis. Economic questions during these months came ever more into the foreground in Germany. The agreement made in summer with England also had favorable political results. The trade connections between these two highly developed countries, which had always been excellent buyers of each other's goods, seemed capable of further developments. I discussed this idea with influential Englishmen, especially during a week-end visit to Lord Runciman, who informed me that he had been requested by Chamberlain to elaborate important questions of concern to Germany. He, as well as Lord Halifax, entertained these ideas most favorably.

I ascertained a certain inclination on Germany's part to co-operate in economic matters, or at least not to stand obtrusively in the way. In January the suspicious Ribbentrop had called me to Berlin in order to question me about a decoded message from the Japanese Ambassador to his Government about a conversation which he had had with me, in the course of which I was supposed to have made some heretical assertions. The Minister for Foreign Affairs, to whom I spoke on this occasion about my economic plans, received these coolly in the beginning, but at a second interview, four days later, on a further increase of Anglo-German trade, he displayed most lively interest. I could not definitely say whether this change was due to the fact that during those days a communication had arrived from Mussolini concerning a conversation held with Chamberlain, in which it was alleged the Prime Minister had asked the Duce for his assistance in improving the relations between Great Britain and Germany. But the connection seems highly probable. Hitler's speech on January 30, anniversary of the "Assumption of Power," laid strong emphasis on economic questions. His remarks seemed to have more significance, and in his appeal he insistently stressed the phrase "export or die."

The impressions of a more favorable atmosphere in Germany were strengthened on my return to London. The press attaché at the Embassy, Dr. Hesse, was called to Berlin by Ribbentrop. He received confidential instructions to get in touch with Chamberlain's chief-of-press, Stewart, who was well known to him, on the matter of a general approach to the British Government. A proposal for a non-aggression pact was also to be made. The Minister for Foreign Affairs declared himself ready to come to London to sign it. Stewart then arranged a meeting for Dr. Hesse with Sir Horace Wilson, who maintained a sympathetic attitude. Great Britain, however, made no other efforts in these overtures—it may be that political events in Czechoslovakia brought them to an end, or it may be that this approach through non-official channels was not to British liking. What seemed to confirm the latter version was a remark made by Lord Halifax,

A banquet at the German Embassy in Tokyo, November, 1937, to celebrate the signing of the Anti-Comintern Pact by the Italians

who said to me, "Herr von Ribbentrop wants to come to London." I was not able to determine why this otherwise ever-hostile Foreign Minister had taken up a conciliatory attitude. That it was merely an episode was proved quite clearly a few weeks later when Ribbentrop offended the British in the economic field.

The course of events soon offered a double opportunity of translating the initiative, as planned on economic grounds, into action. A representative delegation of the Rhenish-Westphalian Coal Syndicate arrived here to negotiate with the Mining Association of Great Britain. These negotiations were carried through in a most friendly atmosphere, resulting in an agreement regulating a number of difficult questions and removing friction. Agreement was reached on the price of coal to third markets, as also to the limitation of spheres of interest, putting an end to undercuttings in prices and consequent capture of markets. A dinner with friendly speeches closed these negotiations. These private economic agreements received official notice through an emphatically friendly speech by the President of the Board of Trade, Stanley. A further advance was proposed. In Berlin there was to be a dinner of the "Trade Group Industry," with prominent British guests. A meeting of top industrial representatives in Düsseldorf was arranged.

The annual dinner of the Anglo-German Chamber of Commerce gave an opportunity of cementing relations. Dr. Wiehl, Chief of the Economic Department of the Foreign Office, took part on behalf of Germany. Stanley and Hudson attended on behalf of Great Britain. On this occasion, also, friendly speeches were made. Arrangements were made for a visit by the two important Cabinet Ministers Stanley and Hudson to take part in the negotiations of the industrial organizations, and for conversations with German officials. A return visit by the German Minister of Economy was suggested. These attempts, of which I informed Berlin, were received coldly and ungraciously. Funk, they said, was overworked, so that he could not be spared. Nor could a date for a later visit be fixed. But the British Cabinet by no means abandoned their efforts. They gave up Funk's visit and contented themselves with a speech of mine about an unofficial meeting. Stanley's and Hudson's visiting tour was adhered to during the conversations held between Stanley, Leith-Ross, and myself. Such a request could not be refused even by Ribbentrop. He agreed with ill grace, and March 17 was fixed for arrival of the two British delegates.

But the clouds already arising on the political horizon were destined to bring to naught all these efforts to produce a *détente* by economic means. The Czechoslovak question, which continued to smolder, owing to ever-increasing demands by Germany, seemed on the point of a violent eruption. Rumors thickened about Hitler's new plan for a violent blow against

Czechoslovakia. I received confirmation of this on my visit to Berlin, where I went to preside as Chairman of the Society for Eastern Asiatic Art, projected by me when in Tokyo. Hitler and the Diplomatic Corps were to be present. Owing to a renewed attack of influenza then prevalent in London, which tied me to my bed, I could not carry out this plan. After my convalescence I met Hewel by chance in the Foreign Office, he being the connecting link between it and Hitler. It has always been a riddle to me why a special post for carrying out the duties of Minister of Foreign Affairs should have been created, but this was probably due to Hitler's usual tactics of using a "semi-official representative" alongside of the official one. But in any case Hewel was a sensible and comparatively moderate man. He told me that, in his view, ambassadors ought to be kept better informed, which was the reason for his advising me that the Führer was planning a march into Czechoslovakia. But as such decisions were only come to at the very last moment, this plan might be altered, although all signs spoke for the invasion. I could only repeat my warning that a fresh attack, after the promise made in Munich, would mean a serious danger, though I could not go so far as to predict that Great Britain would be certain to declare war if only the outer appearances of hostilities could be avoided. During my few days' stay in Berlin I gathered further unfavorable impressions. Ribbentrop was not to be seen—to me a significant symptom. In any case I did not expect any political enlightenment from him. Funk, too, whom I visited on account of the approaching ministerial visit, usually pleasant and affable, was reticent and hesitant.

I returned to London, oppressed by a feeling of an approaching catastrophe. The political results of renewed aggression were plainly visible. From the National-Socialist train of thought it was impossible to explain the motives for such a dangerous and desperate adventure. The aim of bringing Czechoslovakia into the German sphere of influence and to annul it as a bastion against Germany had been achieved. Slovakia had seceded. President Benes had retired from the political scene, and the shadow Government in Prague offered every kind of co-operation. Hitler's policy showed itself ever more plainly as that of a man running amok. The political storm broke after an interval of a few days. The invasion of Prague set free the waves of indignation and anger, as was to be expected. It is true Chamberlain in the Commons and Halifax in the Lords made statements condemning Hitler's action, but indicated no fundamental change of policy towards Germany. Soon, however, the irresistible forces of British public opinion dragged the Government along. Whilst the secession of Slovakia had been accepted with indifference, the march into Bohemia and Moravia reopened the wounds of Munich, as yet hardly healed and therefore still painful. Hitler's perjury was felt to be an indecency, making impossible further political intercourse with him. The average Englishman had understood the linking of the Sudetenland as a union of Germans with Germans. The incorporation, however, of seven millions of foreign race was considered irreconcilable with the declared principles of National Socialism itself. It was regarded as unadulterated imperialism.

The feelings of the English, which had already taken definite shape in political circles, were instinctively aroused. Germany, by linking up Austria and the Sudetenland, had attained the greatest increase of power that the British were willing to grant. Any further violent and one-sided annexation would be found to increase the preponderance of power of a single country on the Continent to such a degree that the hundred-year-old Continental policy of the island kingdom would be destroyed.

Party tactics heated the atmosphere still further. It became clear to the Conservative voter, and most emphatically so to the party officials, that another political defeat of Chamberlain and the failure of the "appeasement" policy might also mean the defeat of the Conservative party at the next elections. These circles pressed therefore for a very much sharper tone. To this had to be added that the rumors and false reports of Hitler's aggressiveness were made much greater than they really were. The press dished up to its readers sensational reports of an impending invasion of Rumania. Thanks to the German-Rumanian trade agreement, plus an intrigue by the Rumanian Ambassador Tilea in London, the conviction of Government and public was aroused that the German expansion to the southeast was imminent. Rumors of extensive military preparations on the Polish frontier increased the excitement. Whilst during the Rhineland occupation of March, 1935, the mood of electoral circles had acted soothingly upon the Government, which was then resolved upon sharp measures, the very opposite now took place.

Under pressure of this influence Chamberlain made his well-known speech in Birmingham on March 17, which was very sharply phrased. It also indicated the beginnings of an encirclement policy in the statement that Britain would act in unison with equally minded powers. The ministerial visit to Germany was cancelled.

Within four days, from March 15 to 19, a technical breach in diplomatic relations took place. This time the Foreign Office set the bad example by recalling Sir Nevile Henderson from Berlin. Naturally Ribbentrop did the same thing. I left London on March 19, after two stormy and unpleasant interviews with Lord Halifax. His irritation at the breach of the Munich Agreement was understandable, as Hitler's actions could not be justified by even the most threadbare excuses. How deeply the resentment was felt was shown by the fact that he did not even respond to my complaint, made on my own initiative, against Duff Cooper's rude insults of Hitler in the Commons. It seemed a further proof to me of the prevailing bitterness that, quite contrary to the venerable traditions of the British Parliament, customary in this noble House, the Speaker did not censure these insults.

After my arrival in Berlin I had to wait five days for a reception by Ribbentrop. As he had not granted me an interview during my last visit, I came to the obvious conclusion that he was imitating Hitler's methods in not wanting to listen to anything not in accordance with his views of world affairs. But I did not feel justified then in relinquishing my post, as long as hopes existed of avoiding the worst.

5. THIRD PERIOD IN LONDON, SUMMER, 1939

As soon as the crisis had abated and Sir Nevile Henderson had returned to Berlin in the beginning of May, I pressed the Foreign Office to allow me to return to London. Ribbentrop gave his consent after some hesitation, but did not give me an interview except when I had declared that I would not return to London without one. In contrast to his usual reserve towards me, he launched out into provocative tirades. If Poland were to quarrel with Germany, she would be shattered. We were ready for a ten years'—nay, even a twenty years'—war. Britain should abandon her support of Poland.

In London I found the political scene entirely changed. Two facts became clear and grew increasingly clear during the following months: the resolute warlike attitude of the people and the creation of a defensive front against further aggressions on Hitler's part. In entire contrast with the feeling that prevailed in the autumn of 1938, when the broad masses did not want to fight and remained passive, they had now taken over the initiative from the Government and drove the Cabinet on. British public opinion did not aim at starting a war, but only at a resolute attitude towards Germany and an armed intervention in the event of aggression by Hitler. The radical groups in the press and Parliament now pushed themselves into the forefront. British public opinion, so susceptible to emotion, was put into a state of mind that made war the very hub of thought and conversation.

The press brought sensational reports, such as a series of articles in the *Sunday Express* under the heading "The Man Who Murdered Hitler."

According to this, Hitler was said to have been murdered some time ago and to have been represented by his double, long kept in readiness. Göring was reported as wounded by an assassin, while the very same papers reported a speech that he made a few days later, in the very best of health.

The official tenor coincided with the state of mind of the public. The members of the National-Socialist party were expelled without any special reason. Permission to remain in England was withdrawn from German merchants who had been trading in England for several years. Others were refused entry. In the course of the summer military preparations increased. The army and navy followed the mobilization of the air force. France, too, took military precautions. The Polish Army, about 900,000 strong, stood in increased readiness close to the German frontier. The military section could not subside either, owing to continual press reports on conferences with the Allies, financial and military discussions with Poland, credits to Rumania and Turkey, a Turkish military mission to London, pressure on Yugoslavia.

Hitler did not let this opportunity escape for exacting an eye for an eye, a tooth for a tooth, with interest and compound interest. But military measures could be carried out better in secret in a totalitarian country, even though the British Government had received the news in summer that two million men had been aligned on the Polish frontier. The expulsion of the National-Socialist officials from England was answered by an expulsion of totally harmless British merchants from Germany.

Above all, Goebbels could now attune the German press to its highest pitch, even though stronger vituperation was hardly possible; for already in the autumn it had adopted the sharpest possible tone against Britain. It could now complain of encirclement. It could engage in disputes with the British press which gave indeed an abundant supply of material. Thus the German writers adopted the simple recipe of branding every conciliatory word on Britain's part as a sign of weakness and decadence, whilst resolute language was deemed an insolent provocation.

The international field of Guarantee and Pact conferences also played a considerable part, by reason of the fanatical interest with which they were followed by the public. Immediately after the march into Bohemia and Moravia, the Foreign Office prepared a diplomatic counterstroke. On March 21 a British memorandum proposed to the French, Russian, and Polish Governments a conference for the conclusion of a consultative pact in defense against further aggressive actions. Simultaneously, the British Government offered unilateral guarantee declarations to a number of smaller countries which were regarded as threatened. Rumania and Greece readily accepted this assurance, whilst others shrank from such a move into the camp of the Western Powers. On March 21 a treaty was concluded with Poland, one of the most threatened countries, stipulating for mutual help, combined with a guarantee of the *status quo*. Recognizing that proper support and power to such a defensive front was lacking without the entry of the Soviet Union, the Foreign Office sent a corresponding inquiry to Moscow. Thus began the negotiations between the Soviet Union, Britain, and France which were to decide the international scene of early summer of 1939.

Impressive though the construction of this power coalition seemed at first, British diplomacy had put its hands into the wasps' nest of Eastern European politics. In the next few weeks it could be seen clearly that the British Government erred in its estimation of some of the facts. This can be seen in the book of documents by Professor Namier, entitled *Diplomatic Prelude 1938–1939,* published in London in 1948. Contrary to prevailing opinion in London, Poland was by no means inclined to throw herself unconditionally into the arms of the Western Powers, but the cunning Colonel Beck, between his two menacing neighbors, wished to try for safety as soundly as possible. Furthermore, London did not realize that in Poland there was more dislike and anxiety with regard to Russia than there was with regard to Germany. Besides, the pact with Poland was a political creation lacking the skeleton of precise promises of military aid.

These organic deficiencies soon became apparent to such a realistic partner as the Soviet Union. The Union, remembering that it would, in case of war, have to bear the main brunt, insisted on the incorporation of the Baltic States in the Russian sphere of influence, for strategic as well as well as for imperialistic reasons. Above all, Russia broached the question of a march through Poland in case of her participation in a war against Germany. But this touched a dangerous spot in the Eastern European defense front. The Baltic States could not be abandoned by the Western Powers when they stood for the independence of small nations. So, far from allowing the Russian colossus voluntarily into their lands, the Poles resolutely and passionately resisted.

Whilst the negotiations between the Western Powers and their Eastern partners were threatened with increasing difficulties, London provoked the irritation of Moscow by technical mistakes. The dispatch of the tried and expert Sir William Strang to the negotiations which were held in the Russian capital was reluctantly accepted by the Soviet Government, who had expected a negotiator of Cabinet rank. And when subsequently British and French officers were sent to Moscow to take part in the military discussions, leading personalities were not selected. On top of all this the British military mission did not travel to its destination by air, but lost ten days because it travelled by sea. And all this happened despite the replacement of Litvinov by Molotov in May, which signified an undoubted departure of the Kremlin from its westerly course during the last few years. The resumption of German-Soviet trade negotiations in July should have served as a further warning signal. And on top of this the British Government, and especially Lord Vansittart, were informed by members of the German resistance group in the Foreign Office of the coming negotiations and the possibility of a pact. When, therefore, the French and British military missions to Moscow replied with cautious general phrases to Voroshilov's precise questions on the kind and extent of their military co-operations in case of a war, it was not surprising that the Russian Marshal gave the haughty reply that such declarations were of no value.

The British public took an enormous interest in the ups and downs of the Moscow negotiations. Chamberlain's declaration in the Commons on May 26 that unity had been attained in important points was greeted with loud cheers, and Molotov's cold speech a few days later with disciplined disappointment. Intentional insults, such as Zhdanov's letter in *Pravda*, that the British and French Governments did not want an agreement with the Soviet Union on the basis of equality of rights, were accepted. But gradually disappointment made itself felt in the columns of the newspapers, and on July 14 the *Manchester Guardian* summed up the prevailing feelings in London with the sentence, "Here we can perceive that the Russian procrastination is one of method."

These two predominating currents—the course of the negotiations with the Eastern European countries and the determination of going to war in case of further German aggressions—influenced the development of Anglo-German relations in the summer of 1939 on a large scale. Even if the negative basis of Hitler and Ribbentrop had not for the time being enforced reserve upon me, the atmosphere which I found in London had a like effect. Therefore I considered it correct to wait for a resumption of personal contacts until the initiative came from the other side. I had many experiences of the press's falsely attributing to me the initiative for discussions with the Foreign Office. Their reports were often unfavorable to Germany. I also had to avoid unnecessarily weakening my own position in Berlin. At length contact was made at a luncheon, arranged in the home of the Parliamentary Under-Secretary of State, Butler, at which, besides myself, there were present Lord Halifax and our Embassy's Counsellor Kordt. In a conference, lasting several hours, a balance was struck in consequence of the change in the political situation and the possibilities of a *détente*. During this and further interviews I took three standpoints which seemed vital to me in those days: of warning the British side of the dangers which their policy of encirclement would bring; of seeking means of a settlement, or a constructive *détente;* and, above all, of pointing out to the German authorities the gravity of the position and the resolution of the British public.

To Halifax and to other British statesmen and politicians I pointed out above all that Britain, through her unconditional guarantee to Poland, had put herself entirely into the hands of her new allies. Theoretically, it might be possible for some Polish magnate or military party to cause an incident, automatically resulting in a state of war. For raids by adventurers Poland's history of the last twenty years offered sufficient examples, such as the conquest of Vilna by General Zeligowski, the Korfanty's raid in Upper Silesia, and Pilsudski's march on Kiev. I did not then know that Pilsudski had proposed a preventive war against Germany in 1933 and 1936. To this warning of a grant of a blank check to Poland, I added the hint that the construction of a front, now begun by the British Government in opposition to aggression, would be felt by the entire German public like a reinforcement of the encirclement policy. The memory of this lay deep in every German consciousness and would arouse the resolve to avert this danger and prevent a repetition of 1914. As a further obstacle to all attempts at a *détente* there was Chamberlain's ever-tightening ring of declarations, opposed by ever-increasing Polish refusals to grant any concession whatsoever. But the greatest difficulty lay in the press, which whipped up public opinion so that any attempted settlement was at once branded as treason.

Vis-à-vis Berlin, my task consisted in pointing out with all emphasis the gravity of the situation and ridding the authorities of the fatal belief that Britain did not take her duties as a guarantor seriously. How I undertook this may be seen from the following extracts from my reports. On July 10 I reported to the Foreign Office, "In short, it may be said that anti-German sentiment is on the increase, that a readiness for war has hardened, that the feeling is, 'we must not put up with anything further, our honor is at stake, we must fight, the Government must not give way.' The articles in the German press about a decadent Britain, about her lack of will to fight, largely contributed to the British attitude." "It would be wrong to conclude from this that Great Britain was drifting irrevocably into a war. Within the Cabinet, and by a small but influential circle of politicians, efforts are being made to initiate a constructive policy with regard to Germany in place of the negative effects of encirclement." In a subsequent report of July 24 I stated that the prevailing sentiment in the highest Government circles was that "an understanding with Germany was still the most desirable and highest aim against the alternative of a war, waged with the utmost reluctance, but considered inevitable unless an agreement with Germany is achieved."

On July 31 I repeated my warning with regard to prevailing opinion in London: "that Anglo-German tension would move towards war unless an effort were made to reach an agreement." This train of thought was endorsed by detailed press reports from Dr. Hesse, who used all other available channels such as visitors and private letters and passed them on to Berlin.

My greatest difficulty lay in answering the question, how an attempted *détente* on a constructive plan, and without the press, could be started. Such attempts would only have a chance if they were submitted to Hitler direct without the knowledge of Ribbentrop. Finally, I remembered an expression he had once used: that it would be easy to settle all differences with Great Britain if he could have the opportunity of conversing, in German, for about two hours with a sensible Englishman. In my opinion there was a grain of truth in this remark. Hitler reacted strongly to personality, and one important condition for the success of such an interview was the guarantee of direct conversation with someone with a complete mastery of the German language. Chamberlain and Sir Horace Wilson fulfilled neither of these conditions, besides being strongly representative of the old school and liable to suspicion on account of their official status. While looking round for men who might be suitable for such a task I thought of Admiral Lord Chatfield, or of Lord Lothian, Ambassador Designate for Washington, or of the Parliamentary Under-Secretary-of-State in the Foreign Office, Mr. Butler. Lord Chatfield, with whom I had had several conversations, fascinated me by his straight, soldierly, and statesmanlike bearing. Besides, Hitler always got on best with the military men. Lord Lothian, who had always been in favor of an understanding with Germany, commanded respect by his character and appearance. Butler, as representative of the younger generation, combined sagacity with a pleasing manner and an assured bearing. But none of these three had much command of German. If necessary I thought that this condition could be raised, the personal impressions being decisive. I put these ideas to some acquaintances in influential posts. Sir Horace Wilson told me that someone of prominence in economic life was being considered. An exchange of views which I had with Chamberlain, through a middleman, gave no concrete results.

These attempts ended in nothing but the conferences of Herr Wohlthat and myself with Sir Horace Wilson. These conferences brought about the final phases in Anglo-German relations before the outbreak of war.

It was a wide and tangled state of affairs which, in July, 1939, caused the British Government to make a renewed attempt at clarification, on a broad basis, of outstanding points of controversy. This intention met with just as great difficulties as did the purely technical question of initiating and subsequently of continuing the negotiations. Public opinion and the press were hostile to Germany and distrusted her. Only in early July, a short but violent crisis had shaken the world, when the American press reported from Warsaw that Hitler would attack Poland from Danzig. Just as in the Czechoslovak week-end crisis, a week-end was also chosen, although it was just a rumor which was soon exposed by the facts. But the outbreak of an excitement that was almost a panic proved that only a spark was needed to bring about an explosion.

Despite the general hostility to negotiations for a mutual arrangement, the initiative of the Cabinet was probably the result of experience gathered during the last months. The attempts to create a counter-front on Germany's eastern flank resulted in great disappointments. The Soviet Government was more opposed to this front than ever. Its difference with Poland became ever more acute. General Ironside's report on the condition of the Polish Army raised many doubts. The effects of the encirclement policy on peace were seen more and more clearly. A difficult conflict with Japan which threatened British prestige was in progress. Some international *détente* by means of a compromise with Germany, or at least a clarification of the issue between war and peace, seemed desirable.

Chamberlain's Cabinet considered Great Britain's position during the prospective negotiations to be more favorable than it had been in the previous year, owing to completion of rearmament. She no longer had to yield to threats from Hitler, and could take it for granted that he would be aware of his own weaker position.

But above everything else, domestic affairs drove the British Government to seek a rapid clarification of relations with Germany.

A general election was due in the autumn. By then Chamberlain would have to stand before the electors with the clear alternative: either "the compromise with Germany has been successful," or "we must prepare for war with Germany." I was plainly told by both Lord Halifax and Sir Horace Wilson that Parliament and public would accept either of these solutions unanimously. Hitler, too, heard it from the British press magnate Lord Kemsley in a long conversation with him during the Bayreuth Festival.

Thus the British Cabinet had the unusually difficult task of carrying through a dual foreign policy. On the one hand there were the negotiations with Moscow, which had to be kept alive; on the other hand, a compromise on a broad front had to be reached with Germany. If the compromise failed, the formation of an Eastern front would have to be achieved. If it succeeded, the Moscow negotiations would lose their importance. In view of the excited feelings in Britain, contact with Germany had to be made with the utmost secrecy. The first contact was made through Herr Wohlthat, who was in London during these weeks as German delegate to the International Whaling Conference. He enjoyed respect as a collaborator of Doctor Schacht, as a master of the English language, and as an experienced negotiator. By mediation of the Norwegian delegate to the Whaling Conference, Hudson, the Minister for Overseas Trade, approached him and proposed a meeting. Wohlthat, after referring the matter to me, accepted the proposal. During these conversations Wohlthat kept in closest touch with me. Hudson developed far-reaching plans for a joint Anglo-German working arrangement for opening up new markets or expanding existing ones. According to him, there were, in particular, three large territories with enormous possibilities for the participation of both countries—the Empire, China, and Russia. The Empire could not be supplied by Britain alone, nor could China be supplied only by Japan. Here, as also in Russia, there was a possibility for Germany to take part in vast economic activities. Furthermore, Hudson suggested a delineation of mutual spheres of interest and the elimination of competition in third markets. At Sir Horace Wilson's instance, two further conferences followed. That Chamberlain approved of these plans, and had possibly worked them out himself, was shown by the proposal that he should meet Wohlthat so as to endorse the program. Wohlthat, however, did not agree to this suggestion, fearing lest his confidential conversations might thereby assume a political character.

The program developed by Sir Horace Wilson embraced in its entirety the mutual relations of both countries. It was not only confined to the economic sphere, but extended also to political and military matters. It dealt with the Colonial problem and included proposals for the purchase of raw materials for Germany. It provided financial arrangements for the two countries, it referred to a settlement of international debts, and took Hudson's ideas into account. The further working out of the program was left to the German side. The decisive question was: would Hitler authorize the appointment of a suitable person to take charge of the negotiations?

The conversations had only gone thus far when a crossfire began. Somehow or other British journalists had obtained wind of Hudson's initiative (according to our own investigations, *via* the French Embassy), and they now obtained from the Minister some rather unwise statements which were to stir up British public opinion. Of greatest effect was the news, quite without foundation, of a British thousand million loan to Germany. The Prime Minister had to reply to some embarrassing questions in Parliament. But a threat to the Cabinet was avoided, and the conference was not ended.

Ribbentrop reacted at once when my own and Wohlthat's reports reached Berlin. In two telegrams he demanded an immediate report on the political questions which Wohlthat had raised with my permission. Wohlthat had apparently omitted to ask Wilson whether the proposals were to be considered as an abandonment of the negotiations (especially with Moscow) for an encirclement of Germany. I was prepared for such an attack. I referred him to my report and pointed out how Wohlthat had confined himself to economic questions. I summarized the initiative taken by Hudson and Wilson under three headings: (1) Anglo-German tension was moving towards a war; (2) the encirclement policy involved Britain in considerable risks; (3) the state of British rearmament permitted the Government to seek a compromise without being suspected of weakness.

That the importance of the British proposals was recognized by persons less warlike than Ribbentrop was shown by Göring's reaction to Wohlthat's report. As has only recently become known, though his adjutant-in-chief, Göring visited Hitler three times in August, earnestly urging him to avoid getting entangled in a war, seeing that a complete compromise with Britain on the basis of Wohlthat's reported offers would bring to Germany the fulfillment of her claims. Hitler, of course, repulsed him. But this episode is significant, showing that in August Göring did not believe in the inevitability of war, on the assumption that Hitler, in his incalculable manner, took irrevocable decisions only at the last moment. This frees those working unceasingly for peace from charges of quixotic behavior.

During the next few days the Wilson-Hudson ideas were carried into the Embassy from quite another quarter. An important member of the Labor Party, Mr. Charles Roden Buxton, who had nothing to do with the political machine, visited Kordt, the Counsellor of the German Embassy, and had a long conference with him. He, too, held the opinion that the only alternative in Anglo-German relations was "war or an understanding." He also considered attempts at a compromise would be possible only if carried through in secret. His proposals were mainly political, and went further than Sir Horace Wilson's. He proposed a limitation of spheres of interest for both powers. Great Britain would respect the German sphere of activity in Eastern and Southern Europe and would rescind all claims under guarantees given to the countries in those regions. Efforts would have to be made to induce France to rescind her alliance with Russia, and the pact negotiations under discussion with the Soviet Union would be dropped. Germany on her part would have to refrain from all interference in the affairs of the Empire and declare herself ready for European co-operation. She would also have to consent to general disarmament. Although Buxton played no immediate or active part in any negotiations, or even stated with whom he had discussed these ideas, his visit showed how broad was the basis upon which Wilson's offers rested.

To give the discussions an official status, Sir Horace Wilson invited me to a conference. It was held in his private residence on August 3 and lasted for two hours. With circumstantial details he disclosed his program, which had already been proposed to Wohlthat. It fell into three sections: political, military, and economic. The conclusion of a non-aggression as also of a non-interference pact was provided for. The military question was not so much a general disarmament as a policy of armament limitations. The economic negotiations were to be for an increase in foreign trade, keeping in view Germany's special position in respect of the South-East; the increase of supplies of raw materials, the Colonial problem, and finally financial aspects.

The political problem was at the root of our conversation. The proposals raised a question which demanded an answer. I put the question to Sir Horace Wilson: how would such a far-reaching program for negotiations and a pact be brought into consonance with other obligations undertaken by Great Britain? Sir Horace wanted to undo the knot by beginning with a non-aggression agreement. If both powers renounced all aggressive actions as a political method, Great Britain would be set free from the responsibilities which she had undertaken, seeing that they would only come into force in the event of an attack. Germany could then put forward her claims to Poland by way of direct negotiations. His main idea was that by bringing about an Anglo-German agreement on all vital questions, the rigidity of the international situation would be relaxed, so that questions relating to Eastern Europe—to Danzig and Poland, for example—would recede into the background. He expected a minor but nevertheless considerable effect from the non-interference stipulation. The Führer had already made such a stipulation in his speech of April 28. On Britain's part there would be readiness to enter into such a treaty. The Danzig question could also be subject to it.

A detailed *exposé* on the tense situation, resulting from martial preparations on both sides, was added to the agreement program. The possibility of crossfire from the press was also referred to. Indiscretions would severely menace the Cabinet, and Sir Horace Wilson emphasized the conviction that the only antidote would be secret negotiations in Switzerland. The moment an understanding had been attained, the danger-point would be passed. Wilson insisted that Hitler would have to prove, soon and plainly, his readiness for negotiations and that every further aggravation of the situation would have to be avoided. That I was unable to give him any information as to the reception which his proposals to Wohlthat found in Berlin was a disappointment to him. He left no doubts that the alternative to the failure of the negotiations would be a drift towards catastrophe.

Thus ended the conference, kept secret until after the war. I sent a detailed report on the conversations to Berlin on the same day. The action of the British Government, which reached its zenith by this proposal, made me ask myself: were these overtures really serious? Or were they meant to serve merely to gain time while the position in Eastern Europe was clarified? Were the obligations, which Germany was to undertake to bring about an accord, not rather unreal? When I retrospectively surveyed the consequences of the intractable Eastern negotiations and considered that, in view of the coming general election, a clarification with Germany had become necessary one way or the other, I came to the conclusion that I could express my full confidence in Chamberlain and in the initiative of his Cabinet. In view of the ever-increasing threat of war, Chamberlain, as a responsible statesman, felt obliged to make one last and desperate attempt for the preservation of peace. And even if this attempt failed, as the result of Hitler's irresponsibility, the fault would have been clearly proved to be his up to the last moment. During my term of office in London Hitler did not once trouble to respond to Britain's offers, not even for form's sake. He never even replied to them. The historical significance of Chamberlain's last peace efforts consists in this: they placed the onus on Hitler's shoulders.

It was clear to me that only a personal explanation in Berlin could possibly give weight to my reports, perhaps with Wohlthat's co-operation. I therefore applied for leave, which was granted the more readily as Ribbentrop had the intention of removing me again from my post in any case. I said good-bye to Lord Halifax. During a long conversation we discussed the tension between our two countries. The Minister for Foreign Affairs expressed his disappointment at the development of events. After Munich he had felt convinced that peace had been assured for fifty years on the following basis: Germany would be the predominant power on the Continent, with a priority of economic rights in Southeastern Europe, while Britain would be occupied with the care of her empire and the safety of sea communications to the Far East. The march into Prague had destroyed all these hopes. Halifax endorsed the fact that Parliament and public were as ready to undertake a war as to come to a compromise with Germany.

I arrived in Berlin probably on August 13. On the day before, Ciano had had a conference with Ribbentrop in Fuschl and had then returned to Italy. A gloomy and depressed atmosphere prevailed in the Foreign Office. Rumors were current that as a result of conversations with Ribbentrop, Hitler's firm determination had revealed itself. It was to seize the very first opportunity for war with Poland. The Secretary of State von Weizsäcker did not express himself clearly in this respect, but his deep pessimism was obvious. I immediately asked about the effects of my two telegrams concerning Sir Horace Wilson's proposals. Weizsäcker shrugged his shoulders and made a motion as though he were wiping something off the table. And so a proposal which should have been examined with the utmost care, even if not considered trustworthy, was simply thrown into the waste-paper basket by Hitler and Ribbentrop. I learned, furthermore, that Wohlthat's report on his London conversations had been taken as an illustration of British public sentiment. My report on the conference with Sir Horace Wilson had been interpreted as a further sign of Britain's weakness. Had I had any further doubts about this experience, they would have been expunged by Ribbentrop's behavior to me. I called on his secretaries, asking them to fix a day and hour for an appointment. I further requested them to telephone to Obersalzburg for an interview with Hitler. I was informed that Ribbentrop was in his summer residence in Fuschl, near Salzburg, and that I would receive a further communication. The Secretary of State supported my request for an interview with Ribbentrop, by a special letter addressed to the Minister. Subsequently he read out to me the words in his letter which summarized my reports, especially those on the attitude of Britain in the event of a German-Polish war.

A few days later I called upon the Chief of Staff, General Halder, and gave him my London impressions, which he fully shared. Halder emphasized the urgency of a talk with Hitler. I replied that I had already taken the requisite steps, but that for over a year the Führer had shown a disinclination to receive me.

From the Ministry of War I went to the Italian Embassy to look up my former Moscow colleague, as well as friend, Ambassador Attolico. He was just on the point of flying to Rome, where Mussolini had ordered him to come. Attolico was excited and agitated and said without further prelude that he would have to speak to me as "a friend to a friend." During the conference with Ciano, resolutions had been taken which could easily lead to a war with Poland. They had been based on the erroneous supposition that Britain would not take part. I expressed my doubts as to the accuracy of this statement, as Britain's participation in the event of such a conflict would surely have been taken into account. Attolico urged me to change the convictions that prevailed in high quarters. I replied that I was trying to do just that.

During the following days no reply came from the Foreign Minister to my request. It was clear that he did not want to speak to me. That he did not mind offering me a personal insult did not surprise me in any way. But I had not considered him so bereft of intelligence as to refuse to receive me for a formal farewell visit, so incurring the suspicion that he did not want to be told how matters really stood. With the consent of the Secretary of State, I went to Gröditzberg, to await further developments. Before my departure I called upon Kriebel, the head of the Staff Department, and told him that under existing circumstances I had no further desire for employment in the Foreign Service and asked him to be retired. My request was granted a few months later.

As I felt the load of responsibility which I bore and saw no possibility of making a verbal report, I resolved after my arrival in Gröditzberg to place before the Minister in a short *exposé* the standpoint which Britain would adopt in the event of a war with Poland. With the knowledge that Ribbentrop would utilize every defect in the *exposé* to discredit my point of view, I considered its form very carefully. I had, in particular, to beware of making inaccurate prophecies as to Britain's entry into the war. But obviously I had to give a possible instance of how Britain would act under the terms of her treaty obligations. Like a red thread through my *exposé* there was the certainty that Britain, after her numerous diplomatic defeats of past years and after her desertion of Negus, Schuschnigg, and Benes, would be anxious to prove her loyalty to treaties, her strength, and her good name. Britain was not vitally interested in the fate of Danzig, but she would assuredly honor political drafts drawn upon her. That is why Britain would not be a silent spectator in any forcible annexation of Danzig by Germany, not to mention other territories, but would consider the point of the alliance to have arisen.

Analyzing in detail the causes of conflict, I stated definitely: If Poland did not reply by military action to a possible resolution of the Danzig Senate, Britain would stand aloof. If Poland replied to such a resolution of the Senate by military action and invoked the relevant clause in the treaty of alliance, Britain would come to Poland's aid by force of arms. In case of a provocative Polish action, such as a bombardment of a German village, ascertainment of the facts and the conviction of Poland's entire responsibility would be of decisive importance. Otherwise there would be the danger of Britain's taking part in favor of Poland. Should Germany, for military reasons, see herself forced to proceed against Poland, Britain's assistance to Poland would have to be reckoned with. It would be improbable that Britain would remain neutral should Poland be brought to a military defeat within a short time. In that case, too, the decision would not depend on Poland's welfare, but on preservation of her standing in the world. A factor to be taken into account when considering Britain's general attitude would be that she felt the need to counteract the widely disseminated opinion that Britain is decadent, unreliable, and weak. I sent this *exposé* to Weizsäcker with a request to forward it to Ribbentrop. He confirmed a little later that it had reached him.

My official career ended with a significant event. Weizsäcker telephoned to me that Ribbentrop had instructed him to express his disapproval of what I had said in my conversation with Attolico. Should there be a repetition of this, strong measures would be adopted against me. Evidently Attolico had telegraphed to Rome that I had complained about my vain efforts to be received by Hitler and Ribbentrop and the telegram had been decoded. Or else a microphone had been installed in the embassy. That

Ribbentrop's unceasing suspicion of myself never ended until the final period of the war was proved six years later in February, 1945.

Again and again I was occupied with the thought whether Hitler and Ribbentrop really believed that Britain, contrary to the obligations which she had undertaken, would not come to Poland's aid in the event of a German attack. There can be no doubt that they received warnings from the most diverse quarters with regard to Britain's participation in a war. In view of Hitler's fanatical obstinacy and his complete ignorance of foreign countries, such self-deception may have been possible. But not so in Ribbentrop's case, for he had had experience of foreign countries and, in his own reports, had even pointed out Britain's increasing readiness for war. He must have known that Britain would not allow herself to be played with when it came to a question of her own position in the world. But his behavior, when Britain's declaration of war became known, suggests that he had not expected it. As was reliably reported by a witness (the interpreter Schmidt, if I remember right), Ribbentrop is said to have come out of Hitler's room quite overcome by Britain's declaration of war and to have asked, almost beside himself, "What are we to do now?" The explanation may be found in Erich Kordt's book, *Illusion or Reality*, in which he reports that Ribbentrop had forbidden all expressions of the opinion that Britain would participate in the war. Anybody speaking like that was either in the pay of, or under the influence of, the British Secret Service. Possibly Ribbentrop had deceived himself into the belief that nothing could happen to affect Hitler's and his plans of attack. After the conclusion of the Hitler-Stalin Pact this belief would doubtless have been further strengthened. But no matter whether he and Hitler disbelieved that Britain would keep her pledges, or whether they only made a pretense of disbelieving, it is certain that they were responsible for a criminal lack of judgment which, in their own jargon, was "unique."

---

6. CONCLUDING REMARKS

It is quite clear to me that this chapter on my London mission makes unpleasant reading. Although it embraces a highly tragic, dramatic, and fateful epoch in which I took part at a focal point in a responsible post, this account only represents a number of separate incidents, following one another without a connecting *leitmotif*. Lack of co-operation between Berlin's central nerves and the London Embassy; vain efforts of the British

Government to win Hitler over to a policy of moderation; corresponding efforts on my part to convince my superiors of the necessity of coming to an understanding with Great Britain; warning upon warning that renewed aggression would lead to war; attempts to divert Hitler and Ribbentrop from their mistaken view that Great Britain was too decadent and hesitant for a struggle; my awareness that no attention was being paid to my advice, and that I was used as a screen behind which Hitler and his associates concealed their aggressive intentions—all these were frustrating.

Despite personal humiliations, the part I played to the very bitter end resulted in complete failure. Assuredly my opposite, Sir Nevile Henderson, was justified when he complained of "The Failure of a Mission," the significant title which he gave to his book. He, however, had the support of his Government; they fought jointly in a good cause and lost the battle.

It was characteristic of my London mission that there was no cohesion in my work. It was atomized into separate episodes. I came to despair of final results as I realized the growing ill will of the leading men in Berlin. But I had to place the incidents on record just as they occurred.

The tragedy which overwhelmed mankind in September, 1939, is too immense to permit this chapter to end with complaints of personal failures and inadequacies. I therefore consider it my duty to add a few further remarks on how this catastrophe could have been avoided.

To my mind, the outbreak of war between Germany and Great Britain bears the symbol of a real tragedy in the classic sense of the word for mankind in general, apart from the outbreak of the war as such. The circumstances and character of the leading personalities at the time made the catastrophe inevitable, a catastrophe that could have been avoided a decade earlier. The tragedy came because there was nowhere on the world's stage a statesman able to make a lasting peace when the general European situation, the German situation above all, was favorable to permanent peace. When the statesman with the necessary courage and perspicacity undertook the leadership for so herculean a task in Great Britain, the conditions of success were not present. In other words, the tragedy of the Anglo-German war is also the tragedy of Neville Chamberlain.

Serious historians can have no doubt that the responsible Germans during the Weimar period were sincere, honest men who tried to rule their homeland in accordance with the democratic principles of the Western Powers and so to integrate Germany, once again, into the European community. They were ready to bear the load left to them by the régime of William II and by the defeat of Germany in the First World War. But they were forced to insist, and did in fact insist, that President Wilson's Fourteen Points must be taken into consideration, and that the terms of the Treaty of Versailles, which proved too severe and, indeed, impossible to carry out, should be altered by way of peaceful negotiation. In consequence of this general political conception they made the Locarno offer and joined the League of Nations. The Ruhr was occupied. Germany's confidence in the Western Powers, which found expression in the Treaty of Locarno, awakened no response, or if it did, too late and insufficient a response. Large districts of Germany remained under Allied occupation. Equality in respect to armaments was refused. So was disarmament. An appeal to Article 19 of the Covenant of the League of Nations, providing for revision of treaty terms no longer compatible with existing circumstances, was proscribed. The timid effort of two straight and honest men, Curtius and Schober, to bring about an Austro-German Customs Union was stifled in embryo in a drastic manner. During these fourteen years statesmanlike leadership on the part of the Allies was completely lacking. Had Chamberlain been in office during those days, his endeavors to fit Germany into the European comity of nations would have been successful. Only a fraction of the concessions which he was ready to make in 1938 and 1939 would have sufficed to fulfill the hopes and wishes cherished during the Weimar days. His energy and tenacity would have caused France to adopt a similar attitude.

When Chamberlain was called upon to take up the Premiership, an irrevocable development had come to an end. The disappointments in the field of foreign affairs had changed the sympathetic current in Germany into skepticism. Inflation destroyed the fortunes of the middle classes and radicalized a conservative element. The resultant revolution altered the social structure of Germany. The change was hastened by an economic crisis which drove more than one-third of the population on the dole. The result was a cleft between the radicalism of the Right and the radicalism of the Left. It ended in National Socialism and Communism, and so condemned to failure the efforts of the "Third Power," the Brüning, Papen, and Schleicher Cabinets, which received no support from either of the two radical currents. There remained only the choice between revolution of the Right or revolution of the Left. The German nation chose the former, without realizing that both methods would lead to the same result.

With the seizure of power by National Socialism, other principles came into force in shaping Germany's destiny, namely, the laws of revolution. Men of different caliber were washed up to the surface and occupied commanding positions. Fanatical revolutionaries, thoughtless demagogues, disregardful of law, decency, or the well-being of the nation, steered it on a course bound to lead to disaster. It is the German people's tragedy that this company of revolutionaries was not replaced by men of the second and moderate line, as is the usual course of revolutions. It was Chamberlain's tragedy that he came to power too late to carry out his plans, which were sound in themselves; that he trusted men who were not statesmen, aware of their responsibilities, but nihilists, fanatics, and mad revolutionaries.

Let the precept be taken to heart by statesmen of the post-war period, that the erection of a new Europe must be brought about before the voice of post-war Germany, a Germany willing to co-operate, has died away.

VI
War and Catastrophe

---

1. THE SECOND WORLD WAR

So my career as a civil servant came to an end after thirty-seven years. I felt relieved and embittered at the same time: relieved that my connection with a Government which had become abhorrent to me had been severed; embittered by the treatment I had received. I decided to abstain from any intercourse whatever with the Berlin authorities and to retire to the country. Consequently I spent only a few days in the capital twice or thrice a year. I even avoided visiting my old colleagues in the Foreign Office. The only friend whom I met to exchange ideas and information was Moltke, until he was appointed Ambassador to Madrid, where he succumbed to appendicitis a few months later.

On the other hand, I was happy to return to Gröditzberg for good and to devote myself to a long-neglected task. The general condition of the estate was now most satisfactory, as the measures taken by me after the death of my father had been successful. The mortgages had been redeemed entirely, with the sacrifice, however, of the sale of almost one half of the original area. The greater part of the remaining 1,100 hectares consisted of forest, but the 300 hectares of farmland were cultivated so intensely—46 per cent with sugar beets and potatoes—that 120 head of cattle and 200 pigs could be kept. The intensive method of farming was further enhanced by an ample stock of agricultural machines, by a distillery and special cultivation of vegetables. Market gardening was also extended and contributed up to 33 per cent of the proceeds of the estate.

I was able to rely entirely on my employees. Nearly all of them had for decades been in the service of my father and myself. The two keepers, aged forty and thirty, and the farm hands, grandfather, father, and son of one family, worked together during these years in cultivating the grounds. Even with the Polish farm hands satisfactory relations prevailed throughout, as they were voluntary workers hired by their foreman, and not conscript labor. For ten years I had entrusted the administration to a reliable and efficient man who was advised and supervised by my former general manager and friend, Herr Cronemeyer.

Thus, so far as my part in the management of Gröditzberg was concerned, I could limit myself to controlling and supervising. I was the less tempted to interfere amateurishly with the routine as I had, since my childhood, observed that agriculture is one of the most difficult and complicated human activities in which only those men are successful who have a blend of learning, experience, and some sort of instinct to do the right thing at the right moment. But quite apart from the human side of agriculture, the process of production is, compared with industry, subject to a double risk: the risk of manufacturing finished goods and the risk of being frustrated by the vicissitudes of the weather.

Though abstaining from amateurish interference, I had the satisfactory conviction that my presence and my supervising activity were almost indispensable. I felt that wisdom of the old proverb, *"Das Auge des Herrn schafft doppelte Ernten"* ("The eye of the proprietor creates a twofold harvest"). Above all, it fell to my lot to safeguard my interest and those of the estate in the constant friction with a government which aimed at an ever-growing curtailment of the rights of the proprietor. In this respect an episode is characteristic which very nearly led to the expropriation of Gröditzberg and to my expatriation from my home.

Endeavors were made to exploit the productive capacities of Germany to the utmost in quest of complete autarchy. This was the aim of Göring's Four-Year Plan. A quest for all the mineral wealth of the country was in progress. Geologists had discovered copper in the vicinity of Gröditzberg, and though this ore was low grade, amounting only to barely 2 per cent, it was deemed sufficient to start production and to build a copper mine, foundries, and refinery. As the site for the housing of the workmen and their families, Gröditzberg had been chosen. Along the mountain slope and through the forest a model city was to be constructed for 40,000 inhabitants. The plans had been laid out; a miniature replica had been made and was to be exhibited in Goerlitz, a city in Lower Silesia, which Hitler was to visit on the occasion of a rally. What would have been left of my estate had these projects been realized were two comparatively small strips of land east and west of the "Josef Wagnerstadt," as this town was to be christened, thus perpetuating the name of the *Gauleiter* of Silesia.

Thus far matters had progressed when I got wind of the affair in London in the spring of 1938. It now became evident that for months prospectors had been roaming through my estate in search of copper and of an appropriate site for the town. Neither my representative in Germany during my absence in Japan, Herr Cronemeyer, nor anybody else had been warned.

Home on leave of absence from London in the summer of 1938, I called a conference of the authorities concerned, above all the President of the District and ambitious originator of the whole scheme, the President of the Chamber of Commerce in Breslau. I was rather outspoken and condemned the methods employed in this case as a "stab in the back" during my absence on duty. Happily, the surprise, aimed at obtaining Hitler's blessing, failed, as he had no time to visit the exhibition with the miniature replica of the copper city. Thus I gained time to prepare a counterattack, demonstrating to the authorities concerned that the location of the settlement was entirely unsuited for various reasons, such as the long distance from the shafts and the foundry, and that other much more suitable sites were to be found elsewhere. When a closer examination of the exact places where the copper was to be found disclosed the fact that the main arteries led away from Gröditzberg, I won my point. The settlement was to be built elsewhere. Millions of marks were spent in this "gigantic" project without any tangible results. The shafts got flooded, the construction of the foundry had to be slowed down through deficiency of materials, and the copper remained unexploited. This episode was not only of vital importance for me, it was also symtomatic of the methods of the National Socialist Government and its utter disrespect for the rights of the individual citizens.

Having overcome this crisis I managed to avoid further entanglements with the State or party. In my private life also I steered the course which I had followed during the years of my official life. Being a member of the party and attending official functions and festivities, I gave no opportunity for concealed or open attack. On the contrary, the authorities were obviously relieved that one of the more important proprietors of the district was not openly hostile to the party.

Hostility towards the system prevailed amongst the upper classes in town and country. In contrast with this attitude of the former "ruling class," the overwhelming majority of the rural population in Silesia (and in the other Eastern provinces), as well as in the smaller cities, remained loyal to the core to National Socialism to the bitter end. A characteristic episode will illustrate this assertion. Count Yorck von Wartenburg, a brother of Frau von Moltke, the wife of my friend and colleague, had been involved in the plot of July 20, 1944, and had been executed. The disgust over his action developed to such an intensity, even in the village adjoining the Moltkes' estate, where his family had lived for decades, respected and popular, that Frau von Moltke and her children suffered grave inconveniences.

The unbounded affection and loyalty towards Hitler prevalent among broad masses of the population was one of the main reasons which filled me with skepticism as to an attempt to free Germany from the shackles of the Nazi régime by killing Hitler. Even now I am of the opinion that even if he had been killed, a terrible civil war would have followed, simultaneously with successful attacks by the enemy forces against a front which would have been disintegrated by this inner strife. Without being backed by the adversary and unable to promise a more lenient peace in case of the overthrow of Nazism, I am afraid that a still greater number of courageous men would have sacrificed their lives in vain, even if their plot against Hitler had succeeded.

The problem of a conspiracy against the head of the State in time of war is of a highly complicated moral and spiritual nature. Whatever may be said about it, the participants of the conspiracy, when it came, were animated by the highest patriotism. They showed supreme courage up to the last moment of their lives, and faced a cruel death unbroken. Their farewell letters, some of which have been published, will rank among the most exalted human documents.

As I was absent from Berlin and the other centers of the Resistance movement, the problem whether to participate or not did not directly enter my orbit. I was, as I have said, not inclined to take the initiative. Intimations of this opposition reached me twice. Once an acquaintance of mine, a great landowner from Upper Silesia, a former deputy of the Prussian Diet and well known in Berlin social and political circles, visited me in the spring of 1943. He said that friends of his in Berlin requested me to accept the post of Foreign Minister, as some changes were due. I replied that Ribbentrop was still in office and the post not vacant, and that if some sort of revolution or conspiracy were planned and under way I did not believe in this form of improving matters. I would not have given a different answer even if the offer had been based on a more solid foundation. As it was, I harbored the suspicion that my friend was a spokesman of the Union Club, the fashionable club in Berlin where much gossiping and political scheming took place. General Hoeppner, executed after July 20, was a frequent visitor to this club even after his arbitrary and unjust degradation by Hitler.

The second approach was still more tentative, though more serious as to its purpose. An acquaintance of mine, a well-known publicist and journalist, an old member of the party but now disgusted, urged me to come to Berlin and to re-enter the political arena. He visited me—in the summer of 1943—in Gröditzberg and explained that men of my experience ought to be more active and should not retire to the country. He asked me whether I knew General Beck and suggested that I should see him, as he was extremely well informed about everything. I followed up this line and broached the question when we met a few months later in Berlin. I assumed that he would arrange a meeting with General Beck. But as he seemed not so intimately acquainted with the General as to invite us together to a lunch or introduce me, I refrained from further initiative, as I had seen Beck only twice when paying my visits to the War Ministry. I had not the faintest idea that he was involved in the plot, just as I was not initiated into the fact that the opposition had already formed a definite nucleus.

As to the local dignitaries in Silesia, I observed my old tactics of avoiding personal intercourse as much as possible and limiting contact to official gatherings. Once or twice a year, when he came to Gröditzberg, I met the *Kreisleiter,* the party boss of the district, Goldberg, the typical narrow-minded official seething with secret resentment. A more interesting type, whom I studied closely, was the newly appointed *Gauleiter* of Silesia, Hanke. As he was nominated in Hitler's last will of April 30, 1945, as Himmler's successor, a short sketch of his personality may be of interest.

When he was appointed as *Oberpräsident* and *Gauleiter* of Silesia and so had the highest administrative and party posts in his hand, I hoped there might be an improvement of the general situation in the province. Hanke was a good-looking man in his thirties, frank and outspoken, without arrogance. Being a Silesian, he evidently felt a deep attachment for his home province. As Under-Secretary of State in the Propaganda Ministry he had quarrelled with his chief, Goebbels, had resigned his post, and had entered the army as a private. Brave in battle, he had been awarded the Iron Cross First Class and had been commissioned. In France he had been wounded.

When I met him at an official gathering, he said he wished to make contact with the great landowners. His views were moderate and reasonable, his demeanor decent. He was correct and sympathetic to the civil servants of the old school. But before long his attitude deteriorated towards radicalism and sumptuous living. He abused, without any foundation, one of the old civil servants in a great assembly. He relied more and more on the party bureaucracy. He ordered the construction of costly buildings, among them a night club, and he himself had six or seven houses. The longer the war lasted, the more powers were being invested in the *Gauleiters*. In 1944 the entirely useless construction of fortifications along the eastern frontier was entrusted to them. They were appointed commissars of defense with practically unlimited power over life and death. Hanke gradually developed into an Oriental despot who wantonly condemned to death several higher officials, among them the burgomaster of Breslau. He had them shot near the monument of Frederick the Great. Before Breslau surrendered to the Russians after a heroic siege, and in spite of being isolated from the Reich by hundreds of kilometres, Hanke left the town by plane for Czechoslovakia. Nothing has been heard of him since.

Often have I pondered over the almost inexplicable psychological change which Hanke underwent within a few years from a decent soldier-like man to a bloodthirsty and debauched despot. I agree with the explanation offered to me that he became a victim of the absolute power invested in him. Unaccustomed to the exercise of power and responsibility, he got drunk by this potent drug and became a criminal. Or, to repeat an epigram by Lord Acton, "All power tends to corrupt—and absolute power corrupts absolutely."

I also came in contact with another type of Nazi. He was Herr Streck-fuss, the chief of the N.S.K.K., the Nazi Automobile Corps, for Silesia. This was not a full-time job. He was, besides, the owner of a great mill, which had been awarded to him by the Nazis for his merits. As he had been appointed Japanese honorary Consul for Silesia and I was acting as the President of the German-Japanese Society, we had to work in close collaboration. He was a likable sort of person who, having succeeded in rising to the surface economically and socially, enjoyed the amenities of life. He kept me informed about the intentions and hopes cherished in the higher party circles.

Another type of Nazi was the *Landrat* of the district of Goldberg, to which Gröditzberg belonged. Herr Daluege, the brother of the notorious police general and "Protector" of Bohemia. He was an old party man and had developed from an orthodox adherent of Hitler to a fierce antagonist of the régime. He indulged in unrestricted criticism of men and measures prevalent in these days and was, therefore, removed to a less agreeable post. He was replaced by an official of the old school. But the influence of the State officials declined more and more, and the party bureaucracy emerged as the absolute dictator in the lower administrative districts as in Berlin.

I was too much imbued with politics to find full satisfaction in the administration of my estate. The momentous events going on in the world did not allow my utter seclusion. Though firmly resolved not to play an active rôle, I was equally intent on keeping in touch with the outer world and being informed about the trend of events within Germany and beyond her borders. The problem to be solved was how to achieve this without entering the limelight of publicity. As always in my life, I waited for a chance and seized it without forcing the issue.

The starting point was the Red Cross work my wife and I were doing. Requested by the Red Cross organization of the district, we toured almost all the small towns and villages of the *Kreis Goldberg*, delivering lectures about the foreign countries in which we had been living. My wife produced her films and I would add some appropriate remarks. The entrance fees went to the Red Cross fund. One of our first performances, in Goldberg, proved to be quite a success, especially some colored films displaying life in Great Britain, a cattle show, weekends, and London. The *Kreisleiter* beamed with delight and urged us to repeat these performances everywhere. A few days later, however, he rang me up rather meekly, and reported that some party comrades had raised objections to the British films as they gave a much too favorable impression of our arch-enemy. I consoled him and went on showing the film.

Having made our appearances in larger cities of Lower Silesia, I was was asked by some organizations to deliver lectures on a large scale about Russia, Japan, and Great Britain. I favored the *Gesellschaft für Wehrwissenschaft und Wehr Politik*. This was the leading society for military science, conducted in the spirit of the most famous German strategists, Generals Clausewitz, Moltke, and Schlieffen. This circle appealed to me as influential, important, and non-party. But occasionally I also delivered lectures for the *Volksbildungs Werk,* an organization built up by the party for disseminating knowledge about foreign countries and furthering education.

It was, in general, a useful and valuable institution, not at all based on narrow party lines. Scientists, explorers, and technicians from the most different walks of life were admitted as well as the stubborn representatives of the party. The most valuable feature of this institution was its voluntary character. The visitors had to pay entrance fees, and the audience was composed of worn-out housewives who turned up with their shopping-bags, as well as workers, artisans, and intellectuals. I was quite proud that my lectures were almost always crowded in spite of the fact I lack all rhetorical skill or fireworks, though able to speak in a matter-of-fact way and without notes. When inquiring why these people went to my lectures, I was answered that they were sick of party oratory and that they wanted instruction by objective speakers.

From 1942 onwards, when provincial organizations of the German-Japanese Society were set up, I was requested to deliver my lectures for this society throughout the Greater German Reich.

I had to refrain from controversial problems, as criticism was not allowed, and I was not inclined to express opinions which I did not share. Thus, I preferred Far-Eastern topics where little harm could be done. Delivering a lecture about the mental attitude of Russia, Great Britain, and Japan towards conscription and other military problems, I stressed Russia's preparedness and her determination to defend her soil so strongly that some of the officers in the audience—I was speaking in 1941 before the invasion of Russia to a gathering of officers—expressed their disapproval of my overvaluation of the strength of the Soviet Union. In my lectures I broached only one theme of political importance because in this respect my view was identical with the official one. I spoke about the "inevitability of the Russo-German war." Of this I was convinced.

I knew from my own experience that Russia always had been a very difficult partner to deal with, and that after the elimination of the Polish cushion we were rubbing shoulders with this uncomfortable neighbor. I had no doubt that Russia, after her consolidation and after the construction of a heavy industry, would press towards the west and southwest. It was obvious to me that the Hitler-Stalin Pact had been concluded with the mental reservation, "Who cheats whom first?" It was beyond question to me that Stalin was waiting for the exhaustion of both belligerents, Germany's above all, to reap his harvest. It seemed to me, therefore, quite logical that he should grab all territories available—the Baltic countries, Bukovina, and Bessarabia—when he had to face the unexpected outlook of a German victory after France's dramatic breakdown (and with Britain's defeat to be expected). But even under more normal conditions I did not doubt that Russia, in the long run, would never allow the extension of Germany's sphere of influence to Southeastern Europe. So, to me, a Russo-German clash was merely a matter of time, things being what they were. That an armed conflict was avoidable with another German government goes without saying. But to deduce from Russia's punctual fulfillment of her economic obligations, agreed to in the Hitler-Stalin Pact, that the Soviet Union was peacefully minded was, according to my opinion, a mistake. If Russia lives up to her treaty obligations, she has afterthoughts. If she feels it safe to do so, she infringes them.

Naturally, I concentrated my main activities on Silesia. There was hardly a town, big or small, left which had not to submit to one or several lectures from me. Gradually I widened my circle to other provinces. I visited Koenigsberg, Danzig, Stettin, Rostock, Hamburg, Cologne, Essen, Stuttgart, Munich, Leipzig, Bamberg, Bayreuth, Nuremberg, Heidelberg, Frankfurt. I also appeared in Berlin several times. I lectured in Vienna and Linz. Sometimes I saved time enough for a lecturing tour of the occupied countries. Twice I visited Poland from Brest-Litovsk to Warsaw, Lodz, Kielce, Lublin, and Cracow. I enjoyed a trip to France, though in winter—February, 1942—and admired the beauties of the Loire castles and the old cities of Tours, Poitiers, Angoulême, Cognac. I was surprised by the well-being of these districts. The shops were much better provided than German shops; wine and spirits were obtainable everywhere for a comparatively modest price.

Relations between the occupation army and the population, living in perfect harmony with each other up to that time, were becoming more difficult as the Communists were organizing the Resistance movement after the outbreak of the war with Russia. Two German sentries had been shot a few days before my arrival in Tours, and General von Stuelpnagel, commander of the occupation troops in France, was about to resign on account of the shooting of hostages demanded by Hitler. He was replaced by his cousin, later on to be executed as a victim of July 20, 1944.

I could have doubled or trebled my lectures from Finland down to Rumania, but the strain of the voyages was too great and my time too crowded with other duties. The most important feature of all these excurcursions was not my lecture, but the opportunity of getting in touch with the local people at a meal or over a glass of beer before or after the performance. That furnished me with the opportunity of exchanging thoughts and obtaining information from men from the most varied walks of life. I preferred the company of the representatives of the armies with whom I harmonized in my views. I met many generals and staff officers, not only in the occupied countries but also in Germany. Especially in the year preceding the attack on the Soviet Union, numerous armies were being concentrated along the frontier and required some enlightenment. In Gröditzberg I was being visited by prominent army leaders. We were on friendly terms with Field Marshal von Manstein and his wife. Their garrison and domicile was Liegnitz, near Gröditzberg. They visited us whenever he was home on leave. We reached full harmony of opinion, though in the guarded terms which became customary in the Third Reich. The more outspoken things which he wanted to communicate to me were transmitted by his adjutant, who explained the strategical situation on the map and dropped valuable hints on this occasion. In the period after July 20 the terror developed to such height that extreme caution was unavoidable. Even the most reticent men could be forced to disclose secrets under torture.

Less caution was applied by my old friend General von Niedermayer, former unofficial Military Attaché in Moscow, whom I met in Silesia in 1943, as commander of a division consisting of legions formed from different nationalities of Russian prisoners of war. There was an Azerbaidjan, an Usbek, a Caucasian, and several other legions, 25,000 men in all. He trained them at the training-camp Neuhammer, thirty kilometres from Gröditzberg. He came to see us several times, and I went to see him and lectured to his officers. I also attended maneuvers of his men and found them quite efficient soldiers.

Niedermayer, being a Bavarian and, consequently, very outspoken, made no bones about the criminal folly of Hitler's policy and strategy. He was exasperated by the crimes committed by the S.S. and the party in Russia. With equally strong terms he condemned the lack of policy as to the future of Russia. By proclaiming neither a united non-Bolshevik Russian empire nor a looser federation of national states we did not, so he said, appeal either to the imagination of the Russian Army, under the command of General Vlassov, or to his men. And so the real enthusiasm to fight for a cherished ideal was not evoked. Nevertheless his men fought bravely, like the Russians of Vlassov's army, up to the end. That they did so, and that one million Russian soldiers voluntarily enlisted in the German Army, should be a relief to those who are being perturbed by Bolshevik propaganda of the "Monolithic" Soviet State.

When the attempt to invade England was abandoned in the early autumn of 1940 and when Rommel failed to break through to Cairo at El Alamin, I knew that a German victory was impossible. The catastrophe of Stalingrad shook the Germans to their depths and made them conscious of impending defeat. But up to 1944 I could not abandon the hope that at least the full impact of the catastrophe would be spared to Germany. I received so much precise information about new weapons, jet-propelled planes, and large U-boats, that I tenaciously clung to the hope that we would be spared utter annihilation.

But I failed entirely to find an answer to the question of what would be the way out of the Nazi dictatorship. Hitler's wanton invasion of Poland, the crime of his attack on Russia, and the increasing terrorism convinced me that the National-Socialist Revolution could not revert to a normal course. The elimination of one set of gangsters by the purge of June 30, 1934, failed to produce a more moderate type of man. On the contrary, there was no doubt that Hitler had thrown off his mask and, on the verge of lunacy, was headed for disaster. The men appointed and tolerated by him, above all Bormann, sank almost visibly into criminality.

When thinking matters over during the preceding years, I had come to the conclusion that a violent interruption of the revolutionary process in Germany by means of a murder or a counter-revolution, especially during the war, would fail to restore peace within. I felt that this disease had to be cured by organic means. I had pinned my hopes on the return of our soldiers after the war. I knew that they were disgusted with the régime of the party bosses and expected that they would stop it. But would they be able to do so after a victorious war? On the other hand, there was no possible doubt that the Nazis flushed with victory would be entirely unsupportable. The depth of depression was reached with the conclusion that only a defeat would be an efficient cure against this evil. But what a defeat would mean for Germany—about this question I harbored no illusions, although my forebodings have been far surpassed by the reality.

I took refuge in reflections of an historical and philosphical kind. Every nation, so I argued, passes through childhood and manhood to old age, till it has to cede its rôle as great power to a younger competitor. Germany, a late-comer among the European nations, had just become an adult by attaining her national unity only seventy years before. Could it correspond with the eternal laws of Providence to condemn the German nation so prematurely to death and annihilation? Were we already degenerate and ripe for the grave? The National-Socialist Revolution was, after all, only an episode, though a frightful one, in the life of the nation, just as the French and Russian revolutions, both besmirched with crime and terror, were only episodes in the lives of both nations. I could not find traces of a mortal illness in the body of the German nation. In all the theaters of war the German soldier fought with his traditional valor, although lacking enthusiasm, and the civilian population worked unceasingly and heroically in spite of privations and air raids. The only ones who excluded themselves from this community of sacrifices were the gangsters at the top and a comparatively small number of henchmen. Was the German nation as a whole doomed to destruction on account of the folly and the crimes of some fanatic revolutionaries?

What I pondered about most was the question of which spiritual impulses enabled the Germans to sustain this fight to the bitter end. Terror alone was no explanation. A population driven to despair would have found means to break the terror by general strikes, mass demonstrations of housewives, or similar outbursts. But even the pretext of air raids, with the ensuing interruption of communications, was not exploited, and after the heaviest bombardments the overwhelming majority of the workers walked, one or two hours after, to their factories. The planned destruction of homes failed to break the spirit of the Germans. They had to capitulate when the enemies had conquered their country, which they were no longer able to defend through deficiency of arms, ammunition, and planes. During the last two years the armies in the field and the population at home had withstood the onslaught of the modern war without the minimum of adequate defense.

Which was then the moral basis of the will to see it through? At the outbreak of the war the mood of the Germans throughout the country can be accurately described as a blend of gloom, despair, apathy, and fatalism. The defeat of Poland was welcomed by the eastern provinces, who were thus united again with the territories ceded to Poland by the Treaty of Versailles. Especially the abolition of the *Corridor*, the return of German Danzig to the Reich, and the re-establishment of a direct connection with the "Island East-Prussia" were greeted with joy. But an enthusiasm comparable with the feeling after the first victories in 1914 was absent even then. Something comparable was felt throughout Germany after the victory over France and the armistice signed at Compiègne in the same railway car as 1918 after the German defeat. The satisfaction that an ignominy inflicted on Germany had been wiped out was enhanced by the conviction that a reconciliation with the western neighbor was at hand. The meeting between Hitler and Pétain, the repulse of the British attack on Dakar by units of the French Navy, and rumors about the conclusion of a Franco-German alliance pointed to this, just as the friendly relations between the German troops and the French population seemed to refute the old tale of an innate hatred between the nations.

Deep concern, amounting to anguish, was the prevalent feeling aroused by Hitler's attack on the Soviet Union. It was not quelled by the German victories of 1941 and 1942, and it extinguished the last smoldering fire of optimism. From now on only grades of pessimism, from concern to despair, differentiated the overwhelming majority of the Germans. After Stalingrad the feeling of impending disaster oppressed them all. That they nevertheless were able to put up a stubborn fight for two more years, though the deficiency of adequate arms demonstrated to them the hopelessness of their struggle in an ever-increasing degree, was, according to my opinion, due to the conviction that surrender meant certain disaster, whereas a continued fight left a chance open for some more favorable result. This conviction was still being hardened when the Germans were led to believe that the Allies were bent not only on the destruction of National Socialism but on the annihilation of Germany.

This belief was inculcated into them by the Allied demand for unconditional surrender and, later on, by the Morgenthau Plan. At first ridiculed by sensible Germans as clumsy Goebbels propaganda, it dawned upon them, when this propaganda was confirmed by facts, that nothing was left but to fight to the bitter end, in the vague hope that something might turn up to save Germany or at least to spare her the invasion by the Bolsheviks.

During these years of mental strain and anguish a personal disaster befell me. My wife, always of delicate health, had to undergo an operation in December, 1941. It showed that she was suffering from cancer, but the doctors were confident that the germs of this insidious illness had been extirpated by the operation. And, indeed, during the following year my wife felt better than ever before. But then came the final outbreak of the malady, to which she succumbed, after long suffering, on September 12, 1943. All I could do to help her was to have her in Gröditzberg up to the end, thus giving her the feeling of the comfort of her home and the distraction of visits of relatives and friends. The funeral service was held at our picturesque old church situated at the foot of the mountain, and she was interred in the adjoining cemetery. But her rest was to be disturbed by the Russians and the Poles. My adopted daughter, Countess Pueckler, who, having been bombed out in Berlin, had moved to Gröditzberg a year before with her four children, helped me in the new household duties.

Dr. von Dirksen with other members of the Embassy before driving
to Buckingham Palace to present his credentials

Competent and devoted servants made these duties comparatively light.

The narrative about the years spent in Gröditzberg during the war would be incomplete without mentioning my efforts at publishing a book. I wrote in 1940 a book about my mission to Moscow, but the Foreign Office objected to its publication. This negative attitude was entirely justified, as the book did not display enough glowing enthusiasm for the Russian ally in 1940 and not sufficient ice-cold hatred of the Russian arch-enemy in 1941. The two copies which I had, had to be burned when the Russians overwhelmed Silesia.

I also wrote a book about Japan at the request of a Berlin publisher. When it was printed and ready for distribution, it fell a victim of the air bombardment of Leipzig. Of the 5,000 copies, two were left, one of them with the bookbinder, who had to bind it nicely as a present for the Japanese Ambassador Oshima. But the Russians got hold of it when they came. The other copy is somewhere in Berlin. I also contributed to a book which was to contain four essays by "leading" experts about political and military problems of Japan, but this book was also bombed, and, when reprinted, bombed again; another essay which I wrote for a review could not appear, as Goebbels stopped the publication of most non-Nazi literature on account of alleged paper shortage. *Habent Sua Fata Libelli!*

With the closing months of 1944 the impending disaster had to be faced. Up to that time Silesia had been a haven of peace in comparison with the other parts of Germany. It had been spared Allied air attacks, apart from occasional raids on Breslau and heavier bombardments of factories in Upper Silesia. The province had become the air-raid shelter of Germany. Numerous treasures had been transferred thither from Berlin. The great hall in the ruin of the old castle harbored 232 big cases with precious manuscripts and books from the Berlin State Library. The library of the "East European Institute" of Breslau University, with 50,000 volumes, was sheltered in my house and was administered by some librarians. Bombed-out refugees from Western Germany crowded the village and houses belonging to my estate.

After the capture of Warsaw and the invasion of East Prussia the menace of the Russian "steamroller" loomed on the horizon, though we firmly hoped that it might by stopped at the fortifications constructed along the frontiers. Precautionary measures of real extent were out of question. They would have been branded as defeatism, and punished by execution. I managed, however, to get a letter of credit from the Deutsche Bank for a considerable sum. I carried it always with me and it saved me when I had to leave my home. Furthermore, I ordered that my shares and debentures should be evacuated with the other deposits of this bank to its branch at Erfurt, a city situated in the center of Germany and certainly out of reach of the Russians. And then we waited for what the new year, 1945, had in store for us.

---

2. THE RUSSIAN INVASION

We did not have to wait long. Since the first days of January we knew that a huge Russian offensive was imminent. In a broadcast Stalin had threatened that he would smash the German front and invade the Reich for a knockout blow. In Berlin, where I had lectured on January 9, great anxiety prevailed even in higher party circles, so I was informed. I was barely back home when the army bulletin reported the beginning of the offensive on January 12, and important initial successes for the enemy. A few days later, January 18, the first refugees arrived from the eastern frontier of Upper Silesia, most menaced by the Russian thrust from the Baranov bridgehead. It was a well-organized column, teams of horses with their carts, tractors, farm hands, and employes. They came from the estate of my old friend von Reinersdorff, with whom I had discussed the dangers of a Russian breakthrough a few months earlier. They numbered thirty or forty. The next day the wife of a general with children and relatives followed, friends of my niece. They had to leave their home at Oels, thirty kilometres southeast of Breslau, at one hour's notice. So the Russian advance was very fast. And then came Reinersdorff himself with his family and servants, ten people and six horses.

From then on I came to know the plight of the manager of a crowded hotel. Departures and arrivals alternated. Rooms and still more rooms had to be found. The great house seemed to extend beyond expectation. Helping hands were available from amongst our guests, also some food. My staff worked with admirable devotion. The stables and the rooms on the farm were filled to overflowing. The morale of the refugees was admirable: no weeping, no complaints. A sort of emergency evacuation of menaced districts to less menaced ones was being organized by the authorities. The population of the district of Guhrau was shifted to our district, Goldberg. One village of this district was to be billeted in Gröditzberg. That augmented the population of my house by twenty persons. They did their own cooking.

We had our meals for forty persons in two rooms; about the same number of servants in the kitchen, and a great number at the estate. Among my guests old age prevailed. For most of these three weeks I harbored three old ladies aged ninety, eighty-eight, and seventy-three.

The Oder line seemed no insurmountable barrier to the Russians. They had crossed the stream 150 kilometres northwest of Breslau, near Steinau, 60 kilometres northeast of Gröditzberg. They had succeeded in crossing it near Brieg, 30 kilometres southeast of Breslau, 130 kilometres from my home. Stubborn fighting was going on for some days on the left bank. Daily we waited impatiently for the arrival of reinforcements. But my administrator, who had to drive almost daily to the provincial capital, returned with the depressing news that no movement of troops eastwards was to be observed.

The *Landrat,* whom I rang up almost daily, reported rumors that a German High Command would be quartered on my house. Nothing came of it. My most reliable source of information seemed to be the Deputy President of Police. He beamed confidence and optimism. According to him, Gröditzberg was the safest place on earth, a real sanatorium. The Russian attack at Steinau was disposed of for good. The battle on the left bank of the Oder was developing favorably. And as to the new evacuation of districts nearer to Gröditzberg, it was an especially favorable omen, as these were preparatory measures for the billeting of German troops. It began to dawn upon me that the police chief was under strict orders to spread false optimistic news. Months later I learned that this scheme was being practiced everywhere. Whoever mistrusted these lies and started for a "trek" on his own initiative was arrested or shot.

"Trek"—this ominous word from the Boer language spread like wildfire in all conversations and became part of the German language. Whether to pack the trucks with some personal belongings and food, harness the horses, get the tractors going, was now a question of life and death. Whether to trek on one's own account or together with the villagers was also a difficult problem. In some districts the order to stay or to trek was issued by the *Kreisleiter*—generally when it was too late. In other districts the individual villagers were free to act on their own initiative. In my district no orders or directives were given either to stay or to move. But my eighteen horses had been seized for some purposes yet unknown, and I could not dispose of them. Besides, it was evident that the trucks would be overloaded far beyond their capacity. The villagers constantly urged me to let them mount my carriages, as the peasants did not have sufficient teams of horses. That these treks were an awful ordeal became obvious in a short time. News reached us that other treks which we had watched on their march westward had been forced to a halt of several days on account of the congested roads. Bitter cold heightened the hardships. Food ran low; the old people and the infants were dying. When the harsh discipline of the party loosened, we observed eastward treks back towards the Russians.

What was I to do? From my experience in the First World War, I knew that the presence of the proprietor was a guarantee for his property. As I spoke some Russian and was used to dealing with Russians, I might have a chance to tide over the first dangerous impact with the enemy till a normal occupation régime was set up and the German authorities resumed their duties under control of the occupying power. One further reason weighed in the balance against the trek. My wife's cousin, Frau von Oheimb, fell gravely ill. It was impossible to transport her to a hospital and let her fall into Russian hands. In my house she could be nursed by my wife's former nurse, who had taken refuge in Gröditzberg. Happily my friend Herr Cronemeyer arrived when I was being tormented by these doubts. He advised me strongly to stay, and I decided to do so, leaving the loophole open to drive away in Streckfuss's trucks with my staff at the last moment.

Meanwhile, the nearer the Russians came, the more things began to get clearer. The inhabitants of the refugee hotel began to leave. Up to the first days of February we had kept up the appearance of a social gathering, at least in the evening after dinner. Then we were assembled in the drawing-room drinking a glass of good wine—it was no use being avaricious now—and chatted about past times, carefully avoiding complaints about what was happening and going to happen. I could not help drawing the comparison with the members of the old régime during the French Revolution who carefully observed the etiquette even in the Bastille and in the tumbrils transporting them to the guillotine. The next morning some of our guests drove their horses on a voyage into uncertainty and misery.

I had managed to find relatives of the two old ladies and to drive them in one of my cars to a safer place. I had also brought my niece with her children by car to Jessen, where my sister was now living after the death of my brother-in-law. The peasants, gathered in my house, formed their columns and continued their trek; it was growing lonely in the house.

One evening about February 1, I was called to the telephone. Our former parson's daughter had got news from her mother, who lived in a village 20 kilometres away in a northwesterly direction near a station of the railway from Breslau to Berlin, that Russian tanks had broken through to this railway line. Now it was merely a question of time until they would be in Gröditzberg. Already the guns boomed 20 kilometres away towards the city of Haynau; the reflections of fires lit up the night sky. Straggling soldiers, but few of them, sneaked along byways. A big trek of a neighboring village passed our house and deepened the sense of loneliness. Our district had answered individually the question: to trek or not to trek. Five villages, Gröditzberg included, stayed. Others trekked.

From Sunday, February 4, the connections with the outer world broke off; no more telephone, no electricity, no water.

In the afternoon a German patrol, an officer with eight men, nice boys, a so-called *Panzer-Vernichtungstrupp,* squads armed with anti-tank grenades, ordered the house to be evacuated, as he would stay there with his men and there would be some fighting. That was not my idea! To get my house and property burned down for some useless shooting in a lost cause! I argued with the officer. But in vain. So the horses were put before the overloaded carts and we started slowly along the road to the forest. I reckoned that the soldiers would leave soon and we might return. That is what happened. Late in the evening we returned.

Some days of living in No Man's Land began. No more Germans, and no Russians yet. No more rations, no more milk from the dairy, no flour, no connection with the outer world except by daring expeditions of single men to the next village three kilometres away. But, on the other hand, no more controls. Thus, pigs were slaughtered freely, butter made by the owners of cattle. Everybody did whatever he liked. We were pretty busy, too. The wine in my cellar was hidden in bombproof places. Silver was buried somewhere in the park. Provisions of bacon and sausages and other necessities were lowered into more convenient places. Shotguns and rifles disappeared, too. They were to find all these things in due course.

Meanwhile the Polish and Ukrainian farm hands in the village were growing restless. The Poles employed on my estate behaved well and continued their work. Single Russian soldiers were appearing. They roamed about with Polish girls and perpetrated some plundering and beating. Every day I walked through the village cheering up the people. White flags were displayed. News leaked through from a neighboring village that the Russians had shot a man who had tried to protect a girl from being violated. She had managed to escape. I talked to her and she confirmed the story.

The health of old Frau von Oheimb deteriorated steadily, and one day she died. It was still possible to arrange a funeral service at our church, as a refugee parson had remained in Gröditzberg. With him and some of my servants we drove to the church. On the way three Russian soldiers rushed out of a house and stopped the car. I explained to them in Russian that we were going to church. One of them peeped into the carriage and, exclaiming happily *"Vot Popochka!"* ("There is the little Father!") let us proceed. Arriving back at my house, we found everything changed. A horde of Russians had entered and strolled through the rooms in quest of loot. With an incredible alacrity they had forced the locks of the packed trunks, and found in no time what they wanted: watches, cigarettes, woolen underwear, knives, and boots. They were perfect masters at discovering hidden objects and searching trunks. When I arrived, they were busy forcing cupboards and drawers and strewing the contents all over the place. Some of the soldiers, most of them young boys, were drunk. A few waved revolvers at my nose, but soon withdrew.

From now on Gröditzberg was afflicted by a steady flow of such visitors. Gröditzberg is happily situated in a remote corner and was thus spared the rear-guard combats fought out on the main road. Anyhow, with a few exceptions, they had no intention of staying, but hurried on after an hour or two. They were privates without officers. Officers seldom made their appearance, two or three of them together, but they were without privates. Uniforms and arms seemed adequate; fur caps extending well over the ears, fur-lined jackets, and thick trousers. They were a mixed lot, but most of them boys. There were sturdy Siberians, most of them brutal and disagreeable; the average were Russian peasant boys and factory workers, and many Mongols or other Asiatics. One of them entered my room, obviously drunk, shouting happily something "Okolo!" At last I guessed what he wanted: it was *eau-de-Cologne,* not for smelling, but as hard liquor.

Soon I developed quite a definite procedure in handling these unwanted visitors. I did not wait for them in the entrance-hall, but stayed in my studio and had them ushered in by my old servant. Thus they entered somewhat subdued. Then I addressed them in Russian, asked them what they wanted, mentioning by the way that I had been five years in Russia as German Ambassador, and showed them a photograph. It was taken when my wife and I had been invited by Voroshilov to a visit to the house of the Red Army. It displayed us both with our host, some high-ranking generals, Litvinov and Krestinski. This photograph produced a miraculous effect on my visitors. They gazed at it eagerly and submissively, naming the War Commisar, while pointing furiously at others, executed during the purge, muttering, "This is an enemy of the State." Thus being on speaking terms with them I proposed to show them round the house. When passing the great hall, where now the library of the Eastern European Institute was piled up on shelves, I pointed to the works of the Russian classics and of Lenin. I found them sufficiently cultivated to appreciate it. Then I led them down a narrow staircase, opened a door leading into the courtyard, and out they were. Some acquiesced in this abrupt termination of their visit. Some returned by another door.

As more time passed these visits became more frequent, coinciding with the advance of the main body of the Russian Army. The hope that the Russians might be pushed back vanished altogether. Even I, though generally skeptical, had entertained such hopes for a day. One evening the battle line came nearer to Gröditzberg after having been far away for days. Machine-guns muttered, guns roared, occasionally even airmen dropped some bombs. But then the noise died down, and from then on it was quiet. A few days later the Russians advanced with full strength even on the unimportant road which crossed the village. For hours a motorized column passed in perfect order: heavy guns, howitzers, trucks with ammunition, Red Cross cars. From front line, Gröditzberg had been reduced to occupied territory.

From now on I was pinned to my house. I did not dare to go to the estate and the stables, and my administrator would come and report. We had to be on the alert day and night, as the presence of the man at the top was most important. "Are you the boss?" was their first question. There might be some hours' rest, but then several parties might arrive together. The number of the Russians grew. They came with trucks instead of cars or motorcycles. But they did not stay overnight unless they camped in the open. Outrages became rampant. In neighboring villages men were shot. Women were violated and beastly crimes were committed. They spared me, thanks to my way of handling them. But my car and my horses were being stolen. One of my visitors, whom I had satisfied with an old watch (he was evidently an officer from Siberia, with an enormous grey fur cap and a huge mustache), warned me with good intention that those who would follow him would be badly drunk. The villagers were terrified and crowded my house in the evening, hoping for better protection there.

Straggling German soldiers aggravated the perilous situation. In the evening they knocked at the door and, entirely exhausted, asked for food and shelter. I harbored them for some hours, but then they had to leave in the dark of the night. If they had been discovered by the Russians, we and they would have been shot.

On Tuesday, February 21, I felt pretty miserable with acute indigestion and had to lie down. Some Russians were ushered into my room, one of them an officer. He gave the impression of being intelligent and subtle, far above the average. Glibly he started a conversation, describing his adventures, addressing me politely as "Mr. Ambassador." Then he asked for pen and ink and wrote a letter of safe conduct. I wondered whether he was from the High Command or from the G.P.U., the more so when I heard that at the same time another officer had visited the kitchen and talked with my servants. He wrote a similar document, adding the detail that I had been Ambassador to Moscow up to 1933, that I had endeavored to establish friendly relations with the Soviet Union, and that I had been removed from my post when the National Socialists had come to power. I felt relieved and thought that I was out of the wood and that smoother times were ahead. But in the evening things took a dramatic and unexpected turn.

3. THE ABDUCTION

At eleven o'clock in the night my old servant entered my room and reported that some German officers wanted to see me urgently. Assuming that they were stragglers on their way back to the German lines, I ordered that some food should be given them and that then it would be better for all of us if they marched on. As my servant replied that they insisted on seeing me personally, I told him to usher one of them in. A nice-looking young man poorly dressed in civilian clothes entered and told me that he had been dispatched from the German High Command of *Heeresgruppe Mitte* (Central Army Group) through the Russian lines to transmit an order to me. He then read an order that I was immediately to accompany these officers back to the German lines. If I refused I would be shot.

Angrily I replied that if the German authorities wanted me to come back into German occupied territory I would, of course, obey their order, as I had remained at my post not for my pleasure but because I considered it to be my duty. The only question was whether I would be physically fit for such an exertion. How far had we to march? Twenty-three kilometres, the officer replied. By the light of a candle I dressed, put my asthma inhalation apparatus into a game-bag, and took leave of my servant. So I left my home. Two more officers in mufti who had acted as sentries in the meantime joined us. It was a cold night, snow covered the fields, the moon was shining brightly.

When we were about to cross the main road a Russian motorcycle thundered past. We had to take shelter behind a hedge. We left the road and marched across the fields. After an hour's march we reached the neighboring village and sneaked into the house of a peasant for a short rest and to study the map. Then we continued our march in leisurely fashion, as the moon was still high and we had to cross the Russian lines in darkness. Besides, it was hard walking over the ploughed fields.

My companions were nice, tactful, and efficient young soldiers. Employing compass and maps, they found their way unerringly. Two major obstacles—a main road and a railway—were overcome unhampered. A few hours later Russian troops advanced on this road, we were told later on. After having marched for three hours, we came near to the Russian lines. Patches of wood alternated with open fields; curves of soft hills narrowed the dark horizon. We had to advance very cautiously. Profiles of Russian sentries became visible against the background of sky. The watchwords they shouted to each other were audible. Suddenly my companions stopped in a wood and sniffed. The air was heavy with the smell of petrol. Were there motor cars parked near by or a depot? But no clues were to be found. We marched on. Windows of peasant houses were lighted and darkened again. Another critical phase was ahead. We had to cross a village which had been occupied by the Russians the day before. Was it still free as it had been a few hours earlier, when my three companions were on their way to fetch me? I was heaved over some fences and wire gates. I had to jump ditches—one of them unsuccessfully, so that I hurt my knee. But soon the dangerous village was left behind us.

We were nearing the German lines, and again we had to be very cautious so as not to be shot at by German sentries as suspects. The commanding officer employed the most efficient counter-measure: hearing the noise of the approaching sentry, he started cursing and swearing in such unmistakable military terms that the sentry came into the open and let us pass after having heard the watchword of the day—it was "Potsdam." After one more hour's march we had reached the first advanced post in a farmhouse. The village we had reached and which was our goal had an appropriate name: Armenruh, which means "Poor Man's Rest"!

During the long six hours of our march I had done some hard thinking. I was under no illusion that this Wild West exploit had been started to save my precious life for Germany. I guessed that the military authorities, having been informed somehow about my stay in Gröditzberg, did not deem it advisable to leave me in Russian hands, as I might be misused by them to serve their purposes by means of torture or pressure. If I were to be indicted, I could counter the charges by valid reasons. But, on the other hand, I was conscious of the fact that "Field Marshal" Schoerner was commander of the Army Group to which I was being brought. He was a blind henchman of Hitler and by his ruthless tactics was responsible for the lives of tens of thousands of German soldiers. And I knew fully that executions were now a rather common procedure. I just had to take one precautionary measure. In the toilet of Armenruh I destroyed the cordial and appreciative letter which Litvinov had written to me when I left Moscow. Since the Russian invasion I carried it with me in case of emergency. Now it seemed a liability. Two years later, during my de-Nazification it would have been an asset. But all-round affidavits have not yet been invented, and one cannot be prepared for every emergency nowadays.

More than a year later the riddle of my abduction was solved. I heard the story from one of my colleagues who was in a responsible post in Berlin at the Foreign Office during those months. When Ribbentrop heard that I was in the Russian-occupied territories he had one of his fits and suspected that I would start intrigues and, thorough nincompoop that he was, that I would negotiate a separate peace. He resolved to have me tried by a Special Court and ordered the High Command to bring me back at all costs. Having heard that I was back again, he dropped the idea of having me indicted. I got an affidavit about these events from my colleague. It was of decisive influence at the trial of the de-Nazification Court.

My concern that some dramatic events were to follow was soon allayed when I reached the army corps of the district. The general commanding the corps received me hospitably and with full consideration of my difficult position. My three companions took leave from me, radiant with joy, as they had been awarded the First Class Iron Cross for their exploit. But now, with the tension relaxed, my illness started again. Though the doctor tried to dissuade me, I insisted on being transported to the A.O.K. (High Command of the Army). Here I met with a very friendly reception, as Field Marshal von Manstein had been a previous commander, and the officers knew that I was friendly with him. Now my health broke down completely, and I suffered a severe heart attack. I was nursed by a very competent doctor and had sufficient time to ponder over my situation.

The first problem to be solved was to get the most urgent necessities of life: soap, shirt, and so on. The second question was what to do next. The estates of my relatives, all situated in the Eastern territories, were already occupied by the Russians or threatened by them. The front was only a few kilometres away from Jessen, where my sister lived. To start for a journey to my relatives in Western Germany was equally impossible in my state of health and with traffic disorganized by air raids. I resolved to go to Upper Bavaria and take refuge with friends.

I was soon visited by the liaison officer of the Foreign Office at the Army Group. He was very anxious to hear about my adventures without breathing a word that I was under suspicion. Probably he was not informed himself. He was very satisfied with my report, transmitted it to Berlin, and that was all I heard. I had, however, some anxious moments when I started, after the restoration of my health five days later, for my next station, the High Command of the Army Group. I was told to proceed there—it was 200 kilometres away—in a motor car together with an officer who was due for the same destination. As I found out, he was the highest military judge of the army. That was no good omen! I suspected some court-martial would get hold of me. I waited in the motor car for my companion, but he did not appear. After some inquiries I found out that he was still drunk after the farewell dinner of the previous evening and was unable to move.

So for 200 kilometres I drove alone across Bohemia to Kolin, the seat of the High Command of the Army Group. Small squads of men were busy building up road blocks against Russian tanks. Columns of cars and trucks with refugees moved slowly along the roads. The country was peaceful and quiet. Near the small cities the inhabitants in their Sunday best—it was a Sunday—were out for a walk. Everybody answered questions politely in German. It was evening when I arrived in Kolin. In the restaurant of my hotel a gay crowd was singing and having drinks. Here again I was received hospitably by some officers of the Army Group who had served under Manstein. They provided me with a rucksack, some soldiers' shirts, underwear, and other necessities.

After a few days I proceeded to Prague, where I met my colleague, Herr von Luckwald, the representative of the Foreign Office in the Protectorate. He, too, was very helpful, and I was able to buy some useful things, though with difficulty, as everything was rationed and my means were restricted. Prague amazed me as a city. It was almost untouched by war. The streets were crowded with gay young people of both sexes. The Czechs had not been drafted for military service. There was little damage by air raids, though daily alerts forced us down to shelters in the morning. The city, this jewel of Baroque architecture, enchanted me.

As Luckwald explained to me, Bohemia was a State efficiently administered by a ubiquitous secret police under the command of the notorious Deputy "Protector" Karl Hermann Frank, so he thought it advisable to report my arrival to the *Burg,* the seat of the Government, as they would get news of it anyhow and might grow suspicious. The next morning I was requested to go to the *Burg* and see Frank. He made a better impression on me than I had anticipated, though the tough and harsh chief of police loomed unmistakably behind the polite surface. He inquired about my impressions in Silesia and about my intentions as to my future. Hearing that I was suffering from heart trouble, he ordered a specialist from the University to examine me. He promised me a motor car to Bavaria. He kept his word. The professor agreed to let me travel. The owner of a motor car going to Linz in Austria notified me that he would fetch me on a certain day. On the evening before my departure Frank sent me a parcel with sandwiches and a bottle of brandy (with a glass) to my hotel. So I cannot complain of Frank!

When I went to see the Commanding General, tragic news reached me. Both brothers of my wife had died on the same day. The elder, to whom I was very much attached, had been murdered in his house by straggling Yugoslav prisoners of war. The younger—whose estate was only a few miles away—his wife, and three young boys, all committed suicide when the Russian tanks entered his estate. As my wife's sister had lost three of her seven children—two boys had been killed in the war and one daughter had lost her life in an air raid—and two sons-in-law, not much was left of my wife's family.

I left Prague in the car of an Austrian architect, accompanied by a

Bohemian contractor. We rushed out of the city during an air raid, crossed the Austrian border, and reached Linz before dusk.

In Linz friends helped me to continue my voyage to Tegernsee in Upper Bavaria. For one day a heavy snowfall prevented my driving by sledge to the remote little mountain village and summer resort, Bad Kreuth, where Herr Noebel, my old colleague in Tokyo, lived with his family, as well as the daughters of Frau von Oheimb, who had died in Gröditzberg as a refugee. Happily a room was free in Noebel's house, and he offered me his hospitality. So I had a shelter again where I could wait for the coming disaster and, maybe, for a new start in the remaining years of my life.

VII
Refugees

I have been thinking over and over again whether I should add a concluding chapter to this book dealing with the events which happened
during the three years after I had to leave my home. Forming now but a
particle of the grey mass of the ten million expelled from Eastern Germany,
my lot is of no more than average interest. Most of them had to suffer
greater hardships than I, and many of them would be able to describe
them more forcefully. The attempt to describe Germany's fate and the
dangers which it involves for the world seems to me futile and inappro-
priate. I do not want to evoke the reproach of self-pity. Besides, what could
be more convincing in this respect than the excellent books published in
America, and articles and "Letters to the Editor" in Great Britain, describing with frankness and firmness the desperate plight of Germany? While
these lines are being written—July, 1948—it is superfluous to point out
what consequences the annihilation of the Eastern German territories was
bound to entail. The "Battle of Berlin" is proof of that.

Nevertheless, I shall add a few concluding remarks to the foregoing
account of my life. By giving a short survey of the emotions and events
which filled these three years which I spent as a refugee I feel I may render
a service to those who share my fate. Such an account may also serve to
enlighten the outer world with regard to the mental and physical process
which is operating in Germany today.

In spring and summer, 1945, a series of stunning blows struck every
German as an individual and as a member of the community. The consequences of Germany's unconditional surrender and of her utter defeat had
to be faced. This meant burying a lifetime's work and a tradition hundreds
of years old. Even more terrible was the disclosure of the ghastly crimes
committed by the rulers of the Third Reich.

But in spite of this despair, a sigh of relief was breathed throughout

Germany the further the Allied troops advanced. Terror and oppression had become unbearable. Contact with the Western world would now be re-established again. Germany would be granted the opportunity to work and to rebuild what her rulers had destroyed. General Eisenhower's proclamation, insisting that the Allied troops had not come as liberators but as victors, destroyed these hopes and stifled the desire to co-operate. And then the momentous, unbelievable, unintelligible event happened: Eurasia was allowed to penetrate to the heart of Europe. The Red Army advanced to the environs of Lübeck, to Weimar, Dresden, and Vienna. Even today, after having read most of the publications concerning the Conference of Yalta, the decisions made there are unbelievable and unintelligible, whether they be examined from a German or an Allied point of view, whether they refer to European or to Far Eastern affairs.

Equally stunning and unbelievable, from whichever point of view, was the next blow which hit the Germans: the blow struck at the Potsdam Conference: the separation of Eastern Germany from the Reich by a line drawn fifty miles west of Berlin. To this 25 per cent of territory and wealth, severed from the German body, a further 25 percent came under Soviet rule. The Poles were authorized to evacuate the German population from the territories assigned to them. But the protective clause that this evacuation should be "orderly and humane" was not kept, either by the Poles or by the Czechs, who were being authorized to expel three to five million Sudeten Germans, or, of course, by the Russians in East Pussia. During the following year millions of Germans from these territories crossed the borders of Western Germany, all of them destitute and only the physically fittest among them unharmed in their health. The only protective clause of the Potsdam Agreement, that the economic unity of the Reich would be maintained, has never operated, on account of Russian obstruction. But even the three Western occupation zones developed more and more into watertight compartments as they were being governed on the basis of fundamentally different laws and ordinances as to administation, voting, finance, de-Nazification.

Germany's purge of Nazis and men in leading positions deprived political and economic life of the brains which had kept the country working under Nazi rule. While tens of thousands of them, probably hundreds of thousands in all four zones—were kept interned in camps for years, a considerable portion of the population, amounting, with their families, to 25 per cent or so, were debarred from their customary professions and offices and remained for years in anxious suspense. That during these years the feeding of the population never reached the subsistence minimum, that economic life came almost to a standstill as a consequence of an uncertainty caused by dismantling, bureaucratic interference, inflation, and taxation, and that black and grey markets flourished—all this is common knowledge and need only be mentioned in passing.

My new abode, Kreuth, escaped destruction during the anxious days that preceded and followed the capitulation. In spite of the fact that Kreuth and Tegernsee had been declared Red Cross areas on account of their numerous hospitals, the S.S. started to entrench themselves in these places. In the first days of May they entered our house and declared that it formed a part of the main defense line. Most of them, little more than boys, did not seem enthusiastic, but their leaders were tough fellows. In the last moment, however, the imminent danger of total destruction by American bombers was averted from these peaceful mountain resorts by courageous men, among them the Swiss Consul, M. Frey, who argued with the American units. The bombardment was postponed and the S.S. retired.

One lovely sunny morning—May 7—the American troops entered Kreuth, one by one. In small groups they trickled in. My host, Noebel, was summoned to an advanced post to act as interpreter. He started for his mission without hat and coat. He came back to his home fifteen months later. He had in the meantime been arrested and sent to internment camps. When I returned in the afternoon from a walk into the village, a jeep stopped at the door. American soldiers had entered the house, asking for Frau Stein, the mother of Frau Noebel. She had, for many years, lived in the United States with her husband, who was now dead. Her eldest son had been killed as a German officer on the Eastern Front. Her younger son had remained in the United States, but she had been without news from him since the beginning of the war. Coming down the staircase and entering the kitchen, she ran, crying, towards a tall American officer, embraced him, and exclaimed: "Walter! Walter!" It was her younger son who had found out where she was living.

It was months before I was involved in the action of the Military Government providing for the automatic arrest of all officials who had held important posts during the Nazi régime. In the meantime the Russians seized the deposits of the banks, and the branch of the Deutsche Bank in Erfurt, whither my shares and debentures had been evacuated. (Erfurt was in the Russian zone). So I lost my fortune. The expropriation, so far as I was concerned, was complete. Speaking objectively, the loss of one's property is not so vital as one might expect. In my case a radical and swift operation is preferable to the slow and gradual procedure. What really hurts is the loss of one's home and the small personal items recalling the past.

I was shaken more deeply by the news leaking through from Gröditz-berg in the following year. On the morning which followed my abduction, Russian officers of high rank called to see me. They were incredulous when they heard I had vanished from the scene. They searched the house and the estate, and threatened to shoot my employees and servants, putting them in a row against a wall and aiming their rifles at them. During the day that followed the furniture, pictures, and everything were packed neatly in cases and transported to Moscow. The old castle on top of the mountain with the collection of medieval arms, furniture, and pictures was burned down.

Gröditzberg had to undergo the same fate as every village in the Russian and Polish occupied zone. My employees and the wealthy peasants were arrested and exiled to Russia for forced labor. My seventy-six-year-old keeper and his wife were shot outright. My administrator, who was severely wounded when he trod on a mine during the march to the railway station, was finished off by the Russian sentry. My second keeper died from exhaustion on the transport. The rest, together with their fellow victims, altogether 1,800, were transported to the Karaganda Steppe in Cental Asia, 500 miles away from the Chinese frontier. They had to work on a huge dam; their "norm," as the Russians call the daily minimum of labor, was to move nine cubic metres of soil. It is superfluous to describe food, lodgings, and climate. After a few months 700 were left of the original number of 1,800, most of them sick and unfit for work. The survivors were sent to more lenient internment camps and even allowed to return to their families. My gardener and another man from Gröditzberg told me the story.

As the expulsion by the Poles of the remaining inhabitants of Gröditzberg proceeded, information from the expellees became more explicit and direct. Numerous inhabitants had been killed by the occupants or had committed suicide. Still more had succumbed to epidemics. Apart from the losses suffered during the war, at least 15 per cent of the Gröditzbergers had died since the catastrophe. The percentage was about the same in the neighboring villages. It may be regarded as the average loss suffered by the population of Soviet-Polish occupied territories. The loss was probably higher in Pomerania and East Prussia.

In August it was my turn for the automatic arrest. As prisoner Number 1764 I was sent to the "Information Center" in Freising, twelve miles from Munich, together with two colleagues, Ambassador von Schoen and Minister Klee. Several generals and high officials completed the population of eight or ten men in our room in the newly built artillery barracks. In all, two hundred male and fifteen to twenty female internees formed a community and kept good comradeship. An Information Center was on a higher and pleasanter level than the internment camps and without their re-educational background. We were not kept waiting for our interrogations as the prisoners in the camps were. After some introductory talks I was put to work by the interrogator assigned to me, a decent and sensible man who, being a German emigrant, had full command of the language. I was requested to draw up memoranda about my diplomatic activity. I did it with great zeal, as it kept me busy.

I shall always remember with pleasure the month spent in the camp in Freising, not because it was a pleasant time physically or mentally. We resented this arbitrary imprisonment. We had not expected that these methods, familiar to the Nazis, would also be applied by the Allies. In other respects, too, Freising was no recreation. Eight to ten old men were herded together in one locked room, camped on some sort of bedstead, with starvation diet and insufficient washing facilities. But nevertheless these weeks rank among the most interesting periods of my life. By long conversations with the inmates of the camp during the two or three hours we were allowed to be out of doors, in a fenced courtyard, I got the first behind-the-scene story of what had happened during the last years of the war. Every phase of this period has since been X-rayed by the Nuremberg trials and in numerous publications, but at that period these conversations were revelations. In the evening we sometimes delivered lectures to our room inmates or played bridge. From the point of view of re-education, these weeks spent in Freising were, I am afraid, a failure. We endeavored energetically and successfully to keep our spirits up and avoided displaying the least sign of depression or irritation. With an outspoken enthusiasm we cleaned our rooms or changed the straw of the sacks on which we slept. This tough mental attitude and feeling of comradeship grew in proportion with the length of the internment. After all, it is not astonishing that there was little enthusiasm for the occupying powers amongst those who were interned for nothing at all for two years, often to be dismissed with the "White Card," which meant that not even the accusation of having committed the crime of party membership could be levelled against them.

After a month I was told by interrogator that I would be transferred to another place where the interrogations would be dealt with by persons more competent in foreign affairs. A few days later ten internees were transferred in a truck to Frankfurt. My hope that we would proceed to Wiesbaden was, however, disappointed. We stopped at the internment camp at Oberursel, near Frankfurt. There I was to have a taste of an ordinary internment camp. Whereas the treatment in Freising had been decent, Oberursel was just a prison: small cells for one occupant; ill treatment, short of beating, by the guards. My belt, shoe-laces, and even my jacket were taken from me, probably to prevent suicide. So I had to shuffle along the corridor, gripping my trousers in order not to lose them. I wondered whether I would have to stay at this place for days, weeks, or months. To my relief this ordeal ended after twenty-four hours. Two smart-looking

American officers asked me to accompany them in their car. We drove to Wiesbaden and stopped at a luxurious villa. Here I was told by one of the officers that I had been brought to this place at the request of Mr. De Witt Clinton Poole, head of the Investigation Commission of the State Department. I had been on very friendly terms with Mr. Poole when he was Counsellor of the American Embassy in Berlin and I was head of the Eastern Department of the Foreign Office.

Soon after my arrival Mr. Poole greeted me and explained that, having been entrusted by the State Department with the task of investigating the pre-war policy of Germany, he had remembered me, found out my address, and obtained my temporary release from the military authorities. He asked me whether I was prepared to collaborate in his task. I replied that I would do so willingly. I stayed two months in Wiesbaden and spent a most interesting and agreeable time with the commission. Mr. Poole displayed the greatest consideration throughout, and I had many interesting conversations with the members of the mission. The result of this work has been published by Mr. Poole in *Foreign Affairs*.

After two months Mr. Poole and his colleagues finished their task, and the mission returned to the United States. But before leaving, Mr. Poole secured my release from the military authorities, and I was allowed to return to Bavaria. I was fortunate to be spared the usual fate of the old refugee: to lead a useless life. After the capitulation I formed the old resolve to do everything within my power to free my home—the "German East"—from the yoke of the Russians and the Poles. The legal basis for such endeavors existed, as the Potsdam Agreement had drawn the German-Polish frontier only provisionally.

I held the opinion that the only effective means of convincing the Western Allies of the necessity for reuniting the Eastern German territories with the Reich was to prove that a restablishment of a Germany within the borders of 1937 would lower their occupation costs. The task was, therefore, to describe the productive capacity of the German East and to set forth how these territories had fed many millions of Germans in the Western territories in addition to their own inhabitants. This task seems easier than it was in the circumstances prevailing in 1945–46. It took weeks and months of research to find out where the men fit for the job were living; also whether they were willing to shoulder the task in spite of their personal hardships. As the libraries in the East were lost for good, and most of those in the West were bombed or damaged, the elementary means of scientific work were lacking. To get typewriters and paper was an almost insoluble problem.

At last a scientific staff under the able leadership of Professor Obst from the University of Breslau was assembled and was supported by one of the Northwestern *Länder*. A series of fundamentally convincing, strictly scientific memoranda, with accompanying charts covering the single provinces such as Silesia, Pomerania, East Prussia, Brandenburg, was the result of their studies, which I transmitted to the representatives of the powers concerned.

During the year 1946 the last millions of the Germans in the Eastern territories were being evicted by the Poles and crowded into emergency shelters, barracks, and air raid *Bunkers* in Western Germany. All those interested in the fate of their home provinces and their inhabitants were overwhelmed with news and reports of every kind: about the state of agriculture under Polish administration, about the loss of life and the hardships endured by these displaced millions. This material had to be sifted, analyzed, condensed into memoranda. The expellees had to be helped and advised. Thus the clearly defined task which had been assigned to me broadened. I came into contact not only with countless individual Silesians who wrote to me or visited me, but I exchanged thoughts with others who were driven from their home provinces for the same reasons as I had been from Silesia.

Interspersed with this work was the endeavor of most Germans during these years to enter as few jails as possible. I, personally, had, from 1945 onwards, to maneuver between being jailed by the Nazis, the Russians, the Americans, the de-Nazifying Germans, and the Nuremberg prosecutors. I had managed to evade the Nazis and the Russians. The Americans got me for a comparatively short time as prisoner, the de-Nazifying Germans for a comparatively long time, but not as a prisoner. The Nuremberg prosecutors wanted me only for interrogation and the drafting of memoranda.

The Germans displayed their customary thoroughness, even after the catastrophe, as far as de-Nazification was concerned. The court in Traunstein in Upper Bavaria tried me and my old friend, General Koestring, former Military Attaché in Moscow, for two days. The presiding judge acted humanly, cleverly, and thoroughly. The members of the court were composed of two inhabitants of Traunstein, one Jewish inmate of a concentration camp, and a Communist. The Communist proved to be an old acquaintance of mine whom I had known in Moscow. He had a small concession there, and the Embassy had been helpful to him. I therefore found him a staunch supporter. Both Koestring and I were acquitted. The public which crowded the courtroom testified its sympathies for us so unmistakably that it had to be warned by the presiding judge not to indulge in open applause.

Soon after my acquittal I was accosted by a young man, a student, in Traunstein, who told me that he had been among the spectators and listeners during my trial. He requested me, somewhat peremptorily, to write my memoirs. This was his opinion and that of his comrades. They wanted to know, so he explained, how things had been in the past and how important men had acted. Questioned whether he had listened to the proceedings on the first day or the second, he replied that he had been in the courtroom from the beginning to the end. "I and my comrades have been 100 per cent in your favor," he added. This episode, it may be, will encourage me to write my memoirs also in German.

My de-Nazification did not, however, end with my acquittal. The prosecutor, afraid that he might be attacked for letting a Nazi bigwig escape, appealed against the acquittal. He succeeded in blocking the normalization of my life for one more year. I did not get a pension; I was not allowed to vote; I was not allowed to write articles in the American zone when a bright press-control officer scented that I was not yet thoroughly and definitely de-Nazified. On the other hand, the proceedings stopped. The courts of appeal, insufficiently staffed, could not deal with the thousands and thousands of cases which were brought before them. At last the prosecutor retracted his appeal. Now I am without contacts with courts, trials, and prosecutors—for the time being. But this little account of personal experiences may contribute to explain the state of mind with which the Germans view the de-Nazification. It has been the most efficient means of killing the willingness to collaborate. It has created an obduracy amounting to Neo-Nazism among the more radical part of those subjected to this "cure."

As soon as contact with the outer world was re-established I tried to get hold of foreign newspapers and books in order to pierce the wall of spiritual isolation which had surrounded us since the outbreak of the war. Having got a survey of world politics again, I started writing articles for the press.

Even physical contact with the outer world has been granted to me. These lines are being written in Switzerland after a prolonged stay in Ireland. A more harmonious atmosphere for a German to whom the gates have been thrown open into a strange pre-war world cannot be imagined than that prevailing in these two hospitable neutral countries. But the threat of a third world war hovers over them just as heavily as over Germany.

2. EXTINCT SPECIES

An ever-recurrent stream carries me, and every other inhabitant of the globe, back to the one problem of overwhelming magnitude and urgency: the impact of East and West and, inextricably linked up with it, the problem of the "German East."

A few years ago, in 1941, I was invited by the city of Liegnitz, near Gröditzberg, to a festivity commemorating the 700 years' jubilee of the battle of Liegnitz, where a German army, though beaten, had stopped the Mongol hordes of Genghis Khan's successors. For 700 years the German East had defended Western civilization and its way of life against Asia. Now this barrier has been destroyed for good, and the West is anxiously looking around for somebody else to assume these duties. Whoever is acquainted with Eastern power-politics is fully aware of the fact that Eurasia never will be coaxed to cede the strategical advantages of the line Lübeck-Vienna which she has been permitted to occupy for incomprehensible reasons.

Whereas Prussia's function as guardian and outpost of the West against the East has been generally underestimated, the effects of her destruction on the internal state of Germany are overrated. The inveterate and overworked slogan of "Prussianism," "Junker," and so on has obscured the fact that Prussia's mission has been fulfilled since the foundation of Bismarck's German Empire, for from then onwards the principles guiding Prussia have been adopted, though to a certain extent unconsciously and unwillingly, by the whole of Germany. The soldier of every German stock has displayed the same fortitude and discipline as the Prussian. The Prussian type of officer has developed uniformly throughout Germany. The administration, all over Germany, was equally efficient and incorruptible everywhere. Even the fundamental principles of the Prussian philosophy of state were absorbed, in a somewhat mitigated form, by the other German states. Prussia, whose territories in Western Germany were only scattered enclaves before 1866, when Hanover and parts of Hesse were annexed, melted into Germany with the foundation of the Reich. She became more a symbol, the reality of which has now been destroyed. That it is one of the indestructible falsehoods to brand her as hyper-nationalistic and as the cradle of National Socialism has been proved again by the attitude of the representatives of the so-called Prussianism, of the officers, officials, and landowners, towards Nazism. The majority of the many thousands of men who sacrificed their lives to free Germany from this terror belonged to these classes.

Prussia can never be resurrected. Even if the Eastern German territories are again joined to Germany, there will be no Prussia. These territories will form a part of their old mother country as federal states. But the inhabitants of these territories have not been annihilated by the destruction of Prussia. Decimated by the war and the brutalities of the eviction, weakened in health, despoiled of their property, crowded into emergency dwellings, further expropriated by an unsocial monetary reform, scattered all over Western Germany, ten million of them are still living. And whereas ten thousand pariahs can be neglected, ten million cannot. The problem of these ten million expellees will range amongst the most urgent problems of Europe, whatever the lot of the Old Continent may be.

The attempts to assimilate the expellees into their new surroundings have failed. Even if Western Germany were more alluring and hospitable than a revolutionized, war-stricken country can afford to be, even if the clauses of the Potsdam Agreement did not provide the legal basis for the demand of a retransfer of Eastern Germany to the Reich, these ten million would never renounce their claim to return to their homes. Whether Germany be split up into a Western and an Eastern part, they remain a "Third Force" which may play an important rôle in events to come.

So far they are passionately anti-Bolshevik, strongly anti-Russian, wholehearted adherents of the West, longing for Western civilization. But it would be wrong for the West to take this adherence for granted indefinitely. Ninety-five per cent of all the Germans are now living far below the standard of Western civilization as far as food, dwelling, clothes, and all the necessities of life are concerned. The younger generation, starting from scratch, is more detached and even skeptical as to the amenities of this civilization. The all-important question whether, without this civilization, the West can be maintained, remains to be answered. Placed before the alternative of belonging to Western civilization without returning home, or of going back to Eastern Germany without maintaining Western standards, the overwhelming majority of the expellees would choose the latter alternative, provided that Soviet or Polish rule were to be abolished. This rule is up to now the dividing line. If the Russians had not committed the incredible folly of treating Germany more brutally than did Genghis Khan, if they had granted Germany semi-autonomy, like Finland, Eastern Germany, perhaps all Germany, would have joined the Eastern Bloc.

Even now the hate of Bolshevism felt by this "Third Force" is cooled by considerations based on *Realpolitik*. Skepticism lest the Western Powers pull out of Germany one fine day, or barter her for more profitable aims, is unabated. The reflection that, after all, Germany belongs geographically to the East, that the enormous untapped resources of Russia will offer a livelihood, work, and well-being, leads many Germans, however reluctantly, to resignation, and to the belief that it would serve their interests and those of their country best to come to terms with the East. Recollections of the traditional policy of the Prussian kings to live in friendship with the Eastern neighbor are still vivid with the historically minded among the Germans. The longer Germany remains the rubble-heap of the world, the longer the Western Powers continue their policy of imposing their decisions on Germany, without letting her shape her own destiny under their supervision—the more these tendencies will grow. All politically minded Germans are convinced—and this is the primary fact to be reckoned with—that the actual state of affairs is merely a passing show, which will soon be superseded by something else. Equally firmly rooted is the belief that without the Eastern territories neither Germany nor Europe will come to their feet again. The last thesis in the German political creed is the belief that a resurrection of Germany and Europe can only be performed within the frame of the United States of Europe. This is the political catechism of the expellees now, in August, 1948. But it may change before long.

As to the spirit and to the mentality which are animating my compatriots from Eastern Germany, I had ample opportunity of making my own observations, of gathering information from hundreds of letters and visitors. A small percentage of them, those weakened by poor health, old age, or weakness of character, have broken under the strain. The overwhelming majority of them, however, have set to work with dogged determination, spurred on by the compulsion to earn their living. Altogether, the characteristic feature of the Germans will be an enormous energy in every kind of mental and physical work, released by the pitiless struggle for survival. In many respects more progressive than their countrymen of the easygoing and wealthy West, many of the refugees have struggled through towards a livelihood, in spite of heavy odds against them.

To be expatriated from one's home devoid of means, and to be transplanted into new surroundings of a devastated and pauperized country, is probably the most acid test to which an individual or a class can be subjected. The Eastern Germans, for whom the downfall from wealth and influence to poverty and insignificance was especially abrupt, have stood the test. Above all the courage and the adaptability displayed by the women are beyond praise. No lamenting, no complaints, but a courageous resolve to face the inevitable. Harassed by the constraint to gather the insufficient rations and necessities of life, to cook and to clean and mend worn-out garments, they are working day and night. They even manage to keep up the atmosphere of their former surroundings and to offer to the

269

visitor hospitality which is, in spite of mean dwellings, refined by the spirit of which it is being offered; a silver tray or some cups, rescued from the catastrophe of "trek" and pillage, must stand for the comfort and the wealth of bygone days. Their husbands and sons, if not in internment camps or in captivity, are trying to earn some money as woodcutters or farm hands or in some transport business, if they have saved a team of horses from their "trek." There are admirals working twelve hours a day as farm hands, General Staff decorated with the highest orders for personal valor peddling goods. Those who have climbed the first rungs of the economic ladder have the post of administrators of farms, or have leased a farm, or are part-owners of some business. As energy, intelligence, skill, and the struggle for survival are the most powerful forces in the development of human character, I have no doubt that the majority of the ten million people from Eastern Germany will come to the surface again and shape a new life of their own wherever it may be.

As a species, they are extinct. But as individuals they will survive. The German East has been atomized. But its atoms are alive.

Index